Praise for *Puerto Ricans in Illinois*

"An informative, well-documented, and clearly written chronicle of the displacement and resettlement of Puerto Ricans in Illinois, focusing on their community organization and mobilization, social and educational struggles, and cultural and political resilience. Drawing on census data, personal interviews, and ethnographic fieldwork, *Puerto Ricans in Illinois* makes a noteworthy contribution to Puerto Rican and Latino studies as well as to immigrant and ethnic studies more broadly."

—**Jorge Duany**, author of *Puerto Rico: What Everyone Needs to Know*

"In *Puerto Ricans in Illinois*, Maura I. Toro-Morn and Ivis Garcia have crafted a detailed, comprehensive and accessible account of Puerto Ricans in Illinois. Through the use of archival collections, aggregate data, interviews and focus groups, and a profound sociological analysis the authors bring to life the history, peculiarities, struggles, and contributions of Illinois's—and the nation's—second-largest Latino group. There are no better scholars who could bring us this well-crafted book about the Puerto Rican experiences in Illinois."

—**Xavier Totti**, editor of *Centro Journal*

"Toro-Morn and García weave the story of Puerto Ricans into the story of the state, showing us where Puerto Ricans cross paths or join with African Americans, Mexicans, and whites in creating communities in Illinois while also providing a valuable glimpse of Puerto Rican populations in smaller cities and towns. This volume presents a rich analysis of the self-organization of Puerto Ricans in multiple spheres as it documents the shifting contours of Puerto Rican belonging and community in the state. Always present are the reverberations of Puerto Rico's continued status as a U.S. territory in many aspects of Puerto Rican life in Illinois. A terrific new contribution to the study of Latinx in the Midwest!"

—**Theresa Ann Delgadillo**, author of *Latina Lives in Milwaukee*

PUERTO RICANS IN ILLINOIS

Puerto Ricans
IN ILLINOIS

MAURA I. TORO-MORN
AND IVIS GARCÍA

Southern Illinois University Press
Carbondale

Southern Illinois University Press
www.siupress.com

27 26 25 24   4 3 2 1

Cover illustration: Puerto Rican flag within an outline of the state of
Illinois created by Hassan Ameli

Library of Congress Cataloging-in-Publication Data
Names: Toro-Morn, Maura I. (Maura Isabel), — author. |
García, Ivis, — author.
Title: Puerto Ricans in Illinois / Maura Toro-Morn and Ivis García.
Description: Carbondale : Southern Illinois University Press, [2024] |
Includes bibliographical references and index. | Summary: "An engaging,
easy-to-read history of the Puerto Rican ethnic group and their
contributions to the culture, economy, and politics of Illinois"—Provided
by publisher.
Identifiers: LCCN 2021026576 (print) | LCCN 2021026577 (ebook) |
ISBN 9780809338160 (paperback) | ISBN 9780809338177 (ebook)
Subjects: LCSH: Puerto Ricans—Illinois—History. | Puerto
Ricans—Illinois—Social conditions.
Classification: LCC F550.P85 T67 2021 (print) |
LCC F550.P85 (ebook) | DDC 977.3/004687295--dc23
LC record available at https://lccn.loc.gov/2021026576
LC ebook record available at https://lccn.loc.gov/2021026577

Printed on recycled paper ♻

SIU
Southern Illinois University System

Maura dedicates this book to her son,
Carlos Morn–Toro

Ivis dedicates this book to her parents,
Nancy Zambrana and Carlos García

CONTENTS

ILLUSTRATIONS

Tables

ACKNOWLEDGMENTS

Like this book, our gratitude extends from Illinois to Puerto Rico and back. In both Illinois and Puerto Rico, we are indebted to our colleagues, friends, and family members who supported us through the various stages of research and writing. Our heartfelt gratitude goes to our esteemed colleague and friend Dr. Ralph Cintrón, University of Illinois at Chicago, because he encouraged us to collaborate on this book. We are also grateful for the institutional support provided by Illinois State University and the University of Utah.

I (Maura) conducted the research and wrote a significant part of this book while on a yearlong research sabbatical from Illinois State University, whose Office of Research and Graduate Studies supported its publication with a small grant. I am particularly grateful for the support of the following administrators at ISU: Dr. Diane Zosky, interim dean of the College of Arts and Sciences; Dr. Joe Blaney, associate dean of Research, Facilities, and IT; Dr. Joan Brehm, chair of the Department of Sociology and Anthropology; and Dr. Jim Skibo, former chair of the Department of Sociology and Anthropology.

In Illinois, I want to thank my "comadres" Marisa Alicea, Nilda Flores, and Juanita Goergen, who have supported me through various stages of my transnational life. In Bloomington-Normal, a community of women, friends, and colleagues have also sustained me through the writing process by listening patiently and asking good questions. My thanks go to Rocio Rivadeneyra, Juliet Lynd, Adena Meyers, Alejandro Enriquez, Maria Luisa Zamudio, and Wendy Smith for the long and short runs, the marathons, and all the activities and events that gave me the space to think, laugh, have fun, and relax in order to return to writing with a clear mind. The Wednesday Morning Wildflower Cycling Group gave me an opportunity to see the beauty of central Illinois in the summertime. Illinois historian Dr. Roger Biles deserves a special note of gratitude, as he patiently answered my questions. I am immensely grateful to the friendship and support of my colleagues in the Department of Sociology and Anthropology and the Latin American and Latino Studies Program. Virginia Gill, Thomas Gershick, Richard Sullivan, Michael Dougherty, Diane Bjorklund, Alison Bailey, and Lisa Ortiz have provided friendship and support. My students at ISU have also contributed to this effort by sharing with me their stories and introducing me to family members.

The ever-growing Bloomington-Normal Puerto Rican community deserves to be mentioned here, since they contributed to this book by sharing their stories. In Puerto Rico, I am grateful for the support of my family, José Toro, Gilberto Toro (Mariel and Marita), and Miriam Aguilar, and my friend Tixarelly Rodriguez. I have been writing about Puerto Ricans in Chicago since the late 1980s, when I was a student at Loyola University. I have met many families, women, and friends along the way who have shared their stories of moving and living in Chicago. I hope they see themselves reflected in this narrative. Many thanks to esteemed colleagues Madeline Troche (Truman College), Michael Rodriguez-Muñiz (Northwestern University), Amalia Pallares (University of Illinois), Frances Aparicio (Northwestern University), and Lourdes Torres (DePaul University).

Frank Morn and Carlos Morn-Toro have a special place in my heart. Frank cared for Carlos and gave me the space and time to be able to travel all over Illinois to collect interviews. He read drafts of the book and celebrated my progress during the yearlong sabbatical. Carlos, this book is for you, because you are a Puerto Rican in Illinois. It is written with you in mind so that you have a sense of history and belonging and can understand and celebrate your roots.

• • •

(Ivis) wish to thank Will Smiley and Justin Grant Whitney at the University of Utah Writing Center for their copyediting assistance on earlier drafts. The University Research Committee at the University of Utah funded a Faculty Research and Creative

Grant Proposal for Puerto Ricans in Illinois that supported Alexander Barton, a graduate student in City and Metropolitan Planning (CMP), who assisted in archiving files, compiling demographics, analyzing data, and other tasks. Hassan Ameli, a PhD student in CMP, created images for my personal collection and recreated a map of Illinois. Dr. Reid Ewing, the director of the Metropolitan Research Center and former chair of CMP, supported my work in many ways. Carol Bierschwale, the college budget and research officer, was very helpful in managing the funds to hire students. Dean Keith Diaz Moore worked to support a yearlong leave in Puerto Rico and backed the special course I designed (ChicagoLAB), which allowed me to return to Chicago. In addition, Keith Bartolomcau, Christopher Stout, and Luke Leither at the University of Utah offered expert advice.

I am grateful to my husband, Jason Holt, not only for offering encouragement but also for scanning books, helping to find resources, and reading early drafts. I thank my uncle Kike and my aunt Lourdes for opening doors for me to move to the United States. My parents, Carlos García and Nancy Zambrana, have always being there for me. My dad's expertise as a librarian was useful in finding news and photos from La Colección Puertorriqueña at Inter-American University and the Biblioteca Digital Puertorriqueña at the University of Puerto Rico. My brother Carlitos; his wife, Veronica; and my nieces and nephews, David, Sofia, and Alina, always bring joy to my life. I am also grateful to my friends and writing buddies but in particular Dr. Natalia Villamizar-Duate and Dr. Erika Abad.

At the Center for Puerto Rican Studies, I recognize Dr. Edwin Meléndez (executive director), Pedro Juan Hernández (senior archivist), and Anibal Arocho (library manager) for helping me navigate the Chicago and Illinois archival collection. Others at Centro, such as Lindsay Nicole Dumas and Maria Estrella Hernandez, were helpful, too. Moreover, Centro supported the oral history project in Chicago and hired me to do this work, which resulted in several interviews included in this book. Julio Quiros at La Fundación Luis Muñoz Marín helped me find material at this collection. Dr. Aldo Lauria-Santiago, professor of Latino and Caribbean studies and history at Rutgers, identified additional vital sources. Alexandro Molina at the Puerto Rican Cultural Center is also a great friend and supporter of this book whom both Maura and I wish to highlight here.

Acknowledgments

We are indebted to members of the Puerto Rican Agenda who offered full access to the most amazing stories of community development—Eliud Medina, Pablo Medina, Hipólito Roldán, Eduardo Arocho, Billy Ocasio, Jessie Fuentes, and Cristina Pacione-Zayas. Special thanks go to José López (Puerto Rican Cultural Center) for his friendship, leadership, and vision.

At Southern Illinois University Press, we are grateful to Dr. Jeffrey Hancks for guiding us through the initial proposal process and to Kristine Priddy, acquisitions editor, for her quick answers to our many queries and for her support. The careful reading by the anonymous reviewers of the manuscript and the questions they raised allowed us to sharpen our narrative and offer a more polished version of the experiences of Puerto Ricans in Illinois. This book was further supported by the expert editorial advice and careful reading of Mary Margaret Simpson.

Special thanks are also due to Arturo Pardavila, Reboot Illinois, Harper and Brothers, the Puerto Rican Agenda of Chicago, the Kheel Center, the Library of Congress, and the Puerto Rican Cultural Center for sharing materials and images.

This book could not have been possible without the lives and experiences of the many Puerto Ricans who now call Illinois home. This book is for you to share with your neighbors so that they can learn for generations to come why there are so many Puerto Ricans in Illinois.

Puerto Ricans in Illinois

1

INTRODUCTION

The state of Illinois celebrated its bicentennial (1818–2018) with a multimedia campaign organized around the theme "Born, Built, and Grown." Indeed, for over two hundred years Illinois has built and grown as a result of the state's demographic diversity. The state was taken from the Indigenous groups who populated the land and encountered French settlers. Throughout the nineteenth and twentieth centuries, European immigrants (German, Italian, Irish, and Polish, among others) arrived and settled in Chicago and other parts of the state.[1] At the turn of the twentieth century, Mexican immigrants, alongside those from Europe, helped construct the state's railroads. In the middle decades of the twentieth century, Mexican agricultural workers were recruited as part of the Bracero Program to work in the corn and soybean fields throughout the state.[2] Today, Mexican Americans constitute the most significant Spanish-speaking group in the state, making their contributions felt across the land. African American families who moved north from the rural South as part of the Great Migration have also been central to the political economy of the state, although not always acknowledged as such.[3] Finally, the most recent arrival of immigrants from Central and South America and war-torn areas in Africa and the Middle East have made significant contributions to the economy, culture, and political life of the state of Illinois. Puerto Ricans represent an essential dimension of that diversity, but the question needs to be asked: What do the citizens of Illinois know about Puerto Rico and Puerto Ricans?

Residents of Chicago, where there has been a significant presence of Puerto Ricans going back to the middle decades of the twentieth century, may be somewhat familiar with Puerto Ricans.

Fig. 1.1. Steel flags in Paseo Boricua. Photograph by Ivis García.

The heart of Chicago's Puerto Rican community, Paseo Boricua (translated as "Puerto Rican Promenade"), is a lively commercial strip, popular among city dwellers for its restaurants, ethnic stores, and festivals. Curious visitors undoubtedly have inquired about the colossal steel Puerto Rican flags that cross the avenue at two points along Division Street. But do those who like to eat and shop in Paseo Boricua's restaurants and coffee shops know the history of struggles facing those business owners and the families who still live in the neighborhood?

In 2016 the celebrated Chicago Cubs won the World Series, finally closing a 108-year-old record, but how many fans know that some of the major stars on the team today are Puerto Rican? For example, a street in the heart of Humboldt Park has been named for former Cubs player Javier Báez. Even more significantly, the history of Puerto Rican participation in the major leagues threads through Illinois. The first Puerto Rican baseball player to play in the U.S. major leagues was Hiram Bithorn, a right-handed pitcher recruited by the Chicago Cubs who made his major league debut in 1942. He also played briefly with the Chicago White Sox. The most important baseball park in Puerto Rico is named after him, Hiram Bithorn Baseball Park in San Juan.

Do Illinoisans who live in the suburbs know much about Puerto Ricans? What about those who live and work in Peoria, Bloomington-Normal, Champaign-Urbana, Decatur, Spring-field, or Carbondale—what do they know about Puerto Ricans? A Puerto Rican man who immigrated to central Illinois in 2001 told us that when he shared he was from Puerto Rico, he was asked, "What part of Mexico is that?" The persistence of deeply held stereotypes about Puerto Ricans was evident in 2013 after Puerto Rican musician and salsa star Marc Anthony sang "God Bless America" at the Major League Baseball All-Star Game in New York City and baseball fans took to Twitter to protest his performance. One fan wrote, "Is he even an American citizen?" Another asked, "Why is a Mexican singing 'God Bless America'?" In the aftermath of two hurricanes, Irma and Maria, that devastated the island in 2017, one of the major issues in the delivery of aid and help was the perception that Puerto Rico's crisis was not a domestic one. According to the *New York Times*, only 47 percent of Americans know that Puerto Ricans are U.S. citizens.[4]

Fig. 1.2. Cubs second baseman Javier Báez at Wrigley Field.
Photograph by Arturo Pardavila, 2016, Flickr, https://www.flickr.com/photos/apardavila/30534074761/.

This book offers readers an opportunity to learn about the history of Puerto Rico, the migration of Puerto Ricans to Illinois, and the cultural, economic, and political contributions of the Puerto Rican women, men, and families who call Illinois home. We present a narrative to show how Puerto Ricans in Illinois have lived, worked, raised their families, and contributed to the social fabric of their communities since the middle decades of the twentieth century while keeping strong connections to their families and communities on the island. Broadly, this volume seeks to share an understanding of the historical forces that have brought and continue to bring Puerto Ricans to the state of Illinois; the diverse processes of community formation for Puerto Rican families who have migrated at different points in time and to different parts of the state; the struggles Puerto Ricans have faced as workers, students, family members, and community leaders and how they have overcome them; and the contributions Puerto Ricans have made to the cultural, economic, and political life in Illinois.

In 2014 Illinois had the seventh largest Puerto Rican population in the United States, with 211,626 Puerto Ricans living in the state. Chicago was ranked as the third most populous Puerto Rican city, after New York City and Philadelphia. Even more significantly, the Center for Puerto Rican Studies reported that Puerto Ricans in Illinois generated nearly $4.1 billion in purchasing power.[5] This report also showed that in 2014, Puerto Ricans in Illinois had lower unemployment rates, poverty rates, and public assistance enrollment than at the national and island levels. Further, in Illinois, Puerto Ricans fared better in terms of education, employment, and income. A recent report sponsored by the Puerto Rican Agenda and focused on Chicago's Puerto Rican community confirmed that Chicago Puerto Ricans fared better than those in New York City and Philadelphia.[6] In Illinois, Latinos represent 17 percent of the statewide population,[7] while Puerto Ricans represent about 10 percent of that Latino population, second to Mexicans, who represent about 80 percent of all Latinos in the state.[8]

In 2017 the most recently arrived Puerto Ricans in Illinois were in a historic category of their own: climate refugees. Over two thousand Puerto Ricans arrived in Chicago in the aftermath of Hurricane Maria, a category 4 storm that devastated Puerto

Rico, cutting electricity, water, and cellular service for the entire island for months.[9]

In Illinois there are many Puerto Ricans who can trace their roots to the early migrants who came in the 1950s and 1960s. Their children and grandchildren are now second- and third-generation Puerto Ricans living in Illinois. These second- and third-generation Puerto Ricans—some prefer to call themselves Chicago Ricans—raise their families, like their parents did, through hard work and commitment to their communities. For some members of this second and third generation, Puerto Rico is a faraway place, a dreamland that they have never visited and have come to know only through stories of relatives, friends, or the news. And there are those who maintain transnational connections to the island via relationships with relatives. This reflects a complicated existence—*a vaivén* (coming and going), a term coined by anthropologist Jorge Duany to address the constant coming and going of Puerto Ricans.[10] For instance, some highly educated Puerto Rican professionals in Chicago take their children to the island to visit relatives and to learn about Puerto Rico. Working-class Puerto Ricans also travel back and forth as a way to deal with the economic crisis currently shaping the island. In addition, recently arrived Puerto Ricans come to study, work, and live in communities across the state. Some come to attend Illinois's finest educational institutions. In this book, we have interviewed a number of Puerto Ricans who have sustained connections between Illinois and Puerto Rico.

This book draws upon rigorous and time-tested research traditions in the social sciences. First, we collected U.S. Census and American Community Survey demographic data for historical and current profiles of the distribution and composition of Puerto Ricans in Illinois. We also used U.S. Census data to show the occupational profile and educational attainment of Puerto Ricans in Illinois. The U.S. Census provided us an opportunity to compare Puerto Ricans with other racial and ethnic groups in the state. While a reliable source of demographic data, the census contains some limitations that must be mentioned here. For example, changes in how Hispanics—a category that includes Puerto Ricans—were counted limited our ability to share longitudinal trends.

Further, we drew upon interviews, oral histories, and fieldwork that we collected for this and other projects and combed the archives of historical societies in Illinois to find some gems, such as the story of Manuel Cordero in Bloomington. We also conducted interviews and focus groups in Chicago and Waukegan for a report for the Puerto Rican Agenda, and with participants' permission we have used some of their quotes for this project. Ivis García collected interviews in Waukegan as part of the Chicago Area Study through the University of Illinois at Chicago, and as part of the Oral History Project of the Center for Puerto Rican Studies in New York City she gathered oral histories of prominent Puerto Ricans in Chicago, such as José López and Hilda Fontani, among others. In addition, Maura Toro-Morn conducted twenty-five interviews exclusively for this book in Chicago, Elgin, Bloomington-Normal, Peoria, and Champaign-Urbana.

In keeping with Institutional Review Board protocols, for interviews with nonpublic figures we protected the identity of those who spoke with us. Puerto Ricans were eager to share their lives with us, and many offered names of other people in their networks and communities. These interviews were combed for critical issues, and whenever possible, we have included direct quotes from transcripts. Toro-Morn also conducted interviews with key leaders in Chicago in the aftermath of Hurricane Maria. A smaller battery of electronic and phone interviews were also done with Puerto Rican educators and business leaders. Interviews were conducted in the language of preference of informants. Sometimes we started in Spanish and finished in English, while other times informants expressly preferred English. We transcribed and translated Spanish interviews.

Last, scholars of the Puerto Rican diaspora have produced a voluminous body of work that we also utilize in this book. Their work helps further contextualize the Puerto Rican experience in Illinois. The literature about Puerto Ricans in Chicago is particularly relevant here.[11]

As a first attempt to document the experiences of Puerto Ricans in the state of Illinois, this book does not offer an exhaustive analysis of the totality of the experience of Puerto Ricans in the Land of Lincoln. We have relied on networks of friends and professional connections to find and interview Puerto Ricans throughout the state, but some communities were beyond our reach due to time, access, and other limitations. It may strike readers that we have privileged the experiences of Puerto Ricans in Chicago, but that was not our intention. Still, today Chicago represents the oldest and largest community of Puerto Ricans in Illinois. The city has given the state such distinguished political leaders as Senator Miguel del Valle and Congressman Luis Gutiérrez. Chicago represents an integral part of our narrative because of the population density in the city. Plus, Chicago is where many of us who live outside the city find *un pedacito de patria* (a little piece of home) and where we go to consume Puerto Rican culture, whether it is to buy *pasteles* (Puerto Rican tamales) for Christmas or *sofrito* (a vegetable cooking base) or to participate in cultural events. Chicago's ethnic communities offer a first-rate world classroom, and its Puerto Rican community is no exception. For this reason, we draw upon the literature developed in Chicago and use the city as a point of departure. We encourage future generations of scholars to study the development of communities outside of Chicago to produce the scholarly work that will deepen our knowledge of this important ethnic group in the state of Illinois.

About the Authors

Our collaboration represents the dedication of two scholars devoted to the study and analysis of the Puerto Rican experience. Both of us share deep connections to the state of Illinois and to the migration patterns this book addresses. In many ways, each of us represents a subject position found in the literature. We both belong to the ongoing migration of educated and professional Puerto Ricans, but at different points in time. I, Maura Toro-Morn, left the west coast of the island, Cabo Rojo, in the early 1980s to pursue my education in the United States. I completed my doctoral studies at Loyola University of Chicago in 1993, writing my dissertation about the intersection of social class and gender in the migration of Puerto Rican women in Illinois.[12] I have dedicated my academic life to documenting the experiences of Puerto Ricans in Chicago, as evidenced by the volume of work I have published about the topic. Upon completing my graduate work, I joined the faculty ranks at Illinois State University in 1993. For over three decades, I have lived a transnational life in keeping with the experiences of Puerto Ricans in the United States, traveling to Puerto Rico for Christmas celebrations, weddings, graduations, and other family events. Similarly, when my son, Carlos, was about to be born, my mother, Rita, came to Bloomington-Normal to support me. When my mother fell ill, I provided a great deal of care for her transnationally. Still today, our family continues to exist in a transnational state, here and there, at once—a characteristic that has also been found among other Latino immigrant groups.[13]

I, Ivis García—like other Puerto Ricans of my generation—moved to the United States to continue my education, in my case to study at the University of New Mexico in Albuquerque in 2004. My uncle Kike lived in Santa Fe, which made the move a little easier for me. After completing my dual master's degrees in community and regional planning and Latin American studies, I lived and worked in San Francisco; Springfield, Missouri; and Washington, D.C. Then I enrolled in the doctoral program at the University of Illinois at Chicago.[14] My collaboration with Moro-Torn began soon afterward when we worked on a community project for the Puerto Rican Agenda, resulting in the publication of the report *60 Years of Migration: Puerto Ricans in Chicagoland*.[15] Before this project, we edited a special issue of *Centro: Journal of the Center for Puerto Rican Studies* focused on new scholarship about Chicago.[16] *Puerto Ricans in Illinois* represents the culmination of our collaboration.

Before and after the Storms

In the fall of 2017, as we worked on this book, two devastating hurricanes—Irma and Maria—hit Puerto Rico within weeks of each other. While Irma caused a lot of damage, leaving the island without electricity for over two weeks, it was category 4 Hurricane Maria that devastated the island beyond recognition. The details of the storm are well known: Maria entered through the southeastern coast and exited through the north, dumping over twenty inches of rain and battering the island with 150-miles-per-hour winds for over thirty hours. Over six years after the hurricanes, we cannot categorically state that the island has fully recovered, since there are still many families without adequate housing. Maria was a historic storm causing massive devastation, material scarcity, and widespread emotional trauma. Readers need to know that before these events, the economy of Puerto Rico already faced a severe economic crisis, placing the island at the forefront of national and international newspapers. For the last twenty years, Puerto Rico had accumulated a mountain of debt, leaving the island without cash to pay that debt off. The crumbling economy and the implementation of austerity measures were drowned out sporadically by the international success of Luis Fonsi and Daddy Yankee's summer hit, "Despacito," a song that—like the storms— is now in the history books.

Again, we need to emphasize that a quality that has characterized the news coverage of first the island's financial crisis and then the devastation caused by Hurricanes Irma and Maria was a vast lack of knowledge about Puerto Rico, including on the part of people at the highest level of the federal government. The question that needs to be asked is this: What exactly is Puerto Rico in relation to the United States? The answer, although complicated, threads through the history that this book addresses and is important to point out: Puerto Rico has been part of the United States since 1898. Whereas most of the territories colonized by Spain declared independence through revolutionary wars and other means, Puerto Rico remained under Spain's control by the time the Spanish-American War broke out in 1898, making it the country with the most extended Spanish influence in the Western Hemisphere. To be clear, Puerto Rico has never been an independent and sovereign country.

On July 25, 1898, Puerto Rico was invaded by U.S. troops and has been under its control until today. Anthropologist Jorge Duany observes that over one hundred years of U.S. influence has meant "an intense penetration of American capital, commodities, laws, and customs, unequaled in other Latin American countries."[17] That is why there was such a widespread public outrage by Puerto Ricans on the island and on the mainland when the United States failed to adequately address the needs of Puerto Ricans in the aftermath of the 2017 storms. The mayor of San Juan, Carmen Yulín Cruz, became the voice of the residents of Puerto Rico when she issued an SOS over Twitter and stated categorically how ineffective the U.S. response had been.

Indeed, an issue frequently used to call attention to the economic crisis on the island and to the humanitarian crisis after the hurricanes is citizenship. Here lies an important nuance: Puerto Rico is not a state of the United States, yet Puerto Ricans have been U.S. citizens since 1917. Puerto Ricans living in Puerto Rico are U.S. citizens, yet they cannot vote in national elections that elect the U.S. president. Puerto Ricans are subject to the military draft and have fought valiantly in all theaters of war that the United States engaged in throughout the twentieth and twenty-first centuries, but they cannot vote for their commander in chief.

Yet, Puerto Ricans living in any of the fifty states can and do vote in state and national elections. Further, federal government programs, such as social security, apply in Puerto Rico, even though levels of assistance are much lower than those provided to people living in any of the fifty states. So what is Puerto Rico exactly? After over one hundred years of U.S. colonialism, Puerto Rico is a colonial paradox, a Spanish-speaking stateless nation with a robust Afro-Caribbean identity.

Puerto Ricans have historically constructed, reconstructed, and affirmed their distinct nationality as a way to resist U.S. colonialism. According to Lorrin Thomas, Puerto Ricans on the island struggle to preserve their right to self-determination and cultural uniqueness in the face of its colonial relationship with the United States.[18] Puerto Ricans affirm their nationality and patriotism when they migrate to the United States by defining themselves as Puerto Ricans. This leads to the perception that Puerto Ricans are not U.S. citizens, and thus they are mistreated and discriminated against. In other words, Puerto Rican citizenship does not translate to equal rights in either Puerto Rico or the United States.

In the aftermath of Hurricane Maria, Puerto Ricans in U.S. communities mobilized to offer help to people on the island. In New York, Florida, and Illinois, Puerto Ricans first organized through Facebook and other social media outlets, searching for relatives. By calling attention to the developing humanitarian crisis on the island and expressing their frustration at the humiliations leveled by the Trump administration, Puerto Ricans in the United States expressed their cultural and political pride, too. Chicago's relief effort was swift and timely. Puerto Ricans throughout Illinois organized in several ways to aid those on the island and the storm refugees arriving in Chicago. An impressive number of community groups raised funds to help support relief efforts; other groups collected food items, water, and additional supplies; and still others lobbied for changes in laws and policies to help Puerto Rico's recovery efforts.[19]

The mobilization of U.S. communities on behalf of Puerto Ricans is the best example of a diaspora community at work. Puerto Rican scholar Ramón Grosfoguel defines the Puerto Rican diaspora as an imagined community with an "imaginary belonging to a territory that spans the island as well as certain areas in the mainland."[20] In fact, in the aftermath of Hurricane Maria,

Puerto Ricans across the United States organized to send help and flexed their political muscle to call attention to the island's political and economic condition. This moment has become an essential, yet unanticipated, part of this book.

Latino, Hispanic, and Puerto Rican

In 2016 the American Community Survey reported that there were 57,398,719 Hispanics in the United States, or 18 percent of the total population.[21] A decade ago, Hispanics became the largest racial and ethnic group in the country, surpassing African Americans. The label "Hispanic" is used widely by social scientists, policy makers, and journalists alongside national origins (Mexican, Puerto Rican, Cuban, and so on). In 2016, Mexicans represented the largest group in this category, with 36.26 million of the nation's Hispanic population. Puerto Ricans are the second largest group in this category with 5.45 million, not counting the 3.26 million living in Puerto Rico in 2016.[22] Other groups included in this category are Salvadorans, Cubans, Dominicans, Guatemalans, and Colombians. The U.S. Census has reported that each one of these groups has seen a population increase over the past two decades.

The label "Hispanic" was formally introduced in the lexicon of racial and ethnic names in the 1970 U.S. Census when it became the official name for the growing number of people from Mexico, Puerto Rico, Cuba, and other parts of Latin America who resided in the United States.[23] Alongside "Hispanic," there are also the labels "Latino" and "Latinx," which are now preferred by activists and scholars alike.[24] The label "Latino" has been more prominent as an alternative to "Hispanic" since the 1990s. "Latinx" has emerged as a source of contention and a way to capture gender-nonconforming and gender-expansive dimensions of identities.[25] Some find the existence of these pan-ethnic labels confusing.

Why do we have so many labels to refer to these communities? To be clear, "Latinx" and "Hispanic" are pan-ethnic terms used to refer to Spanish-speaking immigrants and their descendants. "Latino" became popular in an attempt to challenge the homogenization that erased nationality differences between these groups. The label emerged in large urban centers, like Chicago, as Spanish-speaking groups came into contact with each other to address the problems they faced. It is a political marker forged among various nationality groups. In Chicago, for example, a pan-ethnic solidarity was formed between Mexicans and Puerto Ricans, leading to the formation of what sociologist Felix Padilla called a "Latino ethnic consciousness," more popularly known today as "Latinidad."[26]

Part of the controversy with these descriptors is about who is doing the labeling. "Hispanic" is a pan-ethnic category that was given by the U.S. Census whereas "Latino" and "Latina," also pan-ethnic categories, are terms that people select when in coalition with each other. In the end, although both categories tend to lump people together who are very different, there is a lot of variance on the ground regarding the labels that people use and adopt for themselves. The Pew Hispanic Research Center has surveyed Hispanic and Latino groups concerning their preferences, and consistently, nationality is the most preferred label by Mexicans, Cubans, and Puerto Ricans.[27] It remains to be seen whether this will be the case in the future, given the high rates of intermarriage between these nationalities. For this book, we will use the label "Hispanic" when using U.S. Census documents or data, but whenever possible we will try to adhere to the desire of those in the Latino community and identify people by nationality, if necessary. Although some people use these terms interchangeably, we prefer to recognize the historical and political history underlying each term.

In this context, it may also be relevant to clarify whether Puerto Ricans are immigrants or migrants. Demographers and international migration scholars distinguish between international movements (immigration or outmigration) and movements that take place within the national borders, also known as internal migrations. Again, since Puerto Rico is part of the United States and Puerto Ricans are U.S. citizens, technically speaking their movement would fall within the category of internal migration, a term we plan to use throughout this book. But there is a significant caveat here. As will be shown in chapter 2, the history of the U.S. colonization of Puerto Rico and the uniqueness of the legal construction of U.S. citizenship place Puerto Ricans alongside the spectrum of "immigrants" rather than "migrants." In other words, although Puerto Ricans are technically migrants, researchers have documented how Puerto Ricans experience migration and other adaptation processes as if they were immigrants.

Illinois at the Crossroads

Illinois is the fifth most populous state in the United States. With 2,178,790 Latinos in 2016, according to the one-year estimates of the American Community Survey, it also ranks fifth in the country in terms of absolute Latino numbers. While Illinois has experienced only modest population growth in recent years (at 3.3 percent, it ranked forty-third out of the fifty states in total population growth between 2000 and 2010), the Latino population increased by 33 percent. Almost all of the growth the state experienced was within its Latino population. And while immigration was a contributing factor behind this growth, 68 percent of the Latino increase was from U.S.-born Latinos rather than from foreign-born migrants.[28] Thus, it can be said that Illinois is at a crossroads of critical demographic movements.

We know that most Latinos settled in Chicago and old industrial cities like Cicero, Berwyn, and Waukegan. The latter three cities have Latino populations of over 50 percent, according to the 2010 census. Puerto Rican settlement patterns mirrored this trend, with large numbers of Puerto Ricans settling in Chicago and other industrial centers. Cities like Zion and Cicero have Puerto Rican populations approaching 5 percent. The number of Puerto Ricans living in Illinois grew from 157,851 in 2000 to 173,982 in 2010, representing an annual growth rate of about 1 percent.[29] The growth rate has accelerated: between 2010 and 2015, the number of Puerto Ricans in Illinois increased by 24,290, representing an annual growth rate of 2.8 percent.[30]

One of the most significant demographic trends since the 1990s is that Latinos are moving out of Chicago and the surrounding suburban counties of Kane, DuPage, Lake, McHenry, and Will. Even so, in 2010, 38 percent of the state's Latino population was living in Chicago. Another 52 percent were living in other cities and counties in Illinois; still, all but 10 percent of Latinos in the state were living in Chicagoland (the counties listed above, plus Cook and Kendall Counties). With 1,295,026 Latinos, Cook County ranks fifth in the country for the counties with the highest Latino population. In fact, 23 percent of the people in Cook County are Latino.[31] Puerto Ricans demonstrate a similar attachment to the counties of Chicagoland. In 2015, 72 percent of all Puerto Ricans in Illinois lived in Cook County, and fully 91 percent lived in Chicagoland. In 2016 there were 209,638 Puerto Ricans in Illinois, representing 1.6 percent of the state's total population.[32]

Illinois is a rather large state covering quite a bit of territory, and when people say "Illinois," all kinds of misconceptions arise. For some, "Illinois" immediately conjures connections to Chicago. Others fail to distinguish between the city and the suburbs. In some imaginations, the rest of the state becomes an invisible mass of land, frequently associated with corn. Downstate Illinois is often reduced to cornfields, a conception that diminishes the geographic diversity of that area, which includes the state capital, Springfield, and other influential cities concerning commerce, popular culture, and economy. There is Peoria, home to a multinational corporation, Caterpillar, Inc. Decatur is home to yet another multinational, Archer Daniels Midland, and Bloomington is the corporate headquarters of the largest insurance agency in the United States, State Farm. Educational institutions are prominent across this geography as well. Whenever possible we try to avoid such categorizations, but the reader must be aware that sometimes the distinctions may be drawn between Chicago, the city with the most substantial number of Puerto Ricans in the state, and other cities with smaller, but significant, communities. Figure 1.3 shows these competing geographic notions.

We consider this history of Puerto Rico a critical departure point in understanding the Puerto Rican–Illinois experience. We take readers through a brief overview of the island's Spanish colonization and its impact, creating a Puerto Rican identity. Since few Americans know or appreciate the effects of the U.S. colonization of Puerto Rico in 1898, we also address that issue in this book. The changes in the political status in the 1950s are critical to understanding what historians have called the "great airborne migration." We will also examine the migration processes of Puerto Ricans to Illinois. Since the middle decades of the twentieth century until now, Puerto Ricans have moved to and from Illinois, some returning to Puerto Rico, others leaving to other parts of the United States, such as Florida or New York City. Puerto Ricans have also moved around Illinois: some have left the city for the suburbs; others have moved from New York to Illinois. It should not surprise readers that Puerto Ricans are found in every county of the state. We share stories of migration drawn from the oral histories and interviews we conducted with

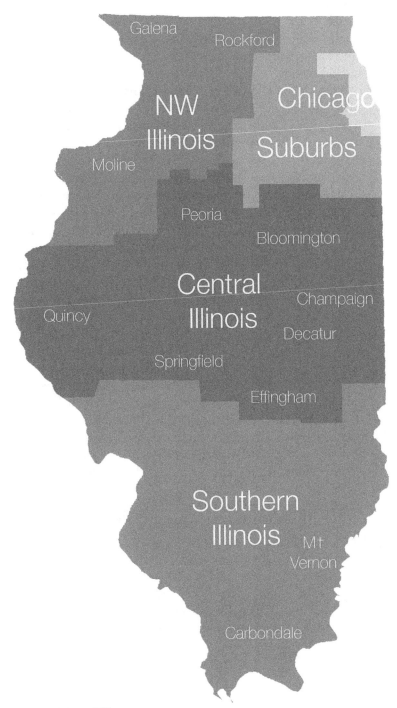

Fig. 1.3. Map of Illinois. Created by Hassan Ameli.

Puerto Ricans and include historical and ethnographic accounts to provide a nuanced narrative of domestic and professional life. We show how Puerto Ricans across Illinois have built resilient and robust families in spite of the discrimination, poverty, unemployment, and underemployment that has plagued many Latino immigrants and minority families in the state.

We will look at the struggles of Puerto Rican students, parents, activists, teachers, and administrators in securing educational opportunities for Puerto Ricans. For both Latino children and adults, education has been a path toward achieving the "American dream." Latino parents who fought to secure a decent job also fought for their children so they could have better opportunities and resources to be able to achieve success. A core component of defending educational opportunities has been to advocate for bilingual education in order to facilitate the transition of Spanish-speaking children. We explore how Puerto Ricans in Chicago founded community organizations to support themselves and describe the development of Puerto Rican communities throughout Illinois. Examining the Puerto Rican riots of 1966 and the creation of Paseo Boricua reveal how Puerto Ricans have built community in Chicago. We also pay attention to cities outside of Chicago to get a glimpse into how people form identity and community in spaces where there are not clear ethnic enclaves but are significant numbers of Puerto Ricans. We provide snapshots of Puerto Ricans living in Elgin, Joliet, Aurora, Waukegan, Cicero, Des Plaines, Peoria, Bloomington-Normal, Champaign-Urbana, Decatur, Springfield, and Carbondale. We also highlight how Puerto Ricans in all of Illinois were able to activate their social capital and political connections to unite and send emergency supplies and collect donations to help rebuild Puerto Rico after Hurricane Maria's devastation.

Puerto Ricans have made significant contributions to Illinois through their hard work and dedication to their families and by participating in the social, political, and cultural life of their communities. Puerto Ricans, like other racial and ethnic groups in the state, represent the future of the country and Illinois.

2

ISLAND PARADOX: *PUERTO RICO, PUERTO POBRE* (RICH PORT, POOR PORT)

In this chapter we offer a brief overview of the history of Puerto Rico as a backdrop to understanding how U.S. colonialism is connected to the migration of Puerto Ricans to the United States. Spain colonized Puerto Rico in 1493 when Columbus reached the island on his second voyage to the New World. When Illinois was founded in 1818, Puerto Rico had been under Spanish control for over three centuries. In the first part of this chapter we offer a sense of what constituted Puerto Rican culture and society at the time of the U.S. invasion in 1898. In order to understand Puerto Rican identity today, it is essential to understand how Puerto Ricans developed a national identity through centuries of Spanish influence and colonization. Our account of this early history is not exhaustive; rather, we focus on key points to examine the colonial conditions that Puerto Ricans encountered as "colonial subjects" of Spain.[1] The spirit of rebellion that ushered independence revolutions in the Americas was evident in Puerto Rico most forcefully in 1868, El Grito de Lares, as the uprising is known, did not result in the liberation of Puerto Rico from Spanish control.

In 1898, thirty years after El Grito de Lares, Puerto Rico, Cuba, and the Philippines found themselves in the crosshairs of one of the most significant moments in the nineteenth century, the Spanish-American War. The United States, a nation with imperial desires of its own, viewed these acquisitions with a great deal of enthusiasm and interest.[2] Eventually, Cuba and the Philippines were declared independent, but Puerto Rico remained under U.S. control. The U.S. colonialization of Puerto Rico had (and continues to have) profound consequences for Puerto Ricans across social classes. But it was the working class and working poor who felt the brunt of the economic policies implemented by the new colonial power as it sought to transform Puerto Rico to serve U.S. interests. For over a century, working-class and working-poor Puerto Ricans have used migration as a survival strategy to resolve the contradictions of their colonial condition. In the second part of this chapter we address the modernization program implemented under the auspices of colonial power in the middle decades of the twentieth century. The modernization program, popularly known as Operación Manos a la Obra (Operation Bootstrap), deepened colonial control of Puerto Rico and institutionalized the migration of Puerto Ricans as a source of cheap labor to address labor shortages existing in the United States at the time. Migration is how Puerto Ricans resolve the consequences of the colonialization process. Puerto Ricans have left en masse for well-known destinations like New York and Chicago and also new destinations.

Paradoxically, under the auspices of Operation Bootstrap, Puerto Rico was transformed from an agricultural to an industrial economy, yet the island also experienced massive migrations. Migration was promoted by the island's intellectual elite and U.S. economic interests as a way to make the modernization program a model worthy of exporting to other parts of the world. From

Fig. 2.1. Christopher Columbus landing in Santo Domingo. Artwork by John Vanderlyn; courtesy of GoodFreePhotos at https://www.goodfreephotos.com.

the 1950s to the 1970s, a substantial number of Puerto Ricans left for the United States, and many of those wound up in Illinois. The modernization program came with a change in status of the island, akin to a cosmetic reconstitution of coloniality. The status is also still somewhat paradoxical: Free Associated State, or in Spanish, Estado Libre Asociado. For readers intrigued with how Puerto Ricans have addressed the status issue, we offer a brief section that describes the most recent plebiscites about the question of status. The last part of this chapter discusses the economic crisis that has swept Puerto Rico in the first decades of the twenty-first century and the socioeconomic problems created by Hurricanes Irma and Maria as the island convulses into an uncertain future. Migration remains a way to resolve the present situation facing Puerto Ricans across social classes. Puerto Rico is today, more than ever, "a nation on the move," as Jorge Duany calls it.[3] The 2008 economic crisis and the natural disasters that followed have added more points of departure and destinations to the Puerto Rican diaspora.

Puerto Rico, Spanish Colony: A Brief Overview

For many years Puerto Rico has been a popular tourist destination in the Caribbean. In fact, tourism represented a significant source of income until the 2017 storms nearly destroyed the island's infrastructure and tourism nearly collapsed. The natural beauty and architectural legacy dating back to Spanish colonialism make the island a favorite of beach bums and history buffs. Journalist Nelson Denis writes in the opening pages of his book, "In the sun-splashed paradise of Puerto Rico, you can lie on a beach in the morning, hike through the rainforest during the day, and spend the evening exploring the ancient walls of a colonial city."[4] Old San Juan is still today one of the best-kept colonial towns in the Americas. Tour guides casually describe the story of the blue cobblestones that today make up the roadways of Old San Juan. One myth is that these bluestones were used by the Spanish conquistadores as ballast for their ship on their voyage to the island. The forts of San Felipe del Morro and Castillo San Cristóbal—both designated as U.S. National Parks—are silent architectural testimonies to the legacy of Spanish colonialism as well. They are military fortifications that today speak to the importance of the island of San Juan Bautista—the Spanish name for Puerto Rico—to the colonial power. These massive structures hide a legacy of exploitation and subordination that took place on the island under Spanish control.

Traveling around the island might also reveal what is left of the coffee and sugarcane plantations that enriched the coffers of the Spanish Crown. In the mountain region, there is a small museum where the lives of Taíno Indians, the Indigenous people who populated the land before Spanish colonization, have been reconstructed for museum viewers. Observers can see replicas of their *bohíos* (housing structures), pottery, and way of life. A more curious tourist might then wander back to the San Juan area and visit the town of Loíza, Puerto Rico's most celebrated black enclave, to gaze at the ethnic and racial mixing that today constitutes Puerto Rican culture and identity.

The colonization of the Americas by Spain is now an epic history of conquest, territorial expansion, and transculturation. The Taíno Indians lived on the island they called Borinquén before Spanish colonization in 1493. We know that they lived in small communities, which they called *yucayeques*, along the coast and that there was a rigid gendered division of labor. Though men held positions of power known as *caciques* (chiefs), women were not excluded from leadership roles. The historical record is consistent that the Spanish invasion and colonization of the island decimated the Indigenous population,[5] as many Taíno Indians died of illnesses brought by the Spanish. The conquistadores also enslaved Taínos and forced them to work, extracting the mineral riches of the island. African slaves were also transported to the island as a source of cheap labor from the mid-1500s until 1873, when slavery was abolished.

The Spanish colonial power allowed significant European immigration to the island. In keeping with patterns found in other parts of the Americas, the Spanish colonial empire was not opposed to racial mixing between Europeans, Indians, and Africans. Although marriage as an institution was a privilege of the elite, the sexual exploitation of Indian and African women produced phenotypes that can be seen in the racial diversity that exists on the island today. In 1899, when the U.S. Census Bureau first attempted to conduct a census of the population in Puerto Rico, the island's racial diversity gave census takers considerable trouble.[6] The United States may offer a point of contrast. In the United States, color and status shaped relations between Europeans and black populations, resulting in the construction of a "color line."

It is important to clarify that racial mixing in Puerto Rico did not entail racial equality.[7] Race mattered then and still matters today in Puerto Rico, but one may not be aware of how much it matters because popular constructions of Puerto Rican identity have employed the notion of Puerto Ricans as descendants of Indian, Spanish, and African heritage, all placed on this mythical, even field.[8] Duany calls this "the canonized discourse on national identity."[9] This imagining of the cultural and racial mixing has become a celebrated quality of Puerto Rican identity. In fact, these notions were repackaged for the 1950s modernization program as *la gran familia puertoriqueña* (the great Puerto Rican family).[10]

This canonized discourse of nationality has been deployed by Puerto Ricans in the diaspora to construct a coherent narrative of national identity as a political affirmation against systematic racialization that they encounter as migrants in the United States. Murals have become a way for Puerto Ricans in U.S. communities to depict and celebrate this aspect of Puerto Rican history and instill pride in their communities. (See figure 2.2.) The history of how that racial mixing came into existence, however, is much more complicated. Puerto Rican scholar Yarma Velázquez Vargas writes that Puerto Ricans have inherited "an understanding of

Fig. 2.2. Cristian Roldan's mural at the corner of Division Street and Washtenaw Avenue, Chicago, of (*left to right*) Taíno Indian, Spanish, and African roots of Puerto Rico. Photograph by Ivis García.

race that was mediated by two colonial regimes, first Spain and then the United States."[11]

The Spanish colonial empire was deeply patriarchal, paternalistic, oppressive, and strictly hierarchical. Across social classes, women were socialized to be "obedient daughters, faithful wives, and devoted mothers."[12] Laws enforced these cultural values. For example, the Spanish Civil Code gave absolute power to the husband as head of the family and administrator of family property. The code also gave the father authority over children. Elaborate laws regulated inheritance, marriage, adultery, and even widowhood. Most of these laws limited the rights of women. As a colony of Spain, the Catholic Church was an institution that influenced family life in significant ways. These social norms guided family life for several centuries.

When gold and other mineral resources were extracted from Puerto Rico, the island became one of the most profitable in the Spanish Empire. The Spanish introduced sugar to Puerto Rico in 1515. By 1887 sugar was the island's primary agricultural industry, but it had a significant coffee industry as well. By the time that the United States arrived on the island in 1898, 446 sugar mills were in operation.

Fig. 2.3. Familia Hernández, including coauthor Ivis García's grandmother as a teenager, on a coffee farm in Lares, Puerto Rico, 1938. Photograph by Juan Heriberto Hernández Arana.

In an agricultural colony like Puerto Rico, social class, race, and gender mattered a great deal. Puerto Rico had a small but very wealthy upper class, known as hacendados (or small-scale owners of farmland), a small middle class, and a considerable mass of working-poor and low-income families, known as *jornaleros* (day laborers). Historian Eileen J. Suárez Findlay explains that "in nineteenth-century Puerto Rico, as in much of Latin America, concepts of honor were based on gendered and racialized beliefs about social ordering, appropriate behavior, and personal worth."[13] For elites, honor was premised on the sexual control of women and the exclusion of poor people and blacks. At the time of U.S. colonization of Puerto Rico, a small but somewhat vocal class of middle-class feminists and liberal activists had demanded social reforms from the Spanish colonial elite. Their advocacy expanded educational opportunities for women and opportunities for political activism, including the right to vote, but these efforts did not materialize. Puerto Rican women had to wait several decades for the right to vote, which they received in 1929, nine years after women in the United States were granted voting privileges.

A few years before U.S. colonization, Spain had instituted concessions to grant more political and economic autonomy to the island, partly because of the many revolts against the colonial power. The grievances against Spain were articulated by many during El Grito de Lares, but one writer in particular, Ramón Emeterio Betances, became the most well-known critic. Betances was a native of Cabo Rojo and a celebrated patriot. He wrote passionately about Spanish oppression and despotism. He observed how, for more than three centuries, Puerto Ricans had paid taxes to the Spanish Crown, but infrastructure on the island was lacking. The colonial empire had also failed to develop schools to educate the Puerto Rican population. Instead, educational opportunities existed only for the elite. The grievances were many because Spain had done too little, too late.

In contrast to most countries in Latin America, Central America, and the Caribbean that waged successful wars of independence from Spain, Puerto Rico remains the only country that never achieved full independence. Instead, Puerto Rico went from one colonial power to the next. The island that the U.S. Army encountered in 1898 was sparsely populated, with about 900,000 people, and the scars of over three centuries of Spanish colonization were visible to the most casual observer. Landless agricultural workers lived close to each other in the coastal areas or scattered throughout the mountainous interior, inaccessible by roads. Social class and racial differences were also a source of confusion for the new occupying empire. As a multiracial society, the lack of overt racial segregation between racial groups mystified (and continues to mystify) Americans who were accustomed to a dichotomous racial world. The project of the new colonial power became not only economic incorporation but, equally important, hegemonic control through changing cultural practices. In the next section, we address the impact of the U.S. colonization of Puerto Rico.

Puerto Rico, U.S. Colony: The First Sixty Years (1898–1958)

What is essential to know about the 1898 U.S. colonization of Puerto Rico? The historical record shows that although U.S. troops invaded Puerto Rico on July 25, 1898, through the town of Guánica, a sleepy little town on the southern coast, the official transfer from one colonial power to the other did not take place until the Treaty of Paris on December 10, 1898. It was then that Spain officially ceded Puerto Rico, Guam, and the Philippines to the United States.[14] The Treaty of Paris stipulated that the U.S. Congress would determine the civil rights and political status of Puerto Rico. Newspapers and magazines spent considerable time and effort in Puerto Rico documenting the U.S. occupation of the island, although they did not use that term. The editor of *National Geographic* wrote in 1924, "No other nation in Puerto Rico has ever created a finer record in colonial administration than our own United States."[15]

The prevalent view of the new colonizing power as evidenced in the books, popular magazines, and cartoons of the time was that Puerto Ricans were a primitive, poor, dependent, childlike people. They delighted in showing the oppression of the Spanish colonists and portraying Americans as the saviors. Suárez Findlay writes that politicians and pundits in the United States proclaimed the new colonial power as a great modernizing agent and a benevolent colonial ruler.[16] Puerto Ricans perceived the U.S. economy, political structure, and cultural practices as emblematic of modernity, and some embraced the reforms they introduced with determination. Yet modernity was an elusive trope that did not materialize until the middle decades of the twentieth century, several decades after the U.S. occupation. For its part, the new colonial empire justified its presence in Puerto Rico "through

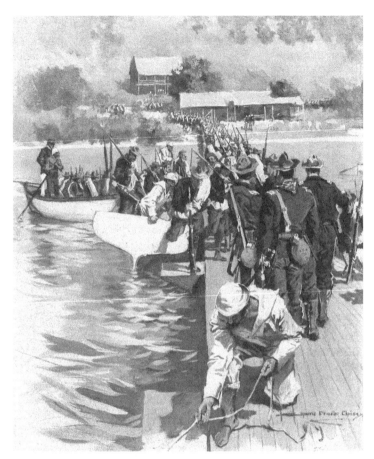

Fig. 2.4. The landing at Guánica, Puerto Rico. Artwork by Howard Chandler Christy; in *Harper's Pictorial History of the War with Spain*, vol. 2 (New York: Harper and Brothers, 1899), 394.

gendered and racialized assertions about Puerto Ricans' alleged lack of modernity and unfitness for self-governance."[17]

The managing of the colony started with a brief period when the military government ruled, but the incorporation of Puerto Rico took place swiftly. The Foraker Act of 1900 and the Jones-Saffron Act of 1917 helped accomplish this. The Foraker Act reconstituted Puerto Rico's political system under the aegis of the new colonial power. Judicial and executive authority of the island resided in a presidentially appointed governor. All government officials were appointed by the U.S. government, including the governor. The Foraker Act also made provisions about landownership, restricting land plots to five hundred acres or less. But these laws were not enforced, which made it possible for U.S. sugar corporations to take over large swaths of Puerto Rican land. The lack of enforcement, along with the lack of transportation to mountainous areas and a preference for sugar production and exportation in the form of U.S. agricultural subsidies, contributed to the corporate development of plantations. This is how independent coffee growers were dispossessed of their land and joined the ranks of *jornaleros*, the agricultural proletariat. These policies resulted in even greater economic despair for working-class and poor families around the island.

The Foraker Act imposed the U.S. political and economic system on Puerto Rico. The U.S. Supreme Court then wrestled with the paradox inherent in the colonization of Puerto Rico. In fact, the court set the legal precedents regarding the political status of the island in a series of opinions known as the "Insular Cases."[18] For example, *Downes v. Bidwell* in 1901 defined the status of the island as a territory of the United States but not part of it. In 1901, some of the Supreme Court justices who had ruled in *Plessy v. Ferguson*—the historical case that institutionalized Jim Crow segregation—ruled that Puerto Rico was not fit to be part of the United States. In other words, the status of the island was defined as an "unincorporated territory," belonging to but not part of the United States. Congress resolved this paradox by imposing U.S. citizenship in 1917 through the Jones-Saffron Act, a task that completed the incorporation of the island as a colonial possession. A week after Hurricane Maria in 2017, when it was clear that the preparations Puerto Ricans had taken were inadequate to meet the devastation that had followed the storm, San Juan mayor Carmen Yulín Cruz stated in a press conference: "We are American citizens; we can't be left to die."[19] Texas and Florida had also been hit by the devastating hurricanes Harvey and Irma in the 2017 hurricane season, yet within a week there had been sufficient relief for those states.

We note that U.S. citizenship created a new paradox: How can Puerto Ricans born in Puerto Rico be U.S. citizens while Puerto Rico is still not a state? The paradox deepens when you consider the meaning of citizenship for Puerto Ricans. The Jones-Saffron Act of 1917 established citizenship as a birthright for Puerto Ricans. What does that mean? It means that all 3.5 million Puerto Ricans living in Puerto Rico are U.S. citizens. It means that Puerto Ricans on the island vote in national presidential primaries, but they do not vote for the U.S. president as those living on the mainland do. It means that male Puerto Ricans aged eighteen to twenty-five are subject to the draft for military service, like their U.S. counterparts. In fact, it is well known that Puerto Ricans have participated in all theaters of war, including World War I, World War II, Korea, Vietnam, Kuwait, Kosovo, Afghanistan, and Iraq.[20] The 65th Infantry Regiment was a unit of the U.S. Army composed entirely of Puerto Ricans. They served during the Korean War and are popularly known as the "Borinqueneers."

Ironically, 2017 marked the centennial of the Jones-Saffron Act, and in an essay written to reflect upon this historic event, Nelson A. Denis argued, "After one hundred years of citizenship, Puerto Ricans know that their homeland was invaded, its wealth exploited, its patriots persecuted and jailed. . . . For Puerto Rico, the legacy of the American Century is a schizophrenic existence. Puerto Ricans

Fig. 2.5. Borinqueneer Jaime Hernández, brother of Ivis García's grandmother. Photographer unknown; Ivis García, personal collection.

are both citizens and colonial subjects of the United States. They have a legislature whose will can be vetoed by Congress. They have been conscripted to take up arms and die on foreign shores for the United States, but they are not permitted to vote for its president." Yet another irony connecting the past and present is that in 1898 a major hurricane, San Ciriaco, destroyed the island and the coffee bean crop. Denis observed, "American hurricane relief was strange. The United States sent no money. Instead, the following year, it outlawed all Puerto Rican currency and declared the island's peso, with a global value equal to the U.S. dollar, to be worth only sixty American cents. Then in 1901, a colonial land tax known as the Hollander Bill forced many small farmers to mortgage their lands with U.S. banks."[21]

The parallels with today's events are rather striking. Hurricane relief was strange then, and it is still now. Newspaper reports and our families' testimonies indicate that, in the hours and days after Hurricane Maria, the United States did not offer any immediate help. It was Puerto Ricans themselves who mobilized to clean roads, assist, and secure food. It would take weeks for any amount of significant help to arrive, and when it did, it was riddled with political strings and wrapped in paper towels. Figure 2.6

Fig. 2.6. Taína
under water.
Photograph by
Ivis García.

shows a painted door in Paseo Boricua that represents a critique of President Donald Trump throwing paper towels in Puerto Rico to hurricane victims. The Taína woman represents Mayor Carmen Yulín Cruz, drowning, begging for help. The response from the federal government was slow and insufficient. For example, a woman in Cabo Rojo who lost the roof of her house and requested help from FEMA told Maura that it took over two months for FEMA to come and appraise her home. Even though she was told she qualified for a loan and was approved for one after she applied, by April 2018 she still had not received the funds.

The first decades of the U.S. occupation of Puerto Rico defy easy categorization. The spelling of the island's name was changed in federal documents from "Puerto Rico" to "Porto Rico" so that English speakers could pronounce it. English was imposed as the official language of instruction on the island until 1948, when Puerto Ricans were able to elect their first governor.[22] The Americanization of the island was also expedited by the presence of various Protestant denominations doing missionary work. Religious groups served to undermine Catholicism and to expedite the promotion of American cultural values and beliefs. The economic changes imposed by the United States singularly wreaked havoc for Puerto Rican families across the social class spectrum. Hacendados found themselves near extinction due to social and economic policies that expropriated their land and political power.[23] Many landowning families lost their land and moved to cities. Daughters in these families were encouraged to pursue education and professional work, leading to the rise of a small class of professional women. Poor and working-class women became integrated into a gender-segregated labor market that was closely related to the needs of U.S. colonial capitalism.[24] Poor women also worked as tobacco strippers, created home needlework, and made straw hats. In the tobacco industry, for example, women worked as leaf strippers, sorters, and packers, work that took excruciatingly long hours and was poorly paid and performed under dangerous conditions. Needlework was also very exploitative, and wages never rose above subsistence levels.[25] Puerto Rican feminist Marcia Rivera observes that U.S. colonialism opened the spectrum of employment opportunities for women while, at the same time, it increased their exploitation as workers. In fact, this is the context that propelled women's involvement in the labor movement. Working-class women "rejected views of feminine fragility, moral superiority, and passivity that were attributed to women by other social classes."[26]

Historians have documented how both needle and tobacco women workers organized labor unions and participated in labor strikes to challenge women's inequality and exploitation as both women and workers. For example, when New Deal legislation threatened to wipe out the home needlework industry because it allegedly did not adhere to U.S. standards, women needleworkers challenged island trade unionists and fought for their right to do homework in the context of their social role as homemakers.[27] Home needleworkers, according to Eileen Boris, defended their work as the only means by which they could provide their families with food.[28] In other words, it was precisely their roles as breadwinners that women workers used to demand higher wages and better working conditions. In the end, New Deal legislation upgraded standards for women needleworkers on paper, but it failed them by not honoring their desire to hold on to the home as their workplace.

Fig. 2.7. Women in a needlework factory in San Juan, Puerto Rico. Photograph by Jack Delano. Library of Congress, U.S. Farm Security Administration/Office of War Information/ Office of Emergency Management/ Resettlement Administration Black & White Photographs. Reproduction number LC-USF34–9058-C.

The rise of a capitalist-based sugarcane plantation economy displaced families whose only means of survival became internal migration. At the turn of the twentieth century, the island coastal regions and mountainous (coffee-growing) areas became points of departure for families moving to the growing urban centers, tobacco farms, and other small manufacturing industries.[29] When employment in urban centers proved limited, Puerto Rican men, in particular, were recruited to do agricultural work abroad, such as in Hawaii, Cuba, and the Dominican Republic. Eventually, Puerto Rican men and women were compelled to migrate to the United States, in particular to the East Coast industrial centers, to meet acute labor shortages due to World War I. This is how New York City became the destination for Puerto Ricans.

Historian Virginia E. Sánchez Korrol's book *From* Colonia *to Community: The History of Puerto Ricans in New York City, 1917–1948*, now a classic in the field of Puerto Rican studies, describes how Puerto Ricans moved to New York City and developed small *colonias* (ethnic communities) throughout the city. She writes that the mechanization of sugar displaced workers and disrupted traditional family patterns, forcing many to leave for New York City. These newcomers encountered a hostile and racially segregated city. She observed that, "while Puerto Rican *colonias* were simultaneously developing in various areas of the city, it was the Harlem community which would assume the lead as the largest and most significant of all the inter-wars settlements."[30]

To invoke Spanish Harlem today is to recall a long history of struggle and survival in the city. The growth of a professional and commercial sector was outstanding in these early *colonias*. In these densely populated communities, the business sector and cultural organizations they supported provided newcomers with a way to affirm their identity to deal with the prejudice and discrimination they encountered. Sánchez Korrol points out that women played a critical role in the formation of these *colonias* as they worked to sustain families by their labor in and out of the family. They also tried to maintain family values in keeping with Puerto Rican culture.

Social scientists in both Puerto Rico and the United States agree that within the first four decades of U.S. control, political and economic changes in Puerto Rico had created social dislocations, widespread poverty, and destitution, problems that affected the well-being of working-class and poor families. Added to these problems was also the political repression that Puerto Ricans encountered as they pressed the new colonial power along political issues. These problems became even more marked in Puerto Rico in the Great Depression years, when the standard of living worsened for families across the social spectrum.[31] Juan González describes how his family lived through such desperate years.[32] His grandmother, who had already lost five children to disease, became a widow, and when she realized that her odd jobs could not provide enough money to support her remaining children, she gave them away to friends, hoping to save them from starvation. He writes, "The psychological scars left in all of them by their long childhood separation were so deep that, decades later, after they'd all been reunited and the family had moved to New York City, the González brothers and sisters never spoke openly of those times."[33] The first president of the University of Puerto Rico, Jaime Benítez, described the decade of the 1930s: "We find that by 1936 we had hit a new low. . . . [We] were puzzled, distressed and angered by the sad and unacceptable plight of our society. We oscillated between frustration and revulsion. At times, incensed by our own helplessness, we felt the compulsion to close our eyes and charge. Some of the best among us did."[34]

Historians Kal Wagenheim and Olga Jiménez de Wagenheim described the period between World War I and World War II as grim years for Puerto Rico. At the most basic level, Puerto Ricans faced starvation, disease, and malnutrition, among other social problems. Internal migration to the growing *arrabales* (squatter settlements) in San Juan had become a way of life for a range of social groups to address the poverty they faced. Luis Muñoz Marín, who would later become one of the architects of the 1950s economic development model that transformed the island from an industrial agricultural economy to a manufacturing one, observed how inequality between the rich and poor threatened the country. Ironically, he was critical of the role the United States had played in creating inequality, calling Puerto Rico "Uncle Sam's second largest sweat-shop."[35]

A few decades later, under the auspices of the Operation Bootstrap development model, Muñoz Marín invited U.S. investors to the island to develop the prototype of what is recognized today as the foundation of globalization processes: export processing zones. Other educated Puerto Ricans, like Jaime Benítez, Pedro Albizu Campos, and Luisa Capetillo, analyzed the social problems that Puerto Ricans faced and mobilized to address them in different ways. Capetillo, for example, a pioneering feminist and labor organizer, called attention to the plight of women workers and helped organize labor unions. Albizu Campos, a Harvard-educated Puerto Rican who became the leader of the nationalist movement in Puerto Rico, called on Puerto Ricans to resist U.S. colonialism and to take arms to fight what he termed "Yankee imperialism." For that, he was jailed and tortured for a significant part of his life. This flurry of activism and national affirmation was met with violence and colonial repression, culminating with the 1937 Ponce Massacre, where police shot at a crowd of civilians, murdering nineteen and injuring another two hundred people.

Fig. 2.8. Painting of the Honorable Luis Muñoz Marín, first elected governor of Puerto Rico. Painting by Estrella Díaz; Wikimedia Commons, https://commons.wikimedia.org/wiki/File:Luis_Mu%C3%B1oz_Mar%C3%ADn.jpg.

Luis Muñoz Marín rose through the ranks of Puerto Rico's political system to propose a form of nationalism that did not seek to cut ties with the United States; instead, it attempted to reconcile—some may say reform—those ties. He was a charismatic leader with a nicely packaged motto: Pan, Tierra, y Libertad (Bread, Land, and Freedom). Muñoz Marín founded the Popular Democratic Party, the party that also reconstituted Puerto Rico's political status as "Estado Libre Asociado." The new political status of the island indeed revealed the paradoxical status of Puerto Rico: Free Associated State. Political optimism accompanied the changes in the political structure of the island as citizens now had a Puerto Rican constitution and could elect their governor. For their part, administrators in Washington were also interested in transforming the colonial model as a way to export the virtues of export processing zones as a form of development.

A generation of Puerto Rican intellectuals helped design the industrialization and modernization program, Operation Bootstrap, which we will discuss in some detail next. But, it was Luis Muñoz Marín, the charismatic leader and promoter, who shared the message of progress and modernization with the masses. He presented himself as a benevolent father who cared deeply for his national family. As a father figure, he promised to change relations with the colonial power by demanding respect. The tropes of *mejorarse* (better oneself) and *buscar ambiente* (searching for a better life) became the popular mantras of the era and were deployed by Puerto Ricans across social classes as a way to think about modernity.[36] The ideas of *mejorarse* and *buscar ambiente* also pushed men and women to leave the island in droves. Many went to New York City, where the early *colonias* had become large community settlements. This movement is known today in the historical archives of the Puerto Rican diaspora as the "great post–World War II migration." Another popular name is the "great airborne migration," since this movement overlapped with the age of airplane travel as a form of mass transportation. Between 1950 and 1960 the number of Puerto Ricans in the United States rose from 226,110 to 892,513. By 1960, over 68 percent of all Puerto Ricans in the United States were living in New York City. These figures also included the number of Puerto Ricans who would later become known as "Nuyoricans," Puerto Ricans born in New York City. Chicago became a port of destination during subsequent decades, although at a smaller scale. Table 2.1 offers a detailed description of how the Puerto Rican community has grown since 1950.

Operation Bootstrap, Modernization, and Migration (1959–Present)

It would be easy to speculate that Hurricane Maria pushed the

Table 2.1. Puerto Rican population in Chicago and New York City

Year	United States	Chicago	Percentage in U.S.	NYC	Percentage in U.S.
1950	226,110	255	0.1	187,420	82.9
1960	892,513	32,371	3.6	612,574	68.6
1970	1,391,463	72,223	5.2	817,712	58.8
1980	2,013,945	112,074	5.6	860,552	42.7
1990	2,651,815	119,866	4.5	896,763	33.8
2000	3,406,178	113,055	3.3	789,172	23.2
2010	4,623,716	102,854	2.2	723,621	15.7

Source: Table created by Ivis García, from U.S. Census of Population and Housing (1950–1990) and U.S. Decennial Census.

island back to where it was before Puerto Rico's modernization program was implemented. When we talked to relatives on the island and read the reports of the loss of infrastructure, rising levels of unemployment, and the stress of living day to day without food and water, we recognized that this assessment was not far from the truth. For many, the aftermath of Hurricane Maria felt like life in the 1940s and 1950s in Puerto Rico.

In the 1950s, under the auspices of the U.S. government and transnational U.S.-owned corporations, Puerto Rico underwent a significant change in its political economy, institutionalizing migration as a survival strategy for Puerto Ricans across social classes. Operación Manos a la Obra was intended to attract capital and jobs to the island to improve the employment prospects and general well-being of Puerto Ricans. In fact, Puerto Rico ushered in the global age of export production as a model for economic development. The government granted incentives to private investors, such as tax exemptions, and subsidized factory space to lure capital to the island. In the 1960s, Puerto Rico was praised around the world for having achieved the elusive goals of modernization and industrialization within less than a generation.

In fact, "in the 1960s, Puerto Rico became the showcase of the Caribbean, tempting other countries in the hemisphere to follow its example and endorse a free enterprise form of capitalism."[37] Indeed, there was a lot of progress and modernization in Puerto Rico in the 1960s and 1970s. Sociologist Zaire Dinzey-Flores points out, "An injection of economic development in the 1950s made the island feel more like the U.S. than its impoverished past. Operation Bootstrap began to modernize Puerto Rico at a whirlwind pace. It brought schools, public housing, electricity, manufacturing, television. . . modern infrastructure, [and] growing social services."[38]

Economic indicators support that story. According to Jorge Duany, "Per capita Gross Domestic Product (GDP), measured in current dollars, practically quintupled, from $278 in 1950 to $1,353 in 1970."[39] There was also a modest decline in unemployment. The rise of the Puerto Rican middle class—primarily achieved through increased earnings and education—was a singular achievement that deserves praise. The modernization program transformed the island into a consumer society. Puerto Rican sociologist Luz del Alba Acevedo offers an intimate portrait of that progress when she writes, "I was born in the era of Operation Bootstrap. . . . I witnessed the rapid and dramatic transformation of Puerto Rico into an industrial and urban center. . . . I did not realize that I was a daughter of Bootstrap until I looked back on my life from the perspective of a migrant."[40]

A house in an *urbanization* (suburban development) was the dream of the growing urban middle class, while a *parcela* (small plot of land) was the dream of the rural working class in the rest of the island. McDonald's, Burger King, and Kentucky Fried Chicken sprung up alongside traditional Puerto Rican cuisine. The contradictions of the colonial model and the new industrialization model were already evident in the 1950s, continuing to reinforce Puerto Rican women and men as a source of cheap labor for the export processing zones in Puerto Rico and for factories and corporations in the mainland. The modernization program resulted in the feminization of the labor force and the institutionalization of migration as a way to survive for Puerto Ricans.

The first stage of the program was labor-intensive light manufacturing. Given the kinds of industries attracted to the island (specifically export-oriented manufacturing), the result was a strong demand for women workers.[41] In the 1950s a survey of Puerto Rican industrial workers established that 79 percent of the women surveyed found their first job in a factory.[42] Puerto Rican writer Esmeralda Santiago tells the story of her mother, who felt compelled to take on outside employment to provide for her family, mainly when her husband was negligent. Culturally, working women encountered stigma and disapproval. Santiago captures her mother's experiences with factory employment: "*Mami* was one of the first mothers in Macún to have a job outside the home. The *barrio* looked at us with new eyes. Gone was the bland acceptance of people minding their own business, replaced by a visible, angry resentment that became gossip, and taunts and name-calling in the school yard. . . . *Papi* seemed to have the same opinion about *Mami*'s job as the neighbor."[43]

According to feminist scholar Palmira Rios, "The disproportionate presence of women in Puerto Rico's manufacturing sector is not an aberration or a chance occurrence but an inherent feature of a developing strategy that has been part of the World War II restructuring of the world economy."[44] More than half of all the jobs created between 1960 and 1980 went to women. Acevedo states that younger, more educated Puerto Rican women workers went into better-paying white-collar jobs in the government, while older, less educated women went into the declining manufacturing industries and low-paying jobs.[45] While the industrialization program incorporated women as workers, the surplus labor (that is, mostly men) was absorbed into the U.S. labor market via migration. Although women's work contributed to the well-being of their families, rising costs of living and declining wages made the economic situation of Puerto Rican working families precarious. Falling employment forced families to find ways to make money to provide for children in areas outside the formal sector. Many unemployed people sought income in the informal sector, including subsistence production, bartering, occupying the land, illegal activities such as crime or drug dealing, and producing goods and services for sale to others.[46] Another result of low wages and high costs of living was the dependency on federal welfare programs for survival, mainly food stamps.

In the 1970s, the island shifted from light manufacturing to capital intensive manufacturing, such as oil refining and petrochemical industries. The 1973 international oil crisis ended this phase of Puerto Rico's development rather abruptly. This is also the time when living standards in Puerto Rico began to erode. Anthropologist Jorge Duany describes the limits of the development model and the 1970s crisis: "The year 1974 marked the beginning of the island's economic deceleration. Annual rates of economic growth declined to an average 3.3 percent during the 1970s and 2.1 percent during the 1980s. Unemployment soared, and wages stagnated."[47] It was evident that the growing costs of labor, energy, and transportation made the island less competitive in the global marketplace. Puerto Ricans dealt with economic stagnation the only way they knew how, by migrating to the traditional points of destination—New York City, Chicago, and Philadelphia, among other cities.

To maintain Puerto Rico's role in the global economy as a tax haven for global corporations, Congress passed in 1976 what is known as "Section 936" in the U.S. Internal Revenue Code, allowing U.S. transnational corporations exemptions from paying taxes on profits reported in Puerto Rico. According to economist Emilio Pantojas-García, the major pharmaceutical corporations took advantage of these exemptions, and they moved their factories to Puerto Rico in full force. The town of Barceloneta became known as "Ciudad Viagra" (Viagra City) since it is the home of Pfizer, the company that produces this drug. Such "miracle drugs" were manufactured on the island and transferred from the island to U.S. markets.[48]

Juan González helps to contextualize what this meant for the average Puerto Rican: "One federal study concluded each pharmaceutical worker in Puerto Rico produced $1.5 million in value for his or her employer in 2002."[49] Puerto Rico is ranked as the most profitable place for investments, above Mexico, China, Brazil, and India. Yet on average, Puerto Rican incomes have remained stagnant. While Puerto Rico is a haven for multinational corporations, the federal government spends nearly $10 billion annually in welfare and transfer payments to address the poverty facing Puerto Rican families. In other words, the average Puerto Rican has not benefited from the wealth created on the island. In 1996, Congress ended Section 936 due in part to changing notions of corporate welfare. Congress offered a ten-year window to phase out the corporate taxes by December 31, 2005. The consequences were disastrous for Puerto Rican workers. This is now known as the beginning of "la crisis Boricua," the deterioration of work opportunities, rising unemployment, loss of public sector jobs, introduction of sales taxes, and rising public debt.[50]

At the turn of the millennium, a new demographic reality emerged: more Puerto Ricans were living in the United States than in Puerto Rico.[51] Put another way, new points of destination have been added to the traditional places of migration. As tax exemptions were eliminated, many corporations left, and the government, another significant source of employment, turned to bonds and loans as a way to meet its obligations. In 2006 Puerto Rico fell into a recession and economic decline with profound consequences for Puerto Ricans across social classes.[52]

Since these changes were implemented, Puerto Ricans have been leaving the island in record numbers. The exodus of the population continued to gain momentum due to the island's high

Fig. 2.9. Painted notice in Paseo Boricua protesting the public debt. Photograph by Ivis García.

Fig. 2.10.
Painted notice
in Paseo Boricua
protesting the
public debt and
relating it to
outmigration.
Photograph by
Ivis García.

unemployment (above 15 percent) and the near economic collapse of its economy, which holds more than $70 billion in public debt.[53] Beginning in 2005, as demonstrated in table 2.2, the number of Puerto Ricans living stateside has exceeded the number of those residing in Puerto Rico. The great migration of the 1950s had always been the benchmark concerning the numbers of people who were pushed by the industrialization model and propelled by job opportunities. Yet the movement taking place in the first two decades of the millennium rival the 1950s great migration in numbers. Since the turn of the new millennium, many more Puerto Ricans have been going to new destinations—like Florida—creating new *colonias*.[54] As table 2.3 shows, while in 1980 the state of New York had 49 percent of all Puerto Ricans in the United States, by 2015 that number had dropped to 25 percent, which is nearly identical to the percentage in Florida. As of 2021, Florida has more Puerto Ricans than the state of New York—where we find the oldest Puerto Rican community.[55] Figure 2.11 shows the top ten states for Puerto Rican population across the United States.

The Status Question

What exactly is the current status of Puerto Rico? Do Puerto Ricans have a say in determining their desired political status for the island? After more than 100 years of colonialization, Puerto Rico continues under the colonial grip of the United States. In fact,

Table 2.2. Puerto Rican population in Puerto Rico and the United States

Year	Puerto Rico	United States	Total
2005	3,668,730	3,781,317	7,450,047
	49%	51%	100%
2006	3,745,007	3,987,947	7,732,954
	48%	52%	100%
2007	3,765,840	4,120,205	7,886,045
	48%	52%	100%
2008	3,781,815	4,216,533	7,998,348
	47%	53%	100%
2009	3,784,396	4,426,738	8,211,134
	46%	54%	100%
2010	3,554,642	4,691,890	8,246,532
	43%	57%	100%
2011	3,542,571	4,885,294	8,427,865
	42%	58%	100%
2012	3,515,844	4,970,604	8,486,448
	41%	59%	100%
2013	3,466,804	5,138,109	8,604,913
	40%	60%	100%
2014	3,404,122	5,266,738	8,670,860
	39%	61%	100%
2015	3,329,046	5,372,759	8,701,805
	38%	62%	100%

Source: Table created by Ivis García, using selected population profile in Puerto Rico from the 2000 U.S. Decennial Census and American Community Survey 1-year estimates (2016)

Puerto Rico has now entered a new phase of colonial administration due to the congressional approval of what is known as the Puerto Rican Oversight, Management, and Economic Stability Act (also known as PROMESA), passed by Congress and signed by President Barack Obama in June 2016.[56] PROMESA created the Junta de Supervisión Fiscal, or Junta for short, which is a board to restructure Puerto Rico's debt, and has made recommendations to address the fiscal situation in Puerto Rico. The austerity measures implemented have been disastrous for Puerto Rican families across

Table 2.3. *U.S. states with the largest Puerto Rican population*

State	1980		1990		2000		2010		2015	
California	93,038	5%	131,998	5%	140,570	4%	189,945	4%	197,399	5%
Connecticut	88,361	4%	140,143	5%	194,443	6%	252,972	5%	280,070	6%
Illinois	129,165	6%	147,201	6%	157,851	5%	182,989	4%	187,159	4%
Florida	94,775	5%	240,673	9%	482,027	14%	847,550	18%	1,069,446	24%
Massachusetts	76,450	4%	146,015	6%	199,207	6%	266,125	6%	317,142	7%
New Jersey	243,540	12%	304,179	11%	366,788	11%	434,092	9%	487,972	11%
New York	986,389	49%	1,046,896	39%	1,050,293	31%	1,070,558	23%	1,084,872	25%
Ohio	32,442	2%	45,911	2%	66,269	2%	94,965	2%	122,908	3%
Pennsylvania	91,802	5%	143,872	5%	228,557	7%	366,082	8%	447,132	10%
Texas	22,938	1%	45,794	2%	69,504	2%	130,576	3%	183,658	4%
United States	2,013,945	100%	2,651,815	100%	3,406,178	100%	4,623,716	100%	4,377,758	100%

Source: Table created by Ivis García, from selected population profile in Puerto Rico and selected population profile in the United States, American Community Survey 1-year estimates (2015).

Fig. 2.11. Map of top ten states with the largest Puerto Rican population. Created by Ivis García, using data from the U.S. Census 2010.

social classes. As this book went to press, a private corporation took over the public electric company, resulting in widespread blackouts across Puerto Rico. The University of Puerto Rico's budget has also been subject to cuts and fiscal measures resulting in student protests. Mora and her colleagues argue that the austerity measures implemented by PROMESA could lead to the contraction of the economy, deepening "la crisis Boricua."[57] Most members of the board are not Puerto Ricans. The current executive director and interim revitalization coordinator is Natalie Jasresko, a woman of Ukrainian descent, raised in Naperville, Illinois.[58]

Puerto Ricans have exercised their right to determine the status question several times. Historically, there have been four general alternatives to the political status of Puerto Ricans: independence, statehood, commonwealth status (a territory according to the U.S. Constitution), and free association (a non-territorial option). Table 2.4 shows the percentage of votes in favor of each political status in five plebiscites categorized on the years of their occurrence: 1967, 1993, 1998, 2012, and 2017.

The first time Puerto Ricans evaluated their political status was in 1967 through a local referendum enacted by the Puerto Rican Legislative Assembly. At the time, the idea was to allow voters to validate or invalidate the commonwealth status, which had been

Table 2.4. Summary of percentage of votes in plebiscites in Puerto Rico on status

Political status	1967	1993	1998	2012[a]	2012[b]	2017
Territorial	N/A	N/A	N/A	46	N/A	N/A
Commonwealth	60.4	48.6	0.1	N/A	N/A	1.3
Non-territorial	N/A	N/A	N/A	54	N/A	N/A
Independence	0.6	4.4	2.5	N/A	5.5	1.5[d]
Statehood	39	46.3	46.5	N/A	61	97.13
Free association	N/A	N/A	0.3	N/A	33	1.5[d]
None of the above	N/A	N/A	50.3	N/A	N/A	N/A
Blank/ void ballots	N/A	N/A	0.3	26[c]	26[c]	N/A
Turnout rate	65.9	74	71.3	71	79	23

Source: Table adapted by Ivis García from "Puerto Rico Status Plebiscites," Wikipedia.

Notes: [a] Voters had two questions to vote on in the 2012 plebiscites. The first question was whether voters agreed to continue with Puerto Rico's territorial status.
[b] The second question asked voters to indicate the political status they preferred.
[c] Because of the almost-500,000 blank ballots, Congress ignored the vote.
[d] Independence and Free association were combined as one option in 2017.

established in 1952. The majority of the votes were cast in favor of the status quo. The political party that supported and represented the commonwealth status is the Partido Popular Democratico; the political party that promoted and supported statehood is the Partido Nuevo Progresista. In the next referendum, which took place in 1993 and was sponsored by the Partido Popular Democratico, the majority of the votes yet again were in favor of the status quo, or the commonwealth, but a large percentage also selected statehood. The 1998 referendum also showed similar support for statehood. This referendum was controversial because it entailed a redefinition of the commonwealth status, which prompted many Puerto Ricans to select a "none of the above" alternative. While the "territorial" commonwealth had only 0.1 percent of the votes, the majority of the votes went to "none of the above," with 50.3 percent.

In the 2012 referendum, free association (a non-territorial form of self-government) was introduced as an alternative to the commonwealth status. There were two questions asked in this referendum, shown in the table as 2012 (a) and 2012 (b). The first

(a) gave voters an option between a territorial and a non-territorial status. The second (b) asked which non-territorial alternative they would prefer: statehood, independence, or free association. A total of 54 percent of voters said no to a territorial status on the first question (a); on the second question (b), a total of 61 percent of the voters cast their vote in favor of statehood, 33.3 percent supported free association, and 5.5 percent independence. There was not a "none of the above" option, but a total of 500,000 ballots were left blank, indicating the discontent of the Partido Popular Democratico with not including the commonwealth status as one of the options. The pro-statehood party passed a resolution to request the U.S. Congress for Puerto Rico to become the fifty-first state in the Union.

The 2017 referendum offered Puerto Ricans two options: statehood or independence/free association. Statehood gained the vast majority of votes, but this referendum, like the previous one, was also cast in controversy, as this time less than a quarter of the people voted. It is important to note that the government of Puerto Rico has held these five plebiscites, but it is the U.S. Congress that ultimately has the power to resolve the status question. Congress has never validated any of these referendums or asked Puerto Ricans for their preference. In other words, these plebiscites have been nonbinding. Also, it is important to mention that Puerto Ricans in the United States were not included in these plebiscites. Yet, the debate about the political status of Puerto Rico animates many conversations across the diaspora. Isar P. Godreau writes that while Puerto Ricans claim a strong national identity with a common history, culture, and language, this does not necessarily imply "a desire for establishing an independent nation-state."[59]

Colonial Paradox in the Twenty-First Century: Economic Crisis and Hurricane Maria

As mentioned earlier, Puerto Rico was recently devastated by two hurricanes—Irma and Maria—leading to a humanitarian crisis of unprecedented proportions for the island. The U.S. federal response to the disaster—or lack of response and empathy—laid bare the paradoxical legacy of over one hundred years of U.S. colonialism.

On September 20, 2017, Hurricane Maria devastated the island's infrastructure, transportation networks, agriculture, and communications systems. The electricity grid collapsed, leaving 80 percent of the island in a complete blackout for over a month.[60] Winds destroyed the agricultural sector, wiping out small and large farm operations. Homes and businesses flooded, leaving families homeless and workers unemployed. Hospitals lacked fuel to maintain generators. Water and food supplies were critically low within one week. It was evident that help was slow in reaching the island. President Trump downplayed the crisis and failed to respond in any significant way for days. His first response came after Carmen Yulín Cruz, mayor of San Juan, held a press conference to call attention to the humanitarian crisis unfolding on the island. Trump responded, not with help, but with tweets. His first tweet alluded to the 2008 economic crisis that left the island nearly bankrupt and signaled to the banks that the debt should be paid. His second tweet made things considerably worse by drawing on long-held stereotypes of Puerto Ricans as lazy. As he put it, "They want everything handed to them." Ironically, Cruz was among those taking refuge in a local coliseum because her home had flooded, like the homes of many other Toa Baja residents.

Other Latin American and Caribbean countries rushed to send aid, but the main obstacle was the 1917 Jones-Saffron Act, a piece of legislation imposed on Puerto Rico in the early stages of U.S. colonization, which prevented direct delivery of aid. Broadly, this act requires that all goods shipped to Puerto Rico arrive from U.S. ports, on U.S. constructed ships, and with U.S. crews. In the aftermath of the crisis, countries that wanted to offer help could not send aid directly to Puerto Rico. On September 28, the Trump administration suspended the Jones-Saffron Act for ten days to facilitate hurricane relief. For ten days there was some relief, but after that, the Jones-Saffron Act continued to obstruct aid from reaching Puerto Rico. In the aftermath of the hurricane, scholars of the Puerto Rican diaspora have called attention to the humanitarian crisis that engulfed Puerto Rico by writing editorials and engaging media outlets to instruct American audiences on the colonial condition in Puerto Rico. Anthropologist Yarimar Bonilla was particularly insightful in a *Washington Post* editorial where she wrote, "As an unincorporated territory of the U.S., Puerto Rico qualifies for aid programs including Federal Emergency Management Agency assistance. However, with a poverty rate nearly double that of Mississippi, failing infrastructure that has been neglected for more than a decade and a public sector that has been increasingly dismantled in response to the debt crisis, the island was already in a state of emergency long before the storm hit. . . . Vulnerability is not merely a product of natural conditions; it is a political state and a colonial situation."[61]

The lack of empathy, the trickle of aid, and now the growing governmental impediments exposed the contradictions of U.S. colonialism. For example, the Jones-Saffron Act has meant that historically Puerto Ricans have paid more for goods and services than any other state, since the cost of transporting goods is added to the prices for products. Ironically, as we reviewed the historical documents for this section of the book, the similarities between how Americans perceived Puerto Ricans then and now are striking. The natural disasters that fell upon Puerto Rico in the twenty-first century have exacerbated the colonial condition of the island and, thus, like trees in the aftermath of the storm, laid bare the legacy of U.S. colonialism.

Concluding Thoughts

Following our overview of Puerto Rican history outlining the complicated situation facing Puerto Ricans today and how it connects to migration to the United States, in the next chapter we address more specifically migration to Illinois. Puerto Rican identity had been forged in over five hundred years of history. The title, "Island Paradox," is a useful way to frame the historical background we offer here. In fact, the history of Puerto Rico is abundant with paradoxes. First, Puerto Rico has never been an independent nation, yet the strong sense of nationality forged through this history is paramount to how Puerto Ricans identified themselves across the diaspora. The modernization program that was designed to modernize Puerto Rico included the paradoxical notion that people had to leave the island for the program to succeed. Similarly, there is also a strong paradox in the political status of the island, in which a nation is supposedly free yet connected to the United States.

The second part of the title, *"Puerto Rico, Puerto Pobre* (Rich Port, Poor Port)," refers to a poem by Pablo Neruda, the famous Latin American poet. In verse, Neruda recognizes the history of colonialism and how it has kept Puerto Ricans "imprisoned" in the past and present. Puerto Ricans have labored to affirm a unique cultural and national background as a form of resilience and affirmation. Evidence of this affirmation can be seen in the murals that now exist in Illinois, principally in Chicago's Puerto Rican community. Migration has been a way that Puerto Ricans have sought to resolve these issues and contradictions, in particular since becoming part of the United States. In the aftermath of the 2017 hurricane season and the reforms introduced by the Junta, the future is even more uncertain for Puerto Ricans across the diaspora.

3

SALIMOS DE AQUÍ (WE LEFT THIS PLACE): MIGRATION TO ILLINOIS

For generations, Puerto Rican poets, writers, and musicians have sought to capture the poetics of migration. In fact, the title of this chapter is drawn from a popular song written and composed by Tito Auger, lead singer and founder of Fiel a la Vega, a Puerto Rican rock-and-roll group popular in the 1990s. "Salimos de aquí" was the band's first hit single in 1996, capturing the existential angst of leaving the island. Yet the national anthem of Puerto Rican migration is the song "En mi viejo San Juan" (In my old San Juan), written by Noel Estrada in the 1940s. The song was originally interpreted by the Trio Vegabajeño. The lyrics have been translated into several languages and performed by musicians around the world. The song's most poignant stanza describes the passing of time and the inability of the Puerto Rican interlocutor to return to the island. Indeed, the passing of time, movements between mainland communities, and return migrations are topics that matter to Puerto Rican migrants in Illinois.

Decades of research about Puerto Rican migration has established that migration to Illinois, principally Chicago, began in the middle decades of the twentieth century. The most significant migration movement brought working-class families to Chicago in the 1950s under the auspices of a labor recruitment contract connected to Operation Bootstrap, the industrialization project discussed in chapter 2.[1] This initial group of men and women, the contract workers, were followed by working-class families in a continuous migration for three decades. Although migration to the city diminished somewhat in the 1980s, Puerto Ricans across social classes continued to move to Chicago and other parts of the state individually and as members of family groups in the last decades of the twentieth century. Some were recruited by a range of corporations with national headquarters in the state, while familial and personal reasons pushed others. We know that today the number of Puerto Ricans migrating to Illinois is small compared with the current mass exodus mostly to Florida. Nonetheless, our research shows that in the first decades of the twenty-first century, a range of economic, educational, political, and familial reasons continue to bring Puerto Ricans to Illinois. As we mentioned in chapter 1, the most recent migrants are those who came to Chicago in the aftermath of Hurricane Maria.

Migration to Illinois has been undertaken by families across the social class spectrum. While working-class families migrated to deal with economic and personal problems engendered by the failures of the modernization program, educated and professional Puerto Ricans have also migrated, pushed by the financial crisis that has engulfed the island since the late 1990s. Some have come as students seeking educational opportunities and have stayed due to employment prospects. Others have been recruited by corporations, while still others left in the aftermath of Hurricane Maria. Gender, social class, and race have been important markers of Puerto Rican migration to Illinois, issues we address in this chapter.

We begin with a demographic overview of Puerto Ricans in Illinois. This includes population distributions across the state and a summary of the socioeconomic profile of Puerto Ricans for selective communities. The socioeconomic profile includes employment status, income, poverty rates, and educational attainment, among other variables. We highlight Elgin, Joliet, Aurora, Waukegan, Cicero, and Des Plaines because they have been known as larger Puerto Rican population centers outside of Chicago.

In the second part of the chapter, we examine the migration stories of Puerto Ricans more broadly. It is common knowledge now that the migration of contract workers to Chicago represents the official beginning of migration from the island to Illinois. When they arrived in Illinois in the late 1940s, there was a small cohort of Puerto Rican students attending the University of Chicago. We find this cohort to be relevant since students also represent a significant migration group to the United States and Illinois. In other words, this helps us highlight how migration from Puerto Rico to the United States has always involved a noteworthy portion of educated Puerto Ricans. In researching this book, we were surprised at the number of recently arrived

Puerto Ricans who left the island for Illinois to further their education. Many come to study and, as is frequently the case, end up staying in Illinois to live and work, to establish families, and ultimately to become permanent residents of Illinois. A historical thread connects the experiences of the Puerto Rican students at the University of Chicago in the late 1940s to those who have come recently. We revisit the recruitment of contract laborers to perform domestic and industrial work in Chicago, a chapter of the Puerto Rican diaspora that exposes the social class and gender biases of the modernization model and the social class exploitation of Puerto Ricans as workers both on the island and in Illinois. The women and men who followed these early contract workers have also encountered various receptions throughout the state. Through fieldwork, interviews, and oral histories, we offer the stories of women, men, and families who followed these early migrants not only to Chicago but also to Bloomington-Normal, Champaign, Peoria, and other parts of the state.

As we noted in chapter 1, it is difficult to document all of the communities in downstate Illinois, but we have selected key cities to highlight. Puerto Rican migration to Illinois has been multidirectional. Some migrated directly from Puerto Rico to other communities in the United States and then migrated to Illinois; others migrated directly from the island to Chicago, where they settled and raised their families; still others migrated to other Illinois cities where they knew that they had employment opportunities. A number relocated from New York City to places like Peoria, where Pedro Rodriguez,[2] one informant, stated his wife had been offered a job. A recently arrived couple, Ana and Raul Rodriguez in Bloomington, migrated in the aftermath of the economic crisis that engulfed the island at the turn of the twenty-first century. More recently, since Hurricane Maria, over 1,324 Puerto Ricans have arrived in Illinois as FEMA evacuees.[3] We also acknowledge the internal migrations within the city of Chicago as a result of gentrification and housing discrimination. In other words, as Jorge Duany declares, Puerto Ricans are genuinely a "nation on the move."[4]

Population Distribution of Puerto Ricans in Illinois

As shown in figure 3.1, in 2016 Puerto Ricans lived in every county of Illinois. The most significant population concentrations are evident in the cities of Chicago, Aurora, Waukegan, Joliet, and Elgin,

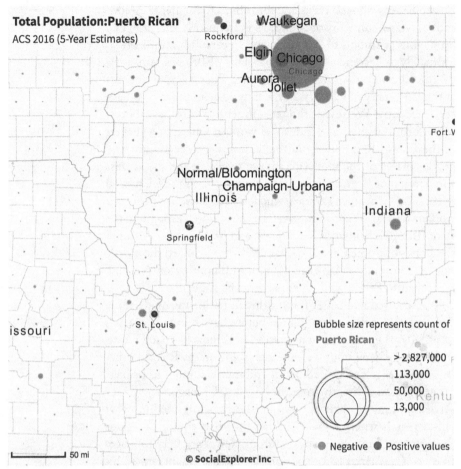

Fig. 3.1. Puerto Rican population in Illinois counties. Created by Ivis García, using data from the American Community Survey's *Population Estimates*, 2015: ACS 5-Year Estimates Selected Population Profiles (Washington, D.C.: U.S. Census Bureau, 2016), https://factfinder.census.gov/.

among others. In central Illinois, Champaign-Urbana, Peoria, and Bloomington/Normal have significant population groups. Table 3.1 offers evidence of Puerto Rican population growth from 1980 to 2015. In 2015 about 80 percent of the Puerto Rican population in Illinois cities was in Chicago. In 1980 the four cities with the most Puerto Ricans were Chicago, Waukegan, Aurora, and Elgin. By 1990 Cicero had become one of the most populous Puerto Rican communities and in 2000 had nearly the same number of Puerto Ricans as Elgin. In 2010, Joliet, Bolingbrook, and Melrose Park started to make the list of cities with a sizable Puerto Rican population, and by 2015 Zion was in the top ten.

Historically, Chicago had been the city with both the highest number and highest percentage of Puerto Rican residents. The number of Puerto Ricans in Chicago topped out in the 1990 U.S. Census at just shy of 120,000, or 4.3 percent of the city's total population. Since then, the number of Puerto Ricans in Chicago has been declining.

An opposite pattern is taking place in cities outside of Chicago. Several Illinois communities, including Franklin Park, Melrose Park, and Zion, now have a greater proportion of Puerto Rican residents than Chicago. Midsized cities like Wheaton, Oak Park, Hoffman Estates, Des Plaines, Champaign, Bolingbrook, and Bloomington recorded modest increases in the Puerto Rican population between 2010 and 2015.

Even in larger cities, the trend has been slow but sustained growth in the Puerto Rican community. The number of Puerto Ricans in Peoria more than doubled between 1980 and 2015, even as the city grew only marginally in the same period. Even fast-growing Joliet added total population at a slower rate than the Puerto Rican community there.

Besides Chicago, some of the cities experiencing the most significant loss in Puerto Rican population include Streamwood, which lost 40 percent of its Puerto Rican population between 2010 and 2015, and Naperville, which lost 48 percent of its Puerto Rican population in the same time period.

Socioeconomic Characteristics
of Puerto Ricans in Illinois

Data for this section come from the American Community Survey (2015 five-year estimates). Here we include employment status, income, poverty rates, and educational attainment, among other variables. Unfortunately, data was available only for eleven cities: Aurora, Bolingbrook, Chicago, Cicero, Des Plaines, Elgin, Franklin Park, Joliet, Melrose Park, Waukegan, and Zion.

The most recent census revealed wide gaps in employment and wage-earning opportunities for Puerto Ricans in cities in Illinois. Puerto Ricans in Bolingbrook and Des Plaines had the lowest rates of unemployment (3.1 and 3.2 percent, respectively) and among the highest median annual household incomes ($75,417 and $62,010, respectively). The median household income in Elgin is also high ($67,534), but this city has a much higher rate of unemployment (12.3 percent).

Table 3.1. Puerto Rican population in Illinois cities, 1980-2015

City	1980 Population	%	1990 Population	%	2000 Population	%	2010 Population	%	2015 Population	%
Aurora	2,253	2.8	2,334	2.3	2,611	1.8	3,867	2.0	5,067	2.5
Bellwood	100	0.5	107	0.5	151	0.7	312	1.6	434	2.3
Bloomington	55	0.1	94	0.2	136	0.2	259	0.3	339	0.4
Bolingbrook	226	0.6	351	0.9	626	1.1	1,254	1.7	1,292	1.7
Carbondale	40	0.2	88	0.3	90	0.4	134	0.5	207	0.8
Champaign	71	0.1	98	0.2	255	0.4	415	0.5	524	0.6
Chicago	112,074	3.7	119,866	4.3	113,055	3.9	102,703	3.8	103,309	3.8
Cicero	327	0.5	1,255	1.9	2,331	2.7	2,782	3.3	2,907	3.4
Des Plaines	115	0.2	199	0.4	419	0.7	615	1.1	744	1.3
Elgin	1,496	2.3	1,895	2.5	2,355	2.5	2,973	2.7	3,103	2.8
Evanston	132	0.2	176	0.2	329	0.4	483	0.6	418	0.6
Franklin Park	79	0.5	164	0.9	466	2.4	829	4.5	769	4.2
Hanover Park	110	0.4	235	0.7	365	1.0	572	1.5	364	0.9
Highwood	33	0.6	29	0.5	22	0.5	29	0.5	10	0.2
Hoffman Estates	155	0.4	243	0.5	332	0.7	584	1.1	817	1.6
Joliet	133	0.2	214	0.3	586	0.6	2,084	1.4	2,166	1.5
Melrose Park	131	0.6	303	1.5	448	1.9	1,095	4.3	1,215	4.8
Naperville	40	0.1	173	0.2	491	0.4	853	0.6	446	0.3
North Chicago	541	1.4	696	2.0	775	2.2	731	2.2	460	1.5
Northlake	98	0.8	131	1.0	279	2.3	522	4.2	244	2.0
Oak Park	155	0.3	275	0.5	329	0.6	555	1.1	601	1.2
Peoria	109	0.1	108	0.1	221	0.2	299	0.3	269	0.2
Pontiac	57	0.5	37	0.3	10	0.1	45	0.4	105	0.9
Rantoul	120	0.6	64	0.4	34	0.3	153	1.2	422	3.2
Rock Falls	40	0.4	33	0.3	63	0.7	91	1.0	100	1.1
Streamwood	114	0.5	196	0.6	382	1.0	555	1.4	336	0.8
Urbana	43	0.1	86	0.2	135	0.4	210	0.5	148	0.4
Waukegan	2,455	3.6	2,561	3.7	2,976	3.3	2,918	3.3	2,795	3.2
West Chicago	62	0.5	96	0.6	150	0.6	186	0.7	264	1.0
Wheaton	71	0.2	126	0.2	169	0.3	290	0.5	327	0.6
Zion	121	0.7	301	1.5	616	2.7	870	3.6	1,209	5.0

Source: Table created by Ivis García, from U.S. Census (1980–2010) and American Community Survey 5-year estimates (2015).

In contrast, Puerto Ricans in Aurora, Cicero, Melrose Park, and Waukegan all have median household incomes below $45,000. Unemployment in these cities is typically high (Cicero has the highest unemployment rate, at 21.2 percent), though Melrose Park is an exception (5.4 percent unemployment).

Families are more likely to experience poverty where unemployment is higher and household incomes are lower. The cities with the highest rates of poverty among Puerto Ricans include Zion (43.9 percent), Cicero (32.6 percent), Waukegan (21.8 percent), Melrose Park (20.1 percent), Aurora (19.3 percent), and Elgin (18.3 percent). The cities with the lowest rates of poverty among Puerto Ricans are Bolingbrook (1.9 percent), Des Plaines (2.6 percent), Franklin Park (4 percent), and Joliet (11.7 percent). Chapter 4 addresses explanations of poverty for Puerto Ricans in Illinois.

There are disparities in educational attainment, too. Some 46 percent of Puerto Ricans in Bolingbrook have a bachelor's degree or higher, compared with just 6.3 percent in Cicero and 7.5 percent in Franklin Park. For most cities, 12 to 16 percent is a typical figure. Waukegan has the highest percentage of Puerto Ricans without a high school diploma (39.9 percent), and Franklin Park and Des Plaines have the lowest (8.5 and 9.9 percent, respectively).

Despite obstacles associated with wage earning and educational attainment, Puerto Ricans generally do not rely on public assistance. Zion is the city with the highest proportion of Puerto Ricans receiving some form of public support. In most cities, between 4 and 7 percent of Puerto Ricans receive some form of public assistance.

In all of the Illinois cities with available census data, Puerto Ricans have a young median age. Melrose Park has the highest median age for Puerto Ricans, but it is still below thirty-three years. In Elgin and Chicago, Puerto Ricans have a median age above thirty. The median age for Puerto Ricans in Bolingbrook is just nineteen years. Puerto Ricans in Joliet, Zion, and Cicero have a median age below twenty-three.

Puerto Ricans in the Suburbs

Anthropologist Gina Pérez reminds us that the movement to the suburbs needs to be understood within the broader context of intra-metropolitan migrations taking place in Chicago.[5] For example, she reported that since the 1980s, Puerto Ricans and Mexicans have moved north and west in the city and have relocated to

Table 3.2. Key socioeconomic indicators in Illinois cities with largest Puerto Rican population

City	% in poverty	Unemployment rate	Median household income	Median age	% Public Assistance
Aurora	19.3	11.7	43,125	29.9	1.2
Bolingbrook	1.9	3.1	75,417	19.2	0.0
Chicago	26.0	14.0	36,588	31.5	6.3
Cicero	32.6	21.2	41,761	22.8	6.7
Des Plaines	2.6	3.2	62,010	28.6	0.0
Elgin	18.3	12.3	67,534	30.1	4.4
Franklin Park	4.0	5.8	64,071	28.7	0.0
Joliet	11.7	5.5	59,531	20.9	3.5
Melrose Park	20.1	5.4	38,750	32.7	2.3
Waukegan	21.8	11.3	30,282	27.9	6.9
Zion	43.9	6.4	No data	21.1	8.2

Source: Created by Ivis García, from the 2000 U.S. Decennial Census and American Community Survey 1-year estimates (2016).

working-class suburbs like Cicero, Addison, and Waukegan. Their movement is informed by a range of social issues and problems that Puerto Ricans and Mexicans have confronted as urban residents such as housing shortages, gentrification, work, policing, and violence.

Elgin

Elgin, a growing city northwest of Chicago, is home to a significant Puerto Rican population. The most recent census reported over 3,100 Puerto Ricans living in Elgin, which is just shy of 3 percent of the city's total population. The Puerto Rican presence in Elgin is due to direct migration from Puerto Rico and from Chicago. Most of the Puerto Ricans in Elgin are from Aguada, a midsize city two hours from San Juan. The migration from Aguada to Elgin began in the 1950s and accelerated in the ensuing decades as family and friends heard of positive experiences from their peers in the bustling manufacturing town.[6]

Table 3.3. Educational attainment in Illinois cities with largest Puerto Rican population

City	Less than 9th grade	9th–12th, no diploma	High school graduate	Some college, no degree	Associate's degree	Bachelor's degree	Graduate/ professional degree
Aurora	16.3%	12.5%	24.0%	25.6%	8.7%	8.6%	4.2%
Bolingbrook	7.3%	7.8%	12.5%	21.4%	5.4%	23.8%	21.8%
Chicago	14.6%	14.1%	29.3%	20.9%	7.0%	9.3%	4.9%
Cicero	12.7%	18.6%	35.8%	16.8%	9.8%	6.3%	0.0%
Des Plaines	3.7%	6.2%	33.3%	28.1%	12.6%	14.4%	1.8%
Elgin	11.2%	19.8%	28.3%	16.9%	5.6%	10.2%	8.0%
Franklin Park	5.8%	2.7%	49.4%	26.5%	8.2%	7.5%	0.0%
Joliet	12.1%	11.5%	35.3%	20.5%	8.2%	8.6%	3.7%
Melrose Park	10.6%	13.4%	33.2%	24.7%	4.4%	7.9%	5.8%
Waukegan	24.7%	15.2%	21.0%	21.7%	2.3%	12.4%	2.7%
Zion	10.7%	6.1%	25.4%	39.8%	6.5%	11.6%	0.0%

Source: Table created by Ivis García, from American Community Survey 5-year estimates (2015).

Unfortunately, Puerto Ricans in Elgin experience some of the highest rates of poverty and unemployment, at 18 percent and 12 percent, respectively. Nonetheless, the median household income ($67,500) of Puerto Ricans is much higher than the average in Illinois. The median age for Puerto Ricans in Elgin is thirty, which is older than for any other city. In terms of educational attainment, 28.3 percent have graduated from high school, 16.9 percent went to college but did not obtain a degree, 5.6 percent completed an associate's degree, and 10.2 percent completed a bachelor's degree.

We interviewed a multigenerational family in Elgin, the Riveras, and their story illustrates the complexities of Puerto Rican migration. Families are involved in a multiplicity of movements intersecting through gender and social class. Carmen Rivera is the grandmother who initially described her move from Chicago to Elgin as an attempt to escape the poor living conditions and urban problems in the city, but before that, Carmen had sought to avoid the situation in Puerto Rico, too, the first move that brought her to Chicago.

> I did not want the kids to grow up in Chicago. I moved initially to Chicago with my daughter. She was twelve years old, and my son was one year old. My sister sent for me in Puerto Rico to live with her and to seek better opportunities for me and my family. That was in 1987 . . . . I quit my job at the Baxter Corporation in Maricao because I was determined to find something better and move permanently to Chicago. I could not start to work right away, so I had to take welfare for two to three months. Through a friend of mine, I found work in a factory.[7]

Carmen's daughter, Letty, married early and left Elgin for Puerto Rico, where Carmen's granddaughter, Olivia, and her grandson, Pablo, were born. Letty and her family relocated back to Illinois when they discovered Pablo had medical problems that could not be adequately addressed in Puerto Rico. Olivia, who has fond memories of her time in Puerto Rico and speaks warmly about her experiences and connections to the island, went to school in Elgin, graduated from Elgin High School, and moved on to pursue her educational goals at Illinois State University. In fact, as we wrote this book, Olivia made family history as the first member of her family to finish college.

As a family, the Riveras have positive memories of the move. One of the women added, "In Elgin, all Puerto Ricans know each other because we are not that many. We live here humbly, but we like it. I am very proud of my contributions to this community. I pay my taxes. I am very proud of my heritage."[8] Migration to the suburbs did not mean a complete disconnection from the island and Chicago. They still travel frequently to Puerto Rico. Carmen was very proud of having taken her granddaughter to the island for a visit. Similarly, she is still connected to her family in Chicago. They visit each other frequently and attend events in Humboldt Park like the Puerto Rican parade and festivals.

Joliet

Joliet, one of the largest cities in Illinois and the seat of Will County, is home to a small but growing contingent of Puerto Ricans. In 1980, the city's 133 Puerto Ricans represented just 0.2 percent of the population. By 1990, the number of Puerto Ricans increased by more than 60 percent, then more than doubled by 2000, growing at a faster rate than the city's population as a whole. The most significant period of growth occurred between 2000 and 2010, when the number of Puerto Ricans living in Joliet more than tripled. By 2015, Puerto Ricans accounted for 1.5 percent of the city's population, numbering nearly 2,200.

Compared to other cities in Illinois, the percentage of Puerto Ricans in Joliet who are in poverty is low (below 12 percent). Unemployment is also relatively low, besting all other communities except Bolingbrook, Des Plaines, and Melrose Park. At 20.9, the median age of Puerto Ricans in Joliet is lower than any other city than Bolingbrook, suggesting a significant number of large families with young children.

In 2015, Jessica Colon-Sayre became Will County's first Latina judge. Colon-Sayre, a graduate of DePaul University, said she has a "passion for what is just and fair" that will not waver.[9] Joliet is also home to Puerto Rican Delicious, a popular bakery.

Aurora

Aurora has been home to a significant and growing Puerto Rican population for decades. In 2010, there were about 3,900 Puerto Ricans in Aurora, up from nearly 2,300 in 1980. Once a major manufacturing center, the decline of industrial jobs in Aurora has affected Puerto Rican families—almost 12 percent are unemployed and more than 19 percent live in poverty. The median household income for Puerto Ricans in Aurora is just over $43,000. Even so, the percentage of Puerto Rican families in Aurora for public assistance is meager (1.2 percent).

Among cities with significant Puerto Rican populations, Chicago, Elgin, and Melrose Park have a Puerto Rican community with a higher median age than that in Aurora. Puerto Ricans in Aurora are generally less likely than their peers in other cities to graduate from high school, and they are also less likely to hold a college degree. In recent years, the number of Puerto Ricans in Aurora has grown significantly. Between 2010 and 2015, the Puerto Rican population grew by more than 31 percent while the total population grew by just over 1 percent.

The Aurora Puerto Rican Cultural Council is a nonprofit organization with 501c3 status since 1998. Initially founded in 1967 by Doroteo Arroyo and Juan M. Ruberte, the organization was known as the "United Puerto Rican Parade Committee," and its primary focus was an annual parade celebrating Puerto Rican heritage in the community. The organization's mission has broadened to include a heritage festival, a pageant, and even a scholarship.[10]

Waukegan

One of the larger cities outside of Chicago, Waukegan was historically an industrial town though, as, with many Midwestern communities, the economy has shifted toward services and healthcare. Income inequality as well as racial and ethnic segregation was prevalent in the city in the 1960s and was the impetus for the Waukegan 1966 riot—a conflict between police and the city's predominantly African American and Puerto Rican south side. Another issue prompting African Americans and Puerto Ricans to riot was the lack of recreation facilities in their neighborhoods.[11]

Today, Waukegan is home to 2,800 Puerto Ricans, just over 3 percent of the city's total population. Poverty and unemployment among Puerto Ricans in Waukegan are high, at 21 percent and 11 percent, respectively. Median household income is lower for Puerto Ricans in Waukegan than in any other major city in Illinois, at just over $30,000. The median age for Puerto Ricans in Waukegan is 28, and about 7 percent of homes receive some form of public assistance. Sixty percent of Puerto Ricans in Waukegan have graduated from high school, and over 17 percent have obtained a college degree.

The Puerto Rican Society in Waukegan is an active and popular community organization. The organization serves food and drinks, organizes cultural activities, and serves as a hangout for Puerto Rican youth and families. A recent activity involved raising funds for families suffering from the effects of Hurricane Maria. During a focus group with several residents of Waukegan, we learned that some Puerto Ricans migrated directly to Waukegan from Puerto Rico, others came from New York, while others just moved from Chicago to Waukegan. The focus group we conducted also included Puerto Ricans who had been born and raised in Waukegan. Here is a sample of their stories:

> I was born in Puerto Rico; then my parents moved to NYC, like, in 1962. Like, 1967 I think we came back over here, Waukegan. I went back to Puerto Rico and lived like twenty years down there. I came back, I used to live in Florida, and from Florida, I came back here.[12]

> My parents came to Waukegan in the '50s. We were all born and raised here in Waukegan. I left for twenty years. I moved around a lot. I moved from Florida, and I came back home to help take care of my sick mother, and now I've been here for thirteen years and worked in Waukegan.

> I was born and raised here. I've lived here all my life. I won't tell you how long because then it will tell you my age [laughter]. But my parents came from Puerto Rico when they were eighteen years old, and, well, they still live in the exact same house. . . where they came and lived here in Waukegan.

> I'm third generation, and, well, I've lived here all my life in Waukegan, and I'm a senior in high school, and I am planning on going to college in Chicago.

> I was born in Puerto Rico. My father and mother migrated to the United States in the 1950s to New Jersey. So, I lived in New Jersey until I got married. Then I lived in New York, and when I got divorced, I moved to Waukegan, and I've been here for thirty-one years. I had lived in Puerto Rico for twelve years. When I was married, we went back to Puerto Rico, so I lived in Ponce for twelve years.

> I was born in Ponce, Puerto Rico. I came here in '54, I think
> it was. . . . I've been here in Waukegan, lived in Waukegan for
> fifty-nine years. I worked at a company for thirty-eight years,
> and then the company left, so. . . and then lately my health
> hasn't been too good.

The pastiche of voices from Waukegan illustrates that many families in this suburb have been long-term residents and have settled with their families to live productive lives. It also shows the variety of reasons these families had to move, work, and return to Waukegan to care for elderly parents, all important life stages.

Cicero

Located due west of Chicago, Cicero was once an industrial center with several steel mills, manufacturing plants, and the Western Electric Hawthorne Works plant. Famously intolerant to people of color, the town underwent a rapid demographic shift beginning in the 1970s as manufacturing jobs declined. In 1980, Puerto Ricans represented only one-half of one percent of the total population in Cicero. By 2015, nearly 3.5 percent of people in Cicero identified as Puerto Rican.

The growth of the Puerto Rican community in Cicero over the last thirty years mirrors the growth of the larger Latino community; nearly 90 percent of people in Cicero identified as Hispanic or Latino in the most recent census. Historically, Puerto Ricans in Cicero and neighboring Berwyn have had roots in the neighborhoods of the west side of Chicago. Puerto Ricans and other Latinos began moving into Cicero in large numbers following World War II.[13]

Nearly one-third of Puerto Rican families in Cicero are in poverty, more than any other major city in Illinois except Zion. And unemployment rates for Puerto Ricans in Cicero are higher than anywhere else; more than 21 percent of the population was unemployed at the 2015 census. Even so, median household income, at just over $41,000, is on par with other cities like Aurora, Chicago, and Melrose Park, and substantially higher than Waukegan. About 7 percent of homes receive some form of public assistance.

Puerto Ricans in Cicero are a young lot; the median age is under twenty-three. They are also less likely than Puerto Ricans in other Illinois cities to attend college. Just under 33 percent have had some college experience, and only 16.1 percent have an associate's or bachelor's degree.

Des Plaines

Des Plaines is located just north of O'Hare International Airport. The city has historically been an enclave for Latino immigrants, but most are from Mexico or Central America. The Puerto Rican population in Des Plaines, though small, has been growing steadily since 1980, when the city's 115 Puerto Ricans represented just 0.2 percent of the population. By 2015, 744 Puerto Ricans were living in Des Plaines, accounting for 1.3 percent of the city's population.

Even before their numbers began to grow, Puerto Ricans were part of local conversations in Des Plaines. The issue of Puerto Rican statehood was discussed frequently and vibrantly in local newspapers in 1976 and 1977. Other topics of discussion included racism in the workplace, blended families, and more inclusive education materials in schools.

A favorite Puerto Rican restaurant in Des Plaines, Santiago's, was involved in fundraising efforts for victims of Hurricane Maria.[14] The restaurant is celebrated for its delicious *jibaritos* (sandwiches made of fried plantains) and tostones (fried plantains).

Puerto Ricans living in Des Plaines boast among the highest rates of educational attainment. Nearly 29 percent of Puerto Ricans in Des Plaines have an associate's degree or higher, more than any other city studied for this book except Bolingbrook. Puerto Ricans in Des Plaines also have among the highest median incomes and lowest rates of unemployment and poverty.

Migration to Illinois Then and Now

Students

Mérida M. Rúa's exceptional ethnography *A Grounded Identidad: Making New Lives in Chicago's Puerto Rican Neighborhoods* highlights the social class, race, and gender dimensions of the Puerto Rican migration to Chicago by juxtaposing the experiences of migrant workers and migrant students. She writes, "Migrant-workers and migrant-students were the roots of Chicago's Puerto Rican community, a community of racial boundaries and understandings distinct from the urban center they came to call home. Female domestic workers, graduate students, and a 'vacationing' social worker, divided by class and status, discovered that wage labor and worker's rights were a common cause."[15] In this section we draw on these categories—migrant students and migrant workers—to further deepen our understanding of the social class, gender, and race dimensions of migration to Illinois.

Migrant students represent a fundamental chapter in the migration of Puerto Ricans to Illinois. The "University of Chicago Cohort," as Rúa calls them, were a small yet leading group of graduate students who migrated to Chicago in the late 1940s.[16] The migration of these graduate students is pivotal because it connects to the successive migrations of students—like the authors of this volume—who left Puerto Rico to pursue higher education in Illinois. Through our interviews, we found that many Puerto Ricans who now live and work in downstate Illinois left the island or other Puerto Rican communities in the United States to come to Illinois to pursue graduate studies. Many have become members of these communities and long-term residents of Illinois. In our view, this affirms that migration from Puerto Rico to the United States has always involved a significant share of educated Puerto Ricans. These migrant students are relevant because of employment opportunities they are offered in colleges and universities around the state. They have become part of the new generation of public intellectuals engaged in challenging stereotypes and prejudice and dismantling racism in Illinois universities and around the nation. Through their research, they have helped document the making of the Puerto Rican diaspora. From the classroom, they have contributed to educating generations of Illinoisans and helped to diversify colleges and universities in Illinois and across the country. The migrant students mattered then and now.

The University of Chicago Cohort included a who's who of the Puerto Rican elite at the time: Elena Padilla,[17] Ricardo Alegría,[18] Muna "Muñita" Muñoz Lee,[19] Ángel Quintero, and Milton Pabón.[20] Of these, Elena Padilla figured prominently in this cohort because she wrote what is today the first empirical study of Puerto Ricans in Chicago. She also became an advocate on behalf of the contracted workers who confronted discrimination and oppression upon their arrival in the city. This makes her, as Rúa proposes, a pioneer in the form of urban ethnography, a branch of anthropological research. In fact, Rúa republished Padilla's doctoral dissertation and placed it at the heart of contemporary discussions about Latinos and new urban studies theory. She argues that Padilla was "a pioneer Latina social scientist who role modeled for us how to engage theory, method, and practice."[21]

The migration of these intellectuals might have been small in number and, some may argue, inconsequential when compared to the waves of working-class men, women, and families who eventually arrived in Chicago in the 1950s and 1960s, but in the broader context of the migrations that followed to Illinois, they are essential. Arguably, they are genuinely the *pioneros* and *pioneras* who first settled in Illinois. We propose that today they represent a meaningful link making visible the subsequent waves of students who made their way to study in Illinois.

The migrant students who came to Illinois from the 1980s through today may not have the social-class pedigree of the earlier wave. They are children of working-class and educated Puerto Ricans who perceived education as a means for social mobility, an essential goal of the modernization program Operation Bootstrap, described in the previous chapter. As the failures of the modernization program plunged Puerto Rico into a deep economic crisis in the 1990s and beyond, the migration of students became more pronounced. As our interviews show, for some migration to Illinois as a student represented their first move out of the island. Others came to study and returned to Puerto Rico to work or moved to work in other parts of Latin America where they secured employment opportunities. Others came to Illinois to investigate their opportunities, returned to Puerto Rico, and then came back to further their education. In the following pages, we draw on some of these interviews. For example, Sandra Flores [22] described how she wound up in central Illinois permanently:

> I came here as an exchange student from the University of Puerto Rico. That was in 1988. I came with one of my college friends. We were both communication majors at the University of Puerto Rico in Rio Piedras. We recognized that our English was not very good and that if we wanted to get ahead and work in public relations, we needed to polish our English. An agency we worked with temporarily was in Virgin Islands, and that made us realize that we needed to work on our language skills. We could read it and write it, but we needed a lot of work with the pronunciation. We decided to apply for national student exchange. The only connection I had to Illinois is that one of my professors had done his doctoral work at Southern Illinois University. He advised us to apply to one of the schools that is known to be one of the best in the state for the field of

communications; that was Illinois State University. It was my very first time I left the island! We lived in the international student dorm. We made friends quickly, but my friend who came with me did not last long. She left within two weeks. When we got ISU, the percentage of Latino students was so low, and that made it very hard for us. One of the things I did was to talk to the professors, and they made accommodations for me. I was here for one semester, and then I returned to Puerto Rico to finish and graduate. I could not stay here financially, and so I had to return [to Puerto Rico]. While I was here [at ISU], I met my future husband. He was also a student here. I then decided to apply to graduate school to do my master's, and that's how I came back to the States. I came back to Indianapolis, but life was very hard. . . . Within a year we got married, and my husband's work moved him to Bloomington.

Similarly, Clara Rivera, who is now a professor at a downstate Illinois university, said, "I came to study, but the scholarship I got from the state of Illinois required me to teach in Illinois for several years, and I ended up staying." Elba Figueroa described how she came to Illinois also to study, specifically to pursue graduate work, and returned to the island once she was finished with her degree, but given the economic conditions in Puerto Rico, she went back on the job market to find herself with a very nice job offer from a prominent university in Illinois.

Aida Fernández's narrative shows how migration is never simply a onetime move. She had been born in the United States but was raised and experienced the most formative years of her life in Puerto Rico, including college, which is when she decided to pursue graduate studies:

I came [to Illinois] in 2012 for graduate studies. . . . I was born on the East Coast. I lived there until I was eleven years old. After, I moved to the west coast of the island with my mom and my younger brother. My other sisters stayed behind [in the United States] because they were older. We moved because my grandmother had Alzheimer's and my mom was the only one that did not work outside the home. We had an uncle in Puerto Rico that had already moved to work. . . . would not have moved from Puerto Rico if I had not gone to graduate school. I came in June to be part of a university program to help you get acclimated with the campus. . . . Then, I took advantage of that and found an apartment for my husband and family so that when they came they don't have to be anxious about living arrangements. My husband came at some point to help me, but he had to return.

Isabel Cintron is an example of how, after migrating to pursue education, one might join the ranks of the teaching profession:

I first came here in 2007 to attend college at Loyola University Chicago. I majored in English and added secondary education as "my plan B" (I wanted, and still hope, to be a novelist). As I continued learning more about pedagogy, I became more and more interested in teaching for its own sake. And I decided to work for Chicago Public Schools because I really wanted to make a difference in children's lives. I wanted inner-city students to have a woman of color before them as an example of what they could do, and I wanted to bring my love for literature to the classroom.

Lulu López, a recently arrived migrant student in central Illinois, described her secondary school experience:

I came to this university because the only two U.S. board-certified music therapists in Puerto Rico studied here at this university. There are others from Argentina and Spain, but only two U.S. board-certified. They both studied here. They recommended that I study here. They said that they offer scholarships, like graduate assistantships. . . . I have come to visit family in Texas, New York, and Pennsylvania, but I was afraid. I was scared about racism because of the Trump administration politics. I was also scared about the cold because I heard bad stories about the weather. It was my first time moving out of my home. But, I was excited about it. . . . I really liked it. People are nice. I feel like home. I feel safe. I have a cohort of friends, graduate students; we are very tight. We support each other. Professors have been good to me. This year during the hurricane my professors asked about my family and showed me concern. I went home for Thanksgiving break, and when I came back I had a meeting with my advisor. She was like, "I was worried that you were not coming back." She was concerned.

We know that some of the evacuees who came to Illinois in the aftermath of Hurricane Maria were students. In fact, when Maura Toro-Morn visited the Hurricane Relief Center in Chicago's Humboldt Park in November 2017, she met a student who had left the island after the storm.

Working-Class Families

Broadly, Puerto Rican migration to the United States has been a working-class phenomenon.[23] As we mentioned in chapter 2, in the aftermath of the U.S. colonization of the island, it was working-class and poor Puerto Ricans who felt the need to find employment opportunities and migrated first to New York City in the early decades of the twentieth century. In the middle decades of the twentieth century, in the midst of Operation Bootstrap, the most substantial number of Puerto Ricans left the island, bound for familiar places like New York City and new sites like Lorrain, Ohio, and Chicago.

Scholars of the Puerto Rican diaspora have created a vast body of work documenting the migration that has been labeled the "great airborne migration" because movement overlapped with the era of airplane travel. Anthropologist Gina Pérez reminds us that the modernization program for Puerto Ricans meant "intellectual and financial freedom for women and economic freedom and development for the nation. Operation Bootstrap was predicated on women's freedoms from the 'traditional constraints'—family, land, and community—in order to achieve the greatest good: economic development."[24] It should not surprise readers, then, to find out that a number of migrants arriving in Chicago in the 1940s and 1950s were women, contracted to do domestic work. For instance, in 1946 the employment agency Castle, Barton and Associates brought 323 women to Chicago and Waukegan to do domestic work in the homes of middle-class and wealthy Illinoisans.[25] Eventually, their migration became known as the "Chicago Experiment," since the government perceived and supported the migration

Woman sewing in a Puerto Rico garment shop. Source: International Ladies Garment Workers Union Photographs (1885–1985). From Wikimedia Commons, https://commons.wikimedia.org/wiki/File:Woman_sewing_in_a_Puerto_Rico_garment_shop.jpg.

U.S. Customs
and Agriculture
inspecting
a woman's
suitcase. El Mundo
Newspaper Project,
University of Puerto
Rico, Rio Piedras
Campus.

of Puerto Rican women of childbearing age as a way to resolve
the inadequacies of the modernization program. Men also were
recruited to work in the steel mills. Labor recruitment became
a state-sponsored way to resolve the unemployment in Puerto
Rico—a characteristic that became even more entrenched in the
era of global migrations.

As Toro-Morn explains, news about opportunities in Chicago
spread quickly around the island, and many working-class
families followed those first migrants. Like other immigrant
groups, families came in stages: sometimes the husband moved
first, secured housing and work, and then brought the rest of the
family.[26] In other instances, families came together. The rural
mountainous town of San Lorenzo sent its share of working-class
migrants.[27] On the west coast, the town of San Sebastián also
figures prominently in the narratives of migration. The Puerto
Rican community in Chicago grew exponentially from the 1950s
to the 1970s due in part to migration from the island. The reception
of this large group of Puerto Ricans deserves some discussion.
Gina Pérez writes that as Puerto Ricans started migrating to
Chicago in the 1950s, local newspapers, like the *Chicago Daily
News*, featured stories about Puerto Ricans in which they were
praised as "good citizens" and as "coming from strong, close-knit
families whose members were self-reliant, eager to work, and
unwilling to receive public aid."[28] In 1961, the *Chicago Tribune*

ran a story about the Medina family and proclaimed them a "model Puerto Rican family."[29] The praise of Puerto Ricans as "hardworking" and "good citizens" with strong "patriarchal families" was intended to immunize them from the pathologies threatening African Americans in the 1950s.[30] In fact, the Chicago media delighted in comparing Puerto Ricans with other ethnic and racial groups, including Puerto Ricans in New York City, who had already gained a national reputation of their own as "violent," "welfare-dependent," "involved in gangs," and coming from fractured families. In the end, these stories of Chicago Puerto Ricans as diligent and kind with strong patriarchal families "provided Illinoisans, but mostly Chicagoans, with an antidote for their racial fears."[31]

But, slowly, these positive reports were replaced with stories of the problems Puerto Ricans encountered in housing, employment, and education. Pérez pinpoints the downfall of Puerto Ricans from the model minority throne: "One year after being christened the modern Horatio Alger, Chicago Puerto Ricans' status as a model minority was seriously challenged by the Division Street Riots in June, 1966."[32] Now, the problems of drugs, poverty, welfare dependency, and gangs placed Puerto Ricans alongside the groups that rendered racial and ethnic minorities as problem people. In the intervening fifty years, Chicago Puerto Ricans have worked hard to transform this negative view of their communities and families and the problems that continue to besiege them.

But not all Puerto Ricans stayed in Chicago; some came downstate. In the archives of the McLean County Museum of History, we found the oral history of Manuel Cordero, a Puerto Rican man from Utuado who migrated to Bloomington in 1956. Bloomington had a long history connected to the circus and was known as a place where performers went to retreat during the winter to practice, and Manuel was recruited to work with the circus:

> I was born in Utuado, Puerto Rico, on June 11, 1939. And I lived with my mother and my father and my brothers—there were several of us. And my mom passed away when I was five years old. And by the time that I was seven years old, I went to live with my brothers. And it was from one brother to another. And I resided with them until I was about seventeen and half[, then] I came to the States. I'm bypassing a few things there. But I did start working by the time that I was 12 years old. . . . There

was a lot of Puerto Ricans in the '50s that were coming to the States because there was work. . . . I decided that I would start to go to New York. But I had a sister that had married a man from Bloomington while he was in the service. And they were living in Texas, and then they eventually moved to Bloomington-Normal. When she heard that I was thinking about going to New York, she says, "You'd be better off if you come to a small place—a small town. Why don't you come to my house?" Which I did. So, I came here on November 6, 1956. She even got me a little job; I couldn't speak English at all. And she got me the job working at a bowling alley. . . . My sister [sent] me every other day or something like that to a little grocery store that used to be at Washington Street. And so here I'm walking with a note to the grocery store. And lo and behold, there comes that man that was there the day before in the barber shop. So he comes in and started walking toward me, and he startled me a little bit. But he approached me again, you know, in a friendly manner, and my English was—I could hardly understand him, what he was saying. Then he kept pointing to the swing, talking about swings and trapeze. That's the only thing I could think. And then I say, "You know," I said to myself, "I don't understand what he's saying." You know, but I say, "If he wants to come with me . . . " So I brought him to my sister's house. I told my sister, . . . "You know what? I really don't know what he wants. He keeps saying 'trapeze,' and this and that and I don't know what he's saying." So they talked a little bit [chuckles]. And my sister just rolled her eyes, and she said, "Oh, Manuel! You know what he wants you to do?" "No!" I say. "He says he wants to teach you how to do trapeze work." "Whoa!" . . . And so, it didn't take too long. We decided that I would give it a try.

Manuel learned the circus trade and traveled all over the United States as a circus performer. Today, Manuel is back in central Illinois.

Other Puerto Ricans followed Manuel to central Illinois in the 1970s and 1980s. Many came to study at Illinois State University. Today, there are over 400 Puerto Ricans who call Bloomington home. Peoria has also attracted its share of Puerto Ricans, in particular working-class Puerto Ricans. One informant we interviewed for this project described how he had lost his job in New York City at the time and a friend told him about work opportunities in Peoria. He explained how his community of support was predominantly his African American friends because there were so few Puerto Ricans in the city at the time. Slowly, when others arrived, he expanded his network of friends. It is important to point out that recruitment of working-class Puerto Ricans to meet labor shortages in what remains of some industries in the state continues. Urban planning scholar Faranak Miraftab's book *Global Heartland: Displaced Labor, Transnational Lives, and Local Placemaking* describes migration of Puerto Ricans to Beardstown, Illinois, in a story cut out from the headlines. Unlike many rural municipalities in the Midwest that are now ghost towns, Beardstown is thriving, notable for its lively business community, residential integration, new schools, and growing populations. In 1987, the Cargill Corporation bought a meatpacking plant from Oscar Meyer. Cargill busted the union jobs and sent company representatives to towns near the U.S.-Mexico border to recruit workers. Immigrants, mostly farmers displaced from Mexico and Central America, were hired to work in the meatpacking facility; later, West Africans were also hired. In 2007, Immigration and Customs Enforcement (ICE) raided the factory, resulting in the deportation of many workers: "ICE arrested sixty-two people, among them fifty-four from Mexico and the rest from Guatemala and El Salvador."[33] At the national level, there has been a continuous narrative charging undocumented immigrants with taking jobs away from native-born residents, yet Miraftab notes that no one had rushed to Beardstown in 1987 to take the eleven-dollars-an-hour jobs in the meatpacking industry. After the ICE raid, the plant went to Puerto Rico to recruit workers, and in December 2007, over fifty Puerto Ricans arrived in Beardstown. In an interesting parallel with the Chicago experiment of the 1950s, Puerto Ricans had not been warned of Illinois winters and the kind of work they would be doing. And as in the 1950s, many Puerto Ricans left before the end of their probationary period of employment. According to Miraftab, "Some could not tolerate the weather or the harsh work; others could not endure the small-town culture or the managers at the manufacturing plant. . . . Workers with legal documentation can be more outspoken and can be more likely to leave."[34]

The Puerto Rican community of Rantoul, Illinois, is also connected to this type of recruitment, as documented by Lisa

Ortiz. Ortiz notes that the migration of Puerto Ricans to Rantoul represents another chapter in the invisible rural-to-rural migrations of Puerto Ricans. A significant group of workers were recruited from the rural town of Jayuya to work at Rantoul's pork plant after a raid by ICE had created labor shortages in the plant. Ortiz documents that migrants' reception in the rural community and their broader migration experiences were marked by significant devaluations from stakeholders in the community.

Decades of research about Puerto Rican migration has shown that leaving the island has never been easy or taken lightly by those who migrate. It is evident that Puerto Ricans in Illinois have engaged in the *vaivén*—that is, the process of coming and going from Puerto Rico to Illinois and back. These migrations are connected to their desires to provide for their families, to address housing and educational quality, and to seek communities that offer more opportunities. The migration stories we shared here are complicated and multigenerational and cut through life stages. Migration is a process that is gendered—men and women do it for different reasons—and the outcomes tend to be different for men and women. Social class has also mattered in the migration of Puerto Ricans. We conclude this chapter by returning to the poetics of migration by sharing a poem written by Puerto Rican Chicago poet Johanny Vázquez Paz, which she dedicated to the people of Humboldt Park who have transformed themselves and their surrounding environments seeking to belong.[35]

A World of Our Own

To the people of Humboldt Park
Between two flags we built
the past of an island exiled to memory.
We put up colonial balconies
and replaced the asphalt with paving stones,
the parks with plazas,
the supermarkets with *colmados*,
American coffee with Café Yaucono,
and hamburgers with steak *jibaritos*.
We changed street names and words in Spanish:
from "desfile" to *parada*, from "patio" to *yarda*,
from "alfombra" to *carpeta*, from "mercado" to *marqueta*,
because we are bilingual *y podemos mezclarlas*.
We put flavor in the food, rhythm

in the music, murals on the walls,
accents on the words, heat into the cold.
We opened *botánicas*, cultural centers,
galleries, museums, restaurants
and anything else we needed
so our children could learn their heritage
of waves returned to shore
mixed with the blood of three races.
We built a world of our own between two flags,
a neighborhood with well-known faces, familiar aromas
and noises kept company by the rumble of the drum.
Our homeland in exile that floats like a desert island
in the deep and vast sea of the city of Chicago.

4

FAMILY AND WORK EXPERIENCES OF PUERTO RICANS IN ILLINOIS

Eduardo Ortiz described the years of hard work and wages he earned in a steel mill in Chicago in the 1950s:

> I started working at U.S. Steel in 1953, and I worked there for 30 years. . . . During those 30 years I worked day and night shifts. I was a laborer for 16 years, and then I worked in a semi-skilled position for another 14 years. The work was hard and dangerous. You had to be alert and have four eyes. There were overhead cranes and moving trucks inside the mill. Some men were killed because it was dark in the mill and trucks would hit them. . . . There were a lot of Mexicans in the mill. . . . When I started in the mill, I was earning $1.70 an hour, and when I retired in 1983, I was making $10.00 an hour. I retired with a pension. . . . After I retired, I lived in Puerto Rico for three years. But Puerto Rico is too hot. I came back to Chicago to be with my kids. I love Chicago.[1]

Rita, seventy-two years old and a Puerto Rican migrant in Chicago, addressed her desire to work:

> After I got to Chicago my husband didn't want me to work, but I wanted to work. I wanted to work because you can meet people, learn new things, and one can leave the house for a while. I saw all the women in the family, his sisters and cousins, working and earning some money and I wanted too. But I had four children, and who was going to take care of them?[2]

And Carla Ponce, a forty-five-year-old professional Puerto Rican woman in Peoria, shared the difficulties she faced at work:

> I was the only Latina working in the office. The only Puerto Rican. Let me tell you, that was my first experience in the

corporate sector. It was terrible! I don't know if it was . . . because I was young, or I was a Latina/Puerto Rican, but I do know that they treated me very poorly. I felt rejected. . . When I started working and living here, I really didn't understand much about race and how people treat you differently because of the way you look. That was my first experience feeling prejudice.[3]

This chapter opens with the experiences of various Puerto Ricans describing their work and family life in Illinois. Historian Lilia Fernández reminds us that Mexicans and Puerto Ricans "served as a viable labor pools to fill American economic needs in the mid-twentieth century." Eduardo's and Rita's experiences, described above, are particularly insightful because they begin to frame the gendered expectations that working-class men and women faced in Chicago. Men were committed to working and supporting their families even in dangerous conditions, whereas for women, employment and family expectations tended to conflict. Rita's experience is a good example of this conflict. Rita wanted to work, but her husband wanted to maintain a traditional gendered division of labor. Our interviews revealed that the realities of family life in Chicago certainly challenged the traditional gendered division of labor among families and pushed women to work outside the home for extended periods of time.[4] Some women, like Rita, wanted a job so that they could provide additional resources for her family, but as a working mother she faced the additional issue of child care. And Carla's story captures the prejudices and discrimination that educated women experienced in the corporate sector in central Illinois. When read together, they allow us to capture some the issues that Puerto Rican women and men faced as workers and as members of families in Illinois.

Using the U.S. Census, we draw a profile of the family composition and occupational distribution of Puerto Ricans in Illinois across time. Demographic data are also useful in comparing Puerto Ricans in Illinois with other ethnic groups, deepening our understanding of how Puerto Ricans fare in relation to those other groups. Fieldwork and interview data complement each section of the chapter with rich and nuanced narratives of the family life and work experiences of Puerto Ricans. Puerto Ricans have worked hard to build secure and stable families in Illinois, but they are not immune to the problems and tensions that have besieged immigrant and minority families over the years. Work stressors, balancing work and family demands, discrimination, and unemployment are problems that have wreaked havoc among immigrant and minority families. Puerto Ricans, like other immigrant families, have shown resiliency in dealing with those stressors, but some problems can be difficult to escape. Poverty is an issue that has afflicted families in both Puerto Rico and the mainland United States, a topic we address in the last part of the chapter.

Puerto Ricans in Illinois live in a range of family types that have served them well concerning their adaptation. As shown in table 4.1, compared with the total female population in the United States, there are far more female-headed households in the Puerto Rican community. And the number of female householders is on the rise. For several reasons, including higher divorce rates, choosing not to marry, or marrying later in life, women are more likely than ever to identify themselves as householders. There is nothing inherently wrong with female-headed households, but these families become vulnerable to poverty.

Unsurprisingly, Puerto Rican men and women are drawn to destinations that provide higher incomes than the island does.[5] Indeed, Puerto Ricans living in Illinois have higher annual median household incomes than those living on the island ($47,379 in Illinois versus $19,977 in Puerto Rico). Even so, a Puerto Rican

Table 4.1. Percentage of Puerto Rican women compared with all women in the United States

Indicators	U.S. all women			P.R. women in the U.S.		
	2000	2010	% change	2000	2010	% change
Female households, no husband present	12.2	21.1	73	26.5	36.3	37
Female householder with related children under 18 years	7.2	49.6	589	18.4	63.6	246
Female-headed households in poverty	26.5	28.9	9	44	42.7	-3
All females living in poverty	13.5	15.1	12	28.2	27	-4

Source: Table created by Ivis García, from 2010 U.S. Decennial Census and American Community Survey 5-year estimates (2015).

Fig. 4.1. Puerto Rican women at San Juan Airport. El Mundo Newspaper Project, University of Puerto Rico, Rio Piedras Campus.

woman who was employed full time earned $3,300 less than the average Illinois woman in 2016. The disparity was even greater for Puerto Rican men, who earned on average $11,800 less than the typical male worker in Illinois. In general, Puerto Ricans had lower household incomes than the Illinois population as a whole, making on average $13,600 less per year than the typical Illinois household.[6]

Puerto Ricans have a strong presence in the labor force, with 64.6 percent involvement (65.2 percent in the population at large). The unemployment rate is slightly higher for Puerto Ricans (8.8 percent) than for the state as a whole (6.3 percent). When compared with the population at large, Puerto Ricans are more likely to be employed in the sectors of retail trade; public administration; arts, entertainment, and recreation; and accommodation and food services. Compared with Puerto Rican men, Puerto Rican women have lower annual median earnings (by about $2,500) and are much less likely to be in the labor force. (More than two in three Puerto Rican men are in the labor force versus only about three in five Puerto Rican women.) Puerto Rican women do, however, have a lower unemployment rate than Puerto Rican men (8.6 versus 9.0 percent).[7]

Family Life in Illinois:
Continuity, Change, and Conflicts

More than three decades of scholarship offer a wealth of stories and research about the experiences and struggles of Puerto Rican families in Chicago. Felix Padilla's now classic 1987 study, *Puerto Rican Chicago*, provides a glimpse of family life in the Windy City for the working-class families who arrived in the 1960s and 1970s. These families relied on each other for everything. Padilla points out how groups of families helped to constitute the first community settlements in Chicago. Families tended to migrate together or in stages and lived close to each other.[8] Congressman Luis Gutiérrez, a celebrated political hero in the Latino/Puerto Rican community in Illinois, describes life in these early barrios:

> In our first apartment down the block at 849 West Willow, I remember about a dozen Puerto Ricans who had just arrived from the island and were living in the basement of the building. Their apartment was smaller than ours, and I thought ours felt cramped, though there was plenty of room for the roaches and the mice. . . . This was Lincoln Park when it was Puerto Ricans living in two- and three-unit apartment buildings, with a few bigger ones here and there, before the traders and investment bankers tore them down or rehabbed them into million-dollar single family mansions. We were doing OK because my mom and dad both worked hard.[9]

According to Gutiérrez, two significant issues continue to shape family life and threaten the well-being of Puerto Rican families in Chicago: gentrification and the limited availability of affordable housing. These issues have a particular impact for aging Puerto Ricans. Ivis García and Mérida M. Rúa found that elderly Puerto Ricans in Chicago are concerned about gentrification and new commercial developments pushing them out of the communities where they have lived and raised their families.[10]

The role families play in moving and settling is still evident today. At O'Hare or Midway after a flight from San Juan has arrived, a familiar scene unfolds: large groups of family members gather to greet other family members. If families come during Christmastime, music and food may be part of the welcoming party. Families and community organizations are also critical during times of emergency. For example, Chicago welcomed Puerto

Rican families displaced by Hurricane Maria. A well-organized cadre of community organizations and city agencies have helped newcomers secure housing, clothes, and schooling for children, among other needs. Puerto Rican community groups and families have been pivotal in orchestrating newcomers' arrival and transition to living in the city, even if they are there only temporarily. For evacuees who have family in Chicago, the most onerous burden falls upon those relatives, who are the primary source of emotional support. In other words, Padilla's assertion that the family is the first shield of help for newcomers was true then and remains true now.

Padilla argued that, in Chicago, Puerto Rican families relied on transplanted cultural notions of *familismo*: the bonds of family and extended kinship networks. According to Padilla, "The cultural traditions of *el campesino* and *jíbaro* [peasants] of Puerto Rico retained their vitality in Chicago's Puerto Rican barrios primarily through family and friendship interactions and communication."[11] While it is true the family networks provided much help in the process of settlement, this idealized view of the family hides some of the issues that Puerto Ricans encountered in Chicago that made the process of settling a complex one for working-class households.[12] For example, Padilla began his narrative of the Puerto Rican family in Chicago by focusing on the Puerto Rican father, the sacrificing figure who unquestionably accepts "the responsibility for the economic welfare of the members of the family."[13] While it is true that men took their responsibilities as fathers and husbands seriously, by magnifying the role of the father, Padilla contributed to the problem feminists have raised in studies of the family: making invisible the work women do on behalf of their families as both mothers and workers.

A generation of feminist Puerto Rican scholars have taken on the task to fill in this gap by documenting how Puerto Rican women supported their families, took additional responsibilities such as employment outside the home, and advocated on behalf of their families in community settings. Furthermore, it was women who did the kin work, as Gina Pérez and Marisa Alicea call it, that sustained transnational family links, allowing families to grow and support each other across time and space. For example, Maura Toro-Morn has shown how some women migrated to do the reproductive, or domestic, work that would allow other women in their families to take jobs outside the home. Through interviews with working-class women in the city, Toro-Morn also found that some working mothers left their jobs in the export processing zones in Puerto Rico to reunite with their families in Chicago.[14] But when it entailed leaving their children behind, Puerto Rican women were reluctant to go. Many resisted leaving Puerto Rico and reuniting with husbands in Chicago. Once in Chicago, it was clear that a number of families could not live on the wages of working fathers alone. Toro-Morn reports that husbands would take on additional work, in keeping with the traditional gendered division of labor. Some women, however, pushed their husbands to accept their working roles. It was evident that women found affirmation in the work they did both in and outside the home, although that did not change their "second shift." In the following passage, a daughter raised in Chicago remembers family life:

> For as long as I can remember my mother and father were always working. The two of them worked in factory jobs, but they were still working in a job—they were not without work. My mother stopped working during the time when the three of us were babies. We were all about a year or so apart, but after we were a little bigger she went back to work. Our parents simply needed to work to care for us. They always wanted to give us everything we needed, and for that they needed two checks.[15]

In keeping with what has been found among other Latino groups, Puerto Rican women contended with the double burden of working for wages and supporting their families. In Chicago, as in other parts of Illinois, working women are still responsible for cooking, cleaning, and caring for the children. Migration may not have altered their gender roles, but given the exigencies of living in the city, many have become quite creative at working through those tensions. Many working-class mothers emerged as activists and advocates on behalf of their own families and communities, contributing to their affirmation and empowerment. We will turn to women's activism in chapters 5 and 6.

Child care has always been an issue for working women. Puerto Rican women in Chicago were very resourceful as they addressed their child care needs. Again, Toro-Morn reports that women developed communal child care centers. A friend or a stay-at-home mom would agree to care for children in exchange for money. Toro-Morn writes that "these informal child care arrangements allowed children to be cared for in a familiar environment, where there was mutual trust . . . and flexibility. Children were cared for in a family setting where language, customs, and Puerto Rican traditions were reinforced."[16]

Here we must recognize how migration is indeed a force that requires complex gendered negotiations between men and women. In other words, as masculinity and femininity are reconstituted in their new place of settlement, we must explore how these identities flex, shift, and are reconstructed across a transnational field. Here, the Puerto Rican experience in Illinois is particularly relevant as an interesting tension that manifests through the experiences of Puerto Rican working-class women. Both Marisa Alicea and Gina Pérez note that Puerto Rican women worked very hard in developing and maintaining kin networks that helped them in the reconstruction of ritual celebrations, care of relatives, and supporting families across a transnational field that included Illinois, Puerto Rico, and other Puerto Rican communities in the United States. Pérez argues that kin work is a meaningful way that women strengthen their networks of solidarity. Kin work helps women sustain strong families across generations. Alicea notes that women derived much pleasure from nurturing these kin networks, even though it added another burden to their lives as immigrant working women. Interestingly, sociologist Elizabeth Aranda has noted that this is a characteristic found among middle-class and educated women in other Puerto Rican communities. She points out that men do some emotional work but that the more significant share of the work is done by women.

Aranda argues that these "transnational ways of belonging" constitute gendered routes to U.S. incorporation. She persuasively makes this transnational work a case for a gendered understanding of assimilation:

If assimilation has been the story of male immigrants, living transnationally is how women attempt to gain independence and mobility (tenets of assimilation) yet also retain their homeland identities (ethnic retention) by recreating homeland culture into hybrid, transnational identities with the intention of transforming, even coopting, their cultural backgrounds so as to redefine them, absent culture's patriarchal undercurrents. In this sense, transnational patterns of living are to women what assimilation is to men.[17]

Second- and third-generation Puerto Ricans in Illinois also offer a window into the complex world of family life and their complicated processes of assimilation. It is evident how second- and third-generation Puerto Ricans grow up in the context of extended families and how the family plays a role in affirming a Puerto Rican identity, a sense of commitment to the community, and the importance of education as a means for social mobility. Rúa captures this complex world in the opening pages of her book *A Grounded* Identidad*: Making New Lives in Chicago's Puerto Rican Neighborhoods*:

> My sense of narratives of place and community and my first "field trips" began on weekends after church on Sunday afternoons when I was a child in Chicago's Puerto Rican neighborhoods. My father, Luis Rúa, a welder by trade, became tour guide as my mother, my *abuela* (grandmother), my two sisters, and I climbed into our gray Buick Regal for his weekly history lesson and his lesson plan for his daughters' futures. . . . He loved the city even when the feelings were not mutual. . . . After he had driven us to places where he had lived . . . we went beyond, to places of his aspirations. . . . [We would] arrive, by one route or another, to one of Chicago's elite campuses, the University of Chicago or Northwestern.[18]

Similarly, Marisa Alicea's auto-ethnographic essay describes how she grew up hearing her relatives say, "*Cuando nosotros vivíamos en la sesentitres* (when we lived on sixty-third) as a prelude to funny and sad stories of how they got lost on their way to work and the difficulties they encountered."[19]

Puerto Rican artist Carlos Flores, who dropped out of school, writes that "it was divine intervention that a camera was placed in my hands during my teens." Intrigued by his own family and community, he took pictures of his world. Now, these pictures are a testament to the hard work and dedication of Puerto Rican families in the initial stages of community formation: "I would photograph my mother cooking *arroz con garbanzoz y patita* [rice with chickpeas and pork] in her kitchen; neighbors working on their automobiles; mothers walking down the street with their children; children playing a baseball game behind their apartment building; and people lounging on a street corner or dancing and eating at a picnic."[20]

Again, we turn to Luis Gutiérrez's autobiography, *Still Dreaming: My Journey from the Barrio to Capitol Hill*, to expose some of the tensions between parents and children:

> I grew up in Chicago listening to my mother say *"Esta no es mi tierra*—This is not my land." She said it a lot in the winters, after snowstorms. In Puerto Rico, you never woke up in the morning, looked out your window, saw a sheet of ice, and wondered how you would get to work. My mom said *esta no es mi tierra* when people broke into our apartment and stole things . . . when my aunt Wilda had her purse snatched off her shoulder in the middle of the day . . . when she saw the Latin Kings gang members hanging out on our corner. . . . *Esta no es mi tierra* was true for my mother. It wasn't true for me. Chicago was my land.[21]

Fig. 4.2. Luis Gutiérrez, U.S. representative for the Fourth Congressional District of Illinois, 1993–2019. Wikipedia, https://en.wikipedia.org/wiki/Luis_Guti%C3%A9rrez.

Generational tensions between parents and children are evident in the Puerto Rican families we and others interviewed in Illinois. Using interviews with second- and third-generation Puerto Ricans in Chicago, Toro-Morn and Alicea found how Puerto Rican parents constructed notions of Puerto Rico as an authentic cultural space to resist the dehumanization they encountered in the city.[22] Home was also the place for the traditional gender socialization of children. In keeping with idealized gendered notions, parents tended to construct a worldview that perceived Puerto Rico as an authentic place, a paradise where there were few dangers, and urban life in Chicago as a dangerous place for both men and women. In their gendered world, young men could fall prey to violence and gangs and daughters could become sexually active and "meter las patas" (a colloquialism in Puerto Rican Spanish that means "screwing up" but in this particular context might mean "getting pregnant out of wedlock"). However, crime and teenage pregnancy are severe problems for Puerto Ricans in both the mainland United States and Puerto Rico, a topic we will address later.

The world of urban dangers placed daughters at a disadvantage because they were expected to stay home and many were policed by other members of the family. Toro-Morn and Alicea write that mothers promoted traditional gender norms even though they were "acutely conscious of the repression, conflicts, and power relations" embedded in these norms.[23] Daughters also recognized the contradictions and inconsistencies of their parents' gender ideologies and actual practices. As Toro-Morn and Alicea put it, "Daughters witnessed a mismatch between traditional gender responsibilities they were expected to carry out and their mothers' lived realities."[24] Daughters and sons resisted and negotiated these gendered notions, some in a way that did not disrupt family relations. A case in point is education. Puerto Rican parents generally frowned upon letting children move away from home but valued education as a goal for upward mobility. Daughters and sons used education as a way to leave home and wrestle with some freedoms for themselves.

Sociologist Lorena García's groundbreaking ethnographic work *Respect Yourself, Protect Yourself: Latina Girls and Sexual Identity* explores the sexual identities of Mexican and Puerto Rican girls in Chicago as they became sexually active, came to terms with their sexual orientations, and struggled with becoming mothers at an early age. In contrast to the immigrant mothers we described earlier, the second- and third-generation mothers García interviewed used four strategies to talk about sex. Some promoted safe sex, while framing sexual knowledge as a form of respect, and others openly shared their own sexual experiences as a way to underscore existing racial and ethnic disadvantages. Some mothers disclosed their daughters' sexual behaviors to other women in their families to seek social and moral support from relatives. Disapproving of the sexual behavior of teenage daughters was also a way to save face as a mother. Some mothers made evaluative statements of white girls' sexuality as a way to safeguard their own daughters' sexuality. Interestingly, this shows how these gendered identities are reconstituted, not only looking inward to Puerto Rican or Mexican norms but, more importantly, in the context of a racial boundary. Mothers would say that white girls "tienen mucha libertad" (have too much freedom) and were "sin vergüenza" (without shame). Mothers did not want their daughters to "act like white girls."

All of these approaches show how race and ethnicity matters in the reconstruction of these gendered norms and identities. These strategies also disclose how mothers were aware of the negative stereotypes that existed about them, and by trying to help their daughters come to their own sexual identities, they, too, gained some sexual respectability. But the most revealing world in García's ethnography is the world of the young women who crafted a sexual ethic of their own, even within the constraints of their families. Many turned to education as a way to gain information and empower themselves, but educational institutions are often ill-equipped to address these issues as they want girls to conform to sexual standards of abstinence. The lesbian girls in her study were by far the most vulnerable, as many were silenced and rejected by their own families and school. García was particularly adamant that twin forces of heteronormativity and homophobia were at play for these lesbian-identified young women.

We do not want to conclude this section without addressing the experiences of the elderly *abuelos* (grandfathers) and *abuelas* (grandmothers), the generation of those who have aged in Illinois and for whom Illinois will be their final resting place. Most immigrants leave home convinced they will return to live their last days in their country of origin, but as is frequently the case, many do not return, primarily due to family obligations. Mérida M. Rúa speaks eloquently about the rituals of death and identity in her ethnography.[25] Since she lived above a funeral home during her research, she describes the rituals of death and dying for Puerto Ricans in the city. Irma M. Olmedo interviewed a number of elderly Puerto Ricans living in a local nursing home and found that they lived by an ethic of *respeto* (respect), a core value of their families and communities that they wished to bequeath to future generations.[26] The women she talked to affirmed the work we discussed: they had tried to balance work and children but at great expense to their spouses. For some, their marriages ended in divorce, an event that placed their families in a vulnerable position. In the end, Olmedo, like Aranda, returned to the notion of accommodation without assimilation to signify that these women accommodated while resisting and maintaining an identity of their own that they used to combat the dehumanization they contended with in the workplace.

The families we encountered in central and southern Illinois were very diverse, but in many ways, they affirm the evidence of research conducted in Chicago. Again, this is a small sample, hardly representative, but very insightful in its own right. The Puerto Rican men and women we interviewed in central and southern Illinois were in long-term marriages. Most of them had adolescent children or were in the throes of raising young children. Since some interviews took place in the summer, we witnessed this household situation firsthand as children interrupted our discussions with requests to go out. We also observed younger adults coming in and out of the house for sports activities. The couples we interviewed were diverse in that most were married to whites. One Puerto Rican man was married to a black woman. Another Puerto Rican man had been married to an African immigrant, but at the time of the interview he was divorced. Two Puerto Rican women were married and then later migrated to Illinois. Two women were single mothers due to divorce. Although our sample is small, many issues addressed in our interviews had also surfaced in other studies of Puerto Rican families. A thread shared by the families we interviewed was their preoccupation with the socialization, family obligations, and identity formations of sons and daughters. Whether in Chicago or central Illinois, Puerto Rican parents idealized Puerto Rico and continued to perceive that their lives in Illinois were dangerous. Second- and third-generation Puerto Ricans raised in central Illinois felt they were also subject to strict sexual boundaries.

Work Experiences of Puerto Ricans in Illinois

The first group of working-class Puerto Rican women arrived in Chicago as contract laborers to do domestic work for upper-middle-class and wealthy women in the city. These *domésticas* encountered a hostile workplace that valued them merely as a source of cheap labor. One employer told a local agency in Chicago, "For sixty dollars, [the Puerto Rican girl] does the work of three people: the nanny, the cook and the maid."[27] In fact, the situation for the *domésticas* got so bad that anthropologist Elena Padilla and her classmates at the University of Chicago mobilized themselves on behalf of these workers. They wrote letters to prominent Puerto Rican figures and, with Muñoz Lee, compiled a report detailing the exploitation and mistreatment of the workers. Men who had been contracted to work in the steel mills did not fare any better; they, too, encountered a hostile work environment where they were subject to discrimination and abuse and were included in the report Padilla and her classmates authored with Muñoz Lee. The report was sent to the Department of Labor in Puerto Rico and several newspapers on the island. In November 1947, graduate students along with several workers picketed the offices of the employment agency that brought the women to Chicago under contract. After the abuses were made public, Padilla and her colleagues helped some of the women get released from their contracts. Many stayed in the city and incorporated themselves into the service and manufacturing sectors. Puerto Ricans have contributed to the workforce of Chicago and, broadly, Illinois in consistent ways. Since their arrival in the city and state, they have worked hard to support their families. Interviews we conducted in central and southern Illinois indicate that workplace prejudice and discrimination continue to shape the work experiences of women and men.

Drawing on the 1960s U.S. Census, Toro-Morn offers us the first full profile of the occupation distribution of Puerto Ricans in Chicago. At the time, 45.7 percent of Puerto Ricans worked as operative and kindred workers, 11.7 percent worked as service workers, 13.7 percent were laborers, and only 5.2 percent worked in clerical occupations. An even smaller 1.2 percent were managers and 1.6 percent were professional workers. A similar distribution existed for women, as 63 percent worked as operatives, 6.8 percent in service work, 8 percent in clerical work, and 2.5 percent in professional work.[28] These categories have changed over the years as the economy shifted from an industrial to a postindustrial—and now global gig—economy, making longitudinal comparison difficult. We know, however, that Puerto Ricans entered Chicago's labor market in positions that quickly disappeared as the city moved to a postindustrial economy. This spelled disaster for many working-class families. Some were able to shift through educational opportunities, but others succumbed to unemployment and poverty.

The 1980s saw some changes in the occupational distribution of men and women as highly educated Puerto Ricans entered the labor market in most white-collar professions. Toro-Morn reports that the percentage of women employed in white-collar jobs went from 12.9 percent in 1960 to 63.6 percent in 1990. Clerical work was a job category that also experienced increases, from 8.1 percent in 1960 to 32.6 percent in 1990.[29] Growth of the Puerto Rican community along Paseo Boricua (Puerto Rican Promenade, a commercial strip in Humboldt Park with many Puerto Rican businesses and organizations) also led to the rise of an entrepreneurial self-employed social class. Toro-Morn noted that several women in her sample had become entrepreneurs and were able to use the ethnic enclave of Paseo Boricua as an essential way to achieve this success.

The Puerto Rican Agenda report issued in 2012 helps us to build a profile of what happened in the intervening years for Puerto Ricans. For example, when compared with Mexicans and Cubans, Puerto Ricans tend to have high unemployment rates. Further, during the 2008 recession, they were hit hardest.[30] Puerto Ricans continue to be employed in retail and other service sectors. Manufacturing still offers Puerto Ricans some employment opportunities but not as many as for Mexican Americans. Second- and third-generation Puerto Ricans have used educational opportunities as a way to move into jobs that tend to be more secure and offer better benefits than those occupied by their parents.

In central and southern Illinois, the experiences of Puerto Rican women and men are varied. Some find themselves employed by white-collar corporations and educational institutions, primary sources of employment in these communities. When taken together, the stories they shared with us revealed that although some Puerto Ricans find themselves fulfilled by work, they cannot escape the problems of balancing work and family demands. This problem seemed to be more pronounced among the women we interviewed.

Poverty and Puerto Rican Families

Poverty in Illinois is a social problem that has historically affected all racial and ethnic groups, but when the demographic data is disaggregated, it is evident that poverty tends to affect some groups more than others. In 2016, 1.7 million people were living below the poverty line in Illinois. Some 14 percent of the population lived below the federally recognized poverty level for a family of four. When seen through a racial ethnic lens, the rates of poverty are staggering: 28.2 percent of African American families live below the poverty level in Illinois, followed by Native Americans with a rate of 25 percent and Latino families at 19 percent. Asian Americans and whites had a poverty rate of 11.6 and 10 percent, respectively.[31] Recently, the state of Illinois has introduced the concept of extreme poverty as a way to further nuance our understanding of poverty. In 2017, over 670,000 people in Illinois were living in extreme poverty. For a family of three, that means living on less than $9,387 per year.[32] People living in desperate poverty struggle to keep a roof over their heads, put food on the table, meet their most basic human needs, and provide for their families every day. The problem of poverty in Illinois has become even more complicated since the 2008 recession and budget crisis that engulfed the state for more than two years.

The Illinois Latino Family Commission, a statewide organization devoted to understanding and promoting the well-being of Latino families in Illinois, commissioned Ivis García Zambrana through the Voorhees Center at the University of Illinois at Chicago to research the plight of Latino families in the state and to write a report on her findings. The report, coauthored with Anna Bachman, offers some valuable information: alongside Florida and New Jersey, Illinois has the lowest poverty levels among Latinos. In 2014 the poverty rate for all Latinos in Illinois was 18 percent. Further, "about 1 in 4 (23%) Latino children live in poverty in Illinois—although high, still lower than any of the other states used for comparison." Poverty rates for Latino elderly in Illinois were at 16 percent, slightly higher than in California (14 percent) but lower than the rest of the states used for comparison. When we disaggregate poverty by nationality, it is evident that in Illinois, poverty continues to be an issue disproportionately affecting Puerto Ricans. Compared with Mexicans and Cubans, Puerto Ricans had the highest percentages of people living in poverty. Some 22 percent of Puerto Ricans in Illinois live in poverty, compared with 18 percent of Mexicans, 13 percent of Cubans, 16 percent of Dominicans, and 14 percent of Central Americans. The rates for the elderly and children in poverty are equally worrisome. For Puerto Ricans, 28 percent of children and 23 percent of seniors live in poverty.[33]

Poverty is a significant obstacle to upward mobility across racial and ethnic groups because it places families, particularly families with children, in a precarious situation. Among single female-headed households, poverty tends to be most prominent in families where children are under eighteen years old. Poverty has reached historically high levels for U.S. women, but poverty rates have dropped notably for Puerto Rican women, both on the island of Puerto Rico and in the mainland United States. The increase in poverty for the population at large is mostly explained by the rise in poverty for non-Hispanic white women over sixty-five years old.

The first Puerto Rican families who arrived in Chicago occupied jobs at the bottom of the city's labor market. These jobs were poorly paid and did not offer the economic security that workers needed to support their families. Working-class women supported their families the way they knew how—by working outside the home, even when husbands protested, and by doing the reproductive labor that sustained their families in Illinois and Puerto Rico. The question that needs to be asked is this: Did the domestic roles of Puerto Rican women change to acknowledge their roles as wage earners? We found that Puerto Rican women faced the double burden of working for wages and coming home to do the work that supported their families. They were not able to negotiate the gendered division of labor in a way that allowed them some freedom and time for themselves, but they wrestled to gain some of that freedom for themselves. In other words, the *abuelitas* that Irma Olmedo interviewed confronted a world of many demands. As Olmedo states, Puerto Rican women had to "learn to handle multiple bureaucracies: schools for their children, hospitals for medical care, landlords for housing, employers for jobs, and merchants for their everyday survival needs. They had to discharge all these responsibilities in English, a new language, and in the face of obstacles such as racism and discrimination. . . . They organized and strategized with cousins, aunts, female neighbors, and others."[34]

The interviews we conducted with Puerto Ricans in central and southern Illinois do not quite tell the full story, but they offer a glimpse of how these families also strive to balance work and family demands. Here we see evidence of how, whether working-class or middle-class, parents struggle raising sons and daughters in their own communities.

Raising Puerto Rican children in Illinois has been difficult for families across the board. To some extent, the problems Puerto Rican families face are similar to those confronting other middle-class parents—gender socialization, discipline, schooling—but we also found that Puerto Rican parents have the additional task of teaching children to be proud of who they are as Puerto Ricans. For example, speaking Spanish in the home, taking family vacations to Puerto Rico, and regularly communicating with family members in Puerto Rico are ways that parents continue to affirm Puerto Rican identity in the family. Will those practices be sufficient for second- and third-generation Puerto Rican youth to sustain their identity? This remains a question that will need to be answered by future research. If rates of intermarriage continue, it is entirely possible that the notion of what it means to be Puerto Rican will change in years to come.

5

EDUCATIONAL STRUGGLES THEN AND NOW

We open this chapter with a quote by Lourdes Santiago describing her public school experiences in Chicago.

> School for me was a joyful experience. I was a teacher's pet. I would always do my homework and sit at my desk quietly. . . . Because of the way I was as a student, the teacher would always call on me to answer questions. . . . Since I was so involved in doing my schoolwork, the teachers pushed me and stimulated me. I was convinced—really believed in my mind—that I would one day succeed. I was so sure that I would become something. It sounded so simple: I will become something as long as I kept going to school and was doing well. In fact, while I was in eighth grade, I was recruited to participate in a program at Clemente High School . . . [but then] everything changed when I turned 15. I was in high school and [fell in love] with my boyfriend. . . . My involvement with the gang was a way of showing my boyfriend I was down, that I was part of the street scene.[1]

Felix Padilla, well-known Puerto Rican scholar, recounted his start in an English-speaking school:

> At the age of 13 I entered the public-school system in the United States. At this time, the school I came to attend in Chicago was, just like its surrounding neighborhood, predominantly white, though each year that passed you could see the student population shift, eventually transforming into the largest Puerto Rican school in the city. . . . What a shock for *un jíbaros* [a rural peasant] . . . . What a shock for someone who did not speak a word of English! Bilingual classes were not yet part

of the school curriculum. . . . Boy was I out of place! . . . And although there was little connection between school and my "self" and though staying in school for me was an important and difficult challenge, I did manage to stay. I had to find a way to remain in school. After all, I was going to be a major league baseball player and, only by playing high school ball, I reasoned, I would get signed.[2]

Sociologist Marisa Alicea, Chicago scholar, remembered her introduction to a bilingual classroom:

I recall vividly the day I was escorted by the school's vice principal to my new fifth grade bilingual classroom. It was the day that started out with my having a lot of quiet nervous energy about the prospect of a new beginning but which ended with the realization that I could accomplish more than my previous teachers and prior education had ever led me to believe. As we waited outside our classroom door, I could hear that not only was the teacher speaking Spanish, she was doing so in the manner in which my family spoke, and I spoke it at home. The sounds of her voice shattered separations I was not consciously aware existed between home and school life. When our teacher came to the door to greet us, it was clear to me from the way she spoke and from her physical features that she was Puerto Rican. I was in awe. It was the first time that I had met a Puerto Rican teacher and that I realized Puerto Ricans could be teachers.[3]

These stories speak powerfully about students' desire to succeed and the role of education as a path to achievement and affirmation. Lourdes said that she "really believed in my mind—that I would one day succeed." Felix was determined: "I had to find a way to remain in school." "I could accomplish more than my previous teachers and prior education had ever led me to believe," said Marisa.

Broadly, the view of education as an important individual and collective value is shared across the Puerto Rican diaspora. But keeping students in school has been an elusive dream for Puerto Ricans living in the United States for many decades. Edwin Meléndez and Carlos Vargas-Ramos report in *Puerto Ricans at the Dawn of the New Millennium* that, although there has been some progress in getting a high school diploma and college education, "the disparity between educational attainment among Puerto Ricans versus non-Hispanic whites and other Hispanic subpopulations has remained constant."[4] Unfortunately, as we will show in this chapter, this is also true for Puerto Ricans in Illinois, where the high school dropout rate remains high compared with whites and where gains in college enrollment and graduation are modest.

In this chapter, we first examine the historical struggles of Puerto Rican parents and community activists to secure educational opportunities for Puerto Rican youth in Illinois, notably Chicago. Puerto Rican parents understand the value of education and care a lot about the education of their children. It was a value Puerto Ricans had internalized from the modernization project that enveloped Puerto Rico in the 1950s, which we discussed in chapter 2. Like other Latino immigrants and African Americans, Puerto Rican parents in Illinois perceive the educational system as a door to the American dream and to opportunities they did not have. In fact, these issues mobilized working parents in the 1960s to advocate for bilingual education programs in the Chicago Public Schools district and the development of schools like Roberto Clemente High School, which we will document in this chapter. These issues continue to animate Puerto Rican parents and activists today. One organization with an important history of educational advocacy in the state of Illinois is ASPIRA, which means "aspire" in Spanish. Originally founded in New York City's Puerto Rican community, ASPIRA came to Chicago in the 1960s and today still plays a vital role in the lives of Puerto Ricans and youth of color in the state of Illinois.

The story of Lourdes that begins this chapter points out two of the most significant problems facing Puerto Rican youth in large urban centers: gangs and school dropouts, topics we also address in this chapter more fully. Those issues mattered in the early stages of community development and still do today. In 2010, the dropout rate among Puerto Ricans in Illinois was about 28 percent, significantly higher than for African Americans (20 percent) and whites (15 percent). Lourdes's story shows how gang membership and the incarceration of Puerto Ricans continue to cut short the dreams and educational aspirations of many Puerto Ricans in Chicago. Across the state, additional issues such as work and family demands curtail the educational expectations of students, too. Aware of the historical legacy of these problems, parents and community leaders continue to organize to address these issues. It is in this context that we also examine how some students persevere through the tumultuous years of high school and manage to graduate. In the state of Illinois and notably in Chicago, alternative high schools have become an essential institution for those who drop out of school. There is evidence to suggest that these schools are not only a pipeline to meaningful careers for Puerto Rican youth but a transformational space to affirm their identities.

The stories of Felix and Marisa, who today are well-known scholars of the Puerto Rican diaspora, allow us to briefly address the experiences of Puerto Ricans in universities across the state of Illinois and offer a preliminary profile of Puerto Ricans who have come to occupy important roles in the ranks of the professorate at institutions of higher learning.

In this chapter, we focus more fully on the educational issues and struggles of Puerto Rican families, using interviews and fieldwork collected exclusively for this book. Again, given that a significant part of the Puerto Rican population in Illinois has lived, worked, and gone to school in Chicago, there is more material about Chicago experiences than those downstate. However, we have collected interviews with parents and students in other regions of Illinois to offer a point of contrast. The educational struggles of Puerto Ricans in the Land of Lincoln could probably fill a book on their own, but our effort here is to provide a broad overview, not an exhaustive one.

Educational Struggles through a Historical Lens

Leaders in the Puerto Rican community of Chicago offer evidence of the poor educational conditions that students faced in the early stages of community formation. Their experiences can be found in the documentary *Chicago's Puerto Rican Story*, produced and directed by Puerto Rican filmmaker Antonio Franceschi. According to José López, a community leader and educator, "The conditions in the schools were horrible. I remember usually finding most Puerto Ricans in the closet rather than in the classroom because they were a problem. They were not looked upon as students, they were looked upon as problems to be dealt with." In the same documentary, well-known Puerto Rican photographer Carlos Flores added, "Coming into the school system, it was kind of interesting because there were no bilingual programs. Basically, what they did at school is that they put you in the back of the room. You spend a lot of time drawing with Crayolas and then when you learn how to speak English you could join the rest of the class."[5]

Puerto Rican congressman Luis Gutiérrez remembers that in the Lincoln Park school he attended, Latino students were punished if they spoke Spanish. Gutiérrez writes in his memoir, "I remember Latino kids being sent to the back of the room, or even the coat room, to play Monopoly and Parcheesi with one another while the rest of us did our ABC's." But "once the teachers decided I could understand them, I didn't have to stay in the corner with the Latino kids who were brought up speaking only Spanish."[6]

This situation is very similar to what Juan González described happening to newly arrived Puerto Rican children in New York City schools. He called it the "sink or swim approach to learning."[7] Students had to persevere in a school system that did not perceive them as worthy learners. Mervin Méndez adds, "There was a lot of labeling mainly because we could not speak English, or we spoke English with an accent." Gamaliel Rodríguez points to a problem that existed in the school system: "They just didn't know anything about us. They changed my name from Gamaliel to Bobby because they could not pronounce my name." Felix Padilla notes that these attitudes and institutional barriers that Puerto Rican students encountered prevented them from continuing as far in school as middle-class white students did.[8] A Puerto Rican community member observed that when he started at Tuley High School, he was one of 1,300 in the freshman class, yet he recalled that only 348 graduated—a dropout rate of over 70 percent.

The 1960s and 1970s was a time of great upheaval, and social activism around the country focused on education. Propelled by the landmark Supreme Court case *Brown v. Board of Education*, people of color collectively mobilized to demand educational opportunities. The prejudices and discrimination that these groups faced were institutionalized and systemic; they encompassed all levels of the educational system from local to state and required additional policy measures and interventions. Educational gains for these groups would not be visible until Puerto Ricans were able to place educators in positions of power to advocate on behalf of students of color and create institutions like ASPIRA.

In Illinois, Puerto Rican community leaders and parents were aware of efforts to address the needs of Spanish-speaking children in other parts of the country. For example, the arrival of Cuban refugees in Florida prompted the development of one of the nation's first bilingual school programs. Similar programs followed in two different school districts in Texas. At the federal level, the passing of the Bilingual Education Act of 1968—popularly known as Title VII of the Elementary and Secondary Education Act—helped raise awareness about the language issues faced by Latino students. This new legislation recognized the rights of a child's native language and its benefits in his or her education. In Chicago, Puerto Rican parents learned about these important cases and mobilized by meeting with key political figures, protesting in the streets, and engaging teachers and local officials.

In Illinois, as well as across the nation, Puerto Rican parents recognized education as the locus of opportunities but were also aware that their children were not being treated fairly. Many were outraged at this treatment and sought to address it on their own and through political activism. Educator Irma M. Olmedo, while interviewing elderly Puerto Ricans about their *memorias* (memories) of the early stages of community life, captured some of the strategies parents used to stay involved and keep educators accountable regarding the education of their children. One of her interviewees stated, "I was in the PTA and never missed the meetings. Two of my daughters were in ASPIRA and my boys were in the ROTC. I would not miss an event with the ROTC and my children. I didn't have a car but something always turned up for me. And as a mother I liked to go to Open House, but not to other events. But, I was always vigilant. And I would tell the principal, don't take anything from my child without my signature. Because I saw how other parents suffered with their children."[9]

Further, Puerto Rican community leaders framed education as an urgent civil right and, through editorials in local newspapers, helped raise awareness and solutions. In Chicago, the local Puerto Rican newspaper, *El Puertorriqueño* (The Puerto Rican), featured several articles a year denouncing public education.[10] For community leaders it was clear that the barrio schools could not accomplish their mission because the conditions were just deplorable. A study conducted by the U.S. Commission on Civil Rights concluded that Chicago schools failed to educate Puerto Rican children.[11] In the 1970s the average schooling for Puerto Ricans was 7.9 years, and only 15 percent completed high school. In comparison, African Americans had an average schooling of 11 years, with 40 percent finishing high school. Parents and community leaders identified the curriculum as a source of problems.

They knew that some teachers were not supportive and, since they didn't live in the community, could not understand the unique sociohistorical location that Puerto Ricans occupied. In short, schools lacked educators and programs to keep Puerto Rican students in schools. Puerto Rican parents in Chicago mobilized to address these issues in different ways. Some advocated in public schools while others advocated in local nonprofit community groups, like ASPIRA.

A turning point in the history of the community was the 1966 Chicago riots. Particularly the Division Street riots of that year represent a moment in the history of the community that publicly exposed the range of problems Puerto Ricans faced as residents in Chicago and the issues of police harassment of Puerto Rican youth. On the fiftieth anniversary of the riot, sociologist Michael Rodríguez-Muñiz noted that the uprising interrupted what was considered normal in the city: the segregation of Puerto Ricans, workplace discrimination, and the mistreatment and devaluation of Puerto Rican youth.[12] Historian Lilia Fernández adds, "The Division Street riots that rocked West Town neighborhood in 1966 left an indelible mark on the Puerto Rican population in Chicago. Whether they had participated in the events or condemned them, Puerto Ricans had become more closely associated with crime, lawlessness, and social disorder. The front-page headlines of local newspapers reinforced for several days that Puerto Rican were a 'problem' for law enforcement and the city more generally. Few told the story of the pressures that Puerto Ricans had been under for more than a decade. The compounded effects of poverty, prejudice, and displacement had made conditions difficult."[13]

Educational opportunities, bilingual education, and neighborhood schools became issues that propelled many to the front lines of activism. Mirelsie Velázquez writes that this is what happened to Maria Cerda. She was a student enrolled at the University of Chicago when she was tapped to become Mayor Richard J. Daley's first Puerto Rican appointed to the Chicago Board of Education in the aftermath of the riots. The Chicago Board of Education had not had African American and Puerto Rican representation since its inception in the 1870s. Cerda reflected on the historic nature of her appointment: "It was a lot of work. At the time I had kids and I had not worked for 10 years. . . . It was really an effort because there were many meetings. It was an exciting period."[14]

Significant community efforts were also placed into creating new community schools that would meet the needs of the youth. For example, Tuley High School saw a massive influx of Puerto Rican students as Puerto Ricans settled in Humboldt Park. In the 1970s, Tuley's capacity was fifteen hundred students, yet it had more than three thousand, leading to problems of overcrowding, lack of infrastructure, and mistreatment from educators. Parents and community members led several sit-ins at the school to raise their concerns about overcrowding and the conditions at Tuley.[15] Carmen Valentín, a graduate of Northeastern University, was one of several leaders in the community who took on this effort by organizing the Coalition for Tuley, a larger group that advocated for better conditions in the school and for the removal of the principal, Herbert Fink, whom they viewed as responsible for the problems of prejudice and discrimination there. In her role as a counselor at Tuley, she encouraged students to mobilize to bring attention to their issues. This is the broader context that led to the development of Roberto Clemente High School.

Roberto Clemente High School: Pride and Struggle

Although very few people in Illinois know that there is a high school in the city of Chicago named after a cherished Puerto Rican baseball hero—Roberto Clemente—most Puerto Ricans in the city are very proud of the school and what it represents. Roberto Clemente High School—renamed Roberto Clemente Community Academy in 2015 and simply called "Clemente" by many—is today a celebrated landmark in the architectural landscape of the Puerto Rican community. The school is near one of the massive steel Puerto Rican flags, at Western and Division, that welcomes visitors to Paseo Boricua. It is difficult to address the history of the school adequately, but when seen through the eyes of some community residents, the school is not only a symbol of the struggle to secure educational opportunities but today a source of great pride. Many important events have been held at the school. In 1998, the Puerto Rican Arts Alliance celebrated its first Cuatro Festival.[16] In 1983, the school hosted a debate among the top contenders for mayor of the city: Harold Washington, Jane Byrne, and Richard M. Daley.[17] Clemente was also featured in *As We See It*, a national television series about racially mixed public schools and what desegregation looked like in everyday life, from dating to academics.[18]

Fig. 5.1. Mosaic of Roberto Clemente in front of Roberto Clemente Community Academy. Photograph by Ivis García.

The school opened to students in the fall of 1974 in the aftermath of the activism that engulfed the community. There was some debate about its location—some advocated for Humboldt Park while others preferred Division Street—but Mayor Daley's administration placed it along Division and established its capacity as four thousand students.[19] The naming of the school proved to be a struggle. In October 1974, the school district board agreed to name new schools after Frederick Nerge, an early settler, and John Ender and Jonas Salk, the physicians who helped to defeat polio. Clemente was included in a list of names not initially considered, but public support, especially from the Puerto Rican community, forced the board to reconsider.[20] It was even more significant that Clemente had died a year earlier in a plane crash as he was flying to Nicaragua to provide relief for earthquake victims.

In its thirty-plus years of existence, the school has been at the center of several controversies. The school became the site of differing educational visions in the 1980s. As a community school, some teachers and community leaders wanted to see more content and connections to the larger colonial context facing Puerto Ricans.[21] But some perceived this content as political propaganda.

As a community school, Clemente has seen its share of gang violence. According to *Kids First—Primero Los Niños*, a study conducted in the 1980s, about 40 percent of students reported being physically assaulted by gangs at Clemente.[22] The release of the report was followed by a march where hundreds of Puerto Rican families carried a mahogany casket, symbolizing the generations of young people who had lost their lives because of gang violence.[23] The study showed that gang violence drove many students to drop out of Clemente, leaving school altogether or enrolling in alternative schools, a topic we address later in this chapter. According to Larry Vaughn from the Alternative School Network, anywhere from 40 to 50 percent of students cited gang harassment as the primary reason for changing schools. In 1987, with about three thousand students, the school had a total of twenty gangs.[24] The problem is ongoing. For example, in 2013, gun violence claimed the lives of three students at Clemente.[25]

The academic standing of the school had been a source of concern, too. Although Clemente has made significant progress in the last twenty years, it scored only two out of ten possible stars in the national GreatSchools ranking in 2017. Further, Clemente students on average perform poorly on the Prairie State Achievement Examination, an annual exam taken by all high school juniors in Illinois, compared with students in the district and state as a whole. Based on state standards for academic achievement, the test assesses proficiency in reading, mathematics, and science.

In 2017, only 756 students were enrolled at Clemente even though Clemente's building has capacity for 3,100 students. The student population has dropped significantly in thirty years because families of color are moving out of the neighborhoods and new families or those that have stayed are choosing other high schools (e.g., charter schools, magnet schools, or public high schools in other neighborhoods, etc.). Roughly 68 percent of the students are Latino/Hispanic, 30 percent are black, 1 percent are white, and 1 percent reported "other." It is well known that many of the students are economically disadvantaged. According to Chicago Public Schools (CPS), 10 percent of students are limited English learners. In 2011, only about half of Clemente students reached graduation, compared with 58 percent across CPS. By 2017, though, the five-year cohort graduation rate at Clemente was 82 percent, exceeding the CPS average of 78 percent.[26]

The school's ability to encourage graduates to enroll in college continues to be a source of concern. Only 49 percent of Clemente graduates enroll in college, compared with 60 percent of all CPS graduates. Some 29 percent of CPS students and 51 percent of all high school students in Illinois meet or exceed ACT college readiness benchmarks, compared with just 6 percent of students at Clemente. CPS ranked Clemente as falling below expectations for student education attainment and below average for student growth. Yet, there are some signs of improvement in the number of out-of-school suspensions. Although still incredibly high, there is evidence that suspensions have declined. In 2016, the school posted an alarming 97.8 suspensions per 100 students. That number dropped to 70.4 per 100 in 2017, still many times more than the district average of 5.8 per 100. Attendance at Clemente—82 percent—pales compared with the district average of 93 percent, but the dropout rate at Clemente (3 percent) is better than in the district as a whole (7 percent).

Community as a Campus

More recently, Clemente has been part of a more massive project known as Community as a Campus (CAAC), an initiative in development since 2009. The CAAC effort was established by the Humboldt Park Community Action Council and adopted as part of a larger community plan. CAAC is focused on revitalization of Clemente and schools that feed into it. Goals include increasing graduation rates of elementary and high school students, increasing the number of graduates who attend postsecondary institutions, and increasing parent involvement in student learning. CAAC is guided by a steering committee and aims to forge ways for parents, students, and teachers themselves to view educators as intellectuals and listeners. It is envisioned as an educational pipeline that supports students from pre-kindergarten through grade 12.

With an emphasis on high academic standards and quality teaching, CAAC includes dual-language teaching, integration of arts, STEM education, and career pathways. CAAC is organized into a Parent Popular Education Institute, a Youth Civic Leadership Development Institute, and a Teacher/Administrator Leadership Institute. Each institute provides an educational pipeline and services for families, including housing, employment, and health care.

The Parent Popular Education Institute mobilizes parents to take part in the education of their children to improve educational outcomes. The goal is to give parents the tools to be effective advocates and to assume leadership roles. Parents learn about such topics as financial literacy, computer skills, culinary arts, and videography. Information is shared about educational opportunities at trade schools, colleges, and universities, as well as other services in the community like health care, healthy foods, and healthy living.

The Youth Civic Leadership Development Institute connects students to after-school programs at the library, to parks and recreation, and to other organizations in the community and the city at large. It develops the leadership skills of young people by giving them decision-making privileges at school boards and commissions. For example, youth from the institute work with CAAC staff and principals as well as the PTA. By increasing participation, CAAC hopes that students can contribute to their communities through a lifetime.

The Teacher/Administrator Leadership Institute is based on the premise that teachers can be co-creators of the educational system and not just deliver information and "do their job." Teachers are the first point of contact with students and need to listen and adjust what they are doing accordingly. Part of the problem, CAAC believes, is that many teachers are disenfranchised, and when that is the case, students become disenfranchised as well. Teachers need to see themselves as capable of transforming students' lives. As José López, educator and community leader, said in a personal interview, "Intellectuals make an effort to not only understand the world but to change it. Intellectuals use their capacity to be agents of change. Teachers can transform students to be lifelong learners." One of the significant issues at Clemente and other schools is that teachers end up leaving their teaching positions. Retention of teachers has become an issue for continuity of vision as well as relationships.

At the widest level, "the ultimate goal is a broad scale experiment in K to 12 education that might eventually be seen as the model for answering some of the fundamental weaknesses in the education of minorities."[27] As Marvin García, a CAAC leader, explained in a personal interview, "Historically, parents have chosen not to send their kids to Clemente, and even administrators would advise parents to take their kids to another school. We are trying to make Clemente the school of choice by improving educational outcomes." Enrollment had been declining precipitously and almost forced the closure of the school in 2013. According to the *High School Progress Report*, in 2015, about 250 new students enrolled at Clemente of 733 total.[28] The changes brought by CAAC and the new Clemente administration have resulted in more students choosing Clemente.

Gangs, Violence, and Teenage Pregnancy: Educational Struggles

In this section, we return to the story of Lourdes Santiago. In 1993 she and Felix Padilla published an ethnographic narrative, *Outside the Wall: A Puerto Rican Woman's Struggle*, that is exemplary of the creative ways used by Latino scholars to develop a body of research that is innovative and cutting-edge. In that work, Lourdes is the primary voice, with sociological captions and commentaries provided by Padilla. Lourdes's story is a captivating one because it addresses a lot of the issues Puerto Ricans still face as a community. It encapsulates the kinds of problems Puerto Rican youth confront in Chicago, cutting short their educational dreams and aspirations. It exposes the historical origins of what sociologists have called the "prison pipeline" in which young men of color are policed, criminalized, and incarcerated—a problem that has become more pronounced today. As a consequence, this also shapes and determines the dreams and aspirations of young women.

As we observed in the previous chapter, Puerto Rican parents in Chicago—and we could add in Illinois in general—have raised their children by strict (some may say traditional) norms executed along gender lines. Anthropologist Gina Pérez explains the underlying issues connected to these parenting strategies and notes that working-class parents perceived urban life as dangerous, "filled with violence, sexual danger, racism, and discrimination."[29] For daughters, fears about sexual dangers range from losing their virginity and becoming sexually active to becoming teen mothers. One of Pérez's informants told her that she was sent to Puerto Rico when she was thirteen "para que no se dañara" (so I wouldn't be ruined). She followed by saying that when girls come back, they get into even more trouble. Pérez's informant, now a mother herself, also worried about her daughter's sexual agency.

These issues are still evident today. In interviews we conducted with third-generation Puerto Rican college students, many spoke about their gender role socialization. In the following passage, a female college student at Illinois State University reflected on the differences between her mother and grandmother and what it meant for her:

> My mom was very fair with us because her mom (my grand-mother) was very strict with her. My mom and my uncle are twelve years apart, but my grandma was so strict. You cannot go to dances; you cannot do this or that. With my uncle, he did whatever he wanted. My mom was like, "That's not fair." My grandma did not talk to her about her menses [period] and birth control. Didn't talk to her about anything. But my mom was so different. With me and my brother, she was very open about that because she was like, "I want you to be able to come to me and talk to me, to feel comfortable." She would tell me, "I don't want you to have sex before marriage, but if that's your choice then you need to know what it means." Honestly, I didn't have sex until I was eighteen years old. That's one of the things I love about my mom. I respect her. She is awesome.[30]

In *Respect Yourself, Protect Yourself: Latina Girls and Sexual Identity*, Lorena García addresses the struggles of second-generation Mexican and Puerto Rican mothers in raising daughters and dealing with their sexual agency. She reports that mothers worried about these issues, and some tended to be "old school" in that they refused to talk about "safe sex" to daughters.[31] There were others who did, transgressing normative family rules about sexuality. For boys, danger tends to gets constituted through street life: after joining a gang, from harassment by the police, and through the unbending criminal justice system.

Return migration to Puerto Rico was also a strategy applied to boys. Pérez reports that two teenage boys dropped out of her GED class because they were sent to live with their maternal grandmother in Puerto Rico; the boys had become involved with gangs.[32] They eventually returned to Chicago because they also got in trouble in Puerto Rico. Another reason that prompted parents to send children to Puerto Rico was education. Additionally, police and the criminal justice system used forced return migration as a way to address problems in Chicago. José (Cha-Cha) Jiménez, once a gang member but today a celebrated community leader, an activist, and founder of the Young Lords organization, described how he became disillusioned with the schools and turned to petty crime and life in the streets for affirmation:

> There was a lot of prejudice in the city, especially against Latinos and African Americans. . . . Once the Puerto Ricans arrived into Lincoln Park [and] got to know each other, the younger ones started forming their own groups. Those groups were more for protection. In the beginning that's how it started. . . . I was in and out of jail for different things. Eventually, I had too many cases that they basically sent me back to Puerto Rico. I was the head of a group at the time, and they wanted to get rid of the head. They gave my mother a choice: since I was still a juvenile, between staying in jail and going to Puerto Rico. I was put in handcuffs and sent to Puerto Rico.[33]

Lourdes Santiago was raised in a stringent environment shaped by traditional Puerto Rican norms and religious beliefs informed by the Pentecostal church. Lourdes remembers that she could not go anywhere. She had household responsibilities of caring and cooking for her family and spent a lot of time in the church—which she enjoyed—but she had no other creative outlet. Lourdes met her boyfriend when she was in eighth grade and he was in high school. She admits that she fell in with him to get out of the house and away from the strict control of her mother. Her mother threatened to send Lourdes to Puerto Rico. But she still defied her mom, and Lourdes and her boyfriend got married while they were still in high school. Lourdes had hoped that marriage and family life would pull her husband away from the gang he was in, but the lure of street life and his leadership in the gang proved stronger. Instead, she became a gang member herself. Her husband was soon incarcerated: "There is no denying it that my husband knew what was happening. In the 1970s, the neighborhood was the site of this little war. Opposing gangs were shooting at one another. There was money to be made through the sale of drugs, and different gangs were competing with one another to control the market. . . . My husband was one of those who was arrested and eventually charged for one such killing."[34] After his imprisonment, Lourdes decided to withdraw from school because, as she put it, "I just couldn't cope with our circumstances."

The dropout issue has lingered in the Puerto Rican community. Part of the dropout crisis is related to gang involvement for boys and teenage pregnancy for girls, problems that are also increasingly evident in other low-income communities. When these issues appear in the popular press, they are frequently framed as problems where Puerto Ricans "lack motivation" and "lack good families," among other long-held stereotypes. We talked to educators about these issues, and they added a list of other problems that compound the dropout crisis. One Puerto Rican educator, for example, described to us the current educational crisis:

> Puerto Rican students, like many of my current students, are faced with difficulties regarding language acquisition and poverty, particularly in neighborhoods that are predominantly Latino. Linguistically, Latinx students are either struggling to acquire English at the level of their peers because they are being raised in predominantly Spanish-speaking households, or they have low levels of literacy in either language because their parents did not teach them Spanish but did not have strong enough English skills to prepare them in English either. As for poverty, it is indeed an issue of money but also of other valuable resources, such as nutritious foods, safe places to study, and study materials/tools like computers. This often affects students from large families in other ways, such as requiring them to work to help support the family, which makes them more likely to fail and/or drop out of school.[35]

Sociologist Nilda Flores-González argues that reducing the school dropout crisis to the lack of motivation of young people misses some important points.[36] She conducted an in-depth ethnographic study in 1993 in a predominantly Puerto Rican inner-city school, Hernandez High, in Chicago. Through this work she reveals that when seen from the perspective of students, the road to becoming a dropout is long; it starts early in their school development and connects through their own racial identity. But it ultimately rests upon educators and the educational system to recognize the complex factors that push some students out. Her work is relevant here because she helps us understand from the perspective of students the many forces that shape their educational journeys. Flores-González points out that at the time of her study, the eight Chicago Public Schools with the highest Latino populations had dismally low graduation rates.

Graduation rates varied between 47.7 percent to 71.1 percent. At the time, CPS did not break down figures by nationality. A charitable look at these numbers means that, at best, more than a quarter of kids in any one school did not complete high school. At the other end of the spectrum is the alarming view that in the 1990s, 50 percent of Latino students dropped out. The Puerto Rican Agenda report shows that dropout rates for Puerto Ricans in Chicago between 2000 and 2010 dropped by 12 percent—but the problem remains still. For example, in 2000, 47 percent of Puerto Rican men and 43 percent of Puerto Rican women did not graduate from high school in Chicago. In the city, in 2010, Puerto Ricans (32 percent) still have higher dropout rates than African Americans (20 percent) and whites (8 percent). Mexicans have the highest dropout rate in the city at 48 percent.[37]

Flores-González argues that navigating the school culture is a primary rite of passage for all young adults, but for Puerto Ricans it comes with added problems and pressures. Hernandez High, the school in her study, had been publicly labeled as a "problem school," ranked low in state educational scores, had a troubled history of gangs and violence, and had been stigmatized as a "dumping ground." Flores-González argues that these factors impacted the students' sense of school identity. She found that some students coped with the stigma attached to Hernandez by defending it, along with their communities and their identities. Some viewed attending the school as an act of defiance. While conducting interviews with young Puerto Rican students at Hernandez, she found that some students—mostly high-achieving students—internalized a "school kid" identity that allowed them to cope with the stressors of school and learning. Within the world of school peer cultures, high-achieving Puerto Rican male students had to confront the threat and fear of gangs at school. According to Flores-González, "Gangs in school impinge on the daily life of non-gang members. While school-oriented students do their best to stay away from gangs, it is impossible to be a student at Hernandez High and not be touched by gang activity. Students say that gangs pose a threat to student safety mainly because there is more than one gang in the school and the potential for fights is always present."[38]

When Hernandez students left the school building, the danger of gangs was ever present for students across the board. Miguel, a student in Flores-González's study, described how he managed. First, he said a person should avoid being alone because "you never know." He added that "getting 'jumped' can be severe and can land you in the hospital." The pressures to join a gang for male students added a lot of stress to their schooling. Students called it achieving a "neutron status" when someone who was not affiliated with a gang managed to maintain cordial relations with its members. In other words, the neutron status meant that one could greet, talk, and even spend time with someone who was gang-affiliated but without becoming a member. Some students might even become "honorary members," which offered protection from beatings. Religion was another strategy used by boys and girls to repel gangs. Those who wore rosaries and pendant crosses were labeled as "church boy" or "church girl."

When gang members started wearing some of these symbols, Flores-González reports that students took to carrying Bibles to school because displays of religiosity helped them escape the recruitment and harassment from those in gangs. At Hernandez High, extracurricular, social, and academic programs allowed the high-achieving students space to affirm a "school kid" identity that connected them to school, enhancing their chances to success and graduate. To be clear, the benefits to the students were many as they became attached to the school, developed meaningful relations with adults, and reported liking school. The "school kids" in Flores-González's study managed to persevere through difficult schooling conditions and graduate with a high school diploma.

Interviews conducted with Puerto Rican college students who went to high school in the suburbs also show that they, too, had to navigate school peer culture but without the additional pressures that those in Chicago faced. Instead, they had to deal with the complexity of attending schools where they were a minority. Here are the observations of two male students:

It was a lot of white people. There were some Latinos and blacks. I remember specifically how the black kids would section themselves off. They had their own community. The groups that were most diverse at my high school were the athletes. It was because they were all a part of the team, so you would see this very diverse group of kids sitting together as a team. That was pretty cool! I was a part of the theater program, which was mostly white. Given how I look, people did not know I was Puerto Rican. They would assume I was white. So, the entire time, people would see me and go "You're white," and I would tell them, "No, I'm not white." They would tell me I was lying! I replied to discount [clarify] who I am, my existence, and my experience based on the color of my skin.[39]

High school wasn't that bad because it was unique in many ways. There weren't a lot Puerto Ricans. There were a couple Mexicans, some African Americans, but it was mostly white. I had my white friends and my Hispanic group. Hispanics bonded together because we were the minority. They were mostly Mexican, a couple were mixed Mexican–Puerto Ricans, and then a few black friends. During the school day, I would mostly hang out with my white friends, but then after school, I was the head of the dance club which was mainly Latinos and African Americans. A couple of my friends who were Mexican came from Bensenville, but they rented in Elmhurst so they could go to the high school.[40]

Not all high school dropouts joined a gang, like Lourdes's husband did. Flores-González points out that deciding to drop out is a long process that for many started in elementary school.[41] It is a hard decision frequently taken after a major turning point. For boys, suspensions and expulsion because of behavioral problems often lead to leaving school. In other words, some students are forced out, while others perceive that the benefits of work and life without school demands are preferable. Some students do not give up on the dream to continue their schooling, and that is why alternative neighborhood schools have become an institutional option for youth in Illinois, specifically Puerto Ricans in the city. They are a lifeline for Puerto Rican students who drop out or are pushed out by institutional forces. In the next two sections, we address the role that organizations like ASPIRA and alternative high schools have played in the lives of Puerto Rican youth.

ASPIRA

One of the most important organizations that has helped keep Puerto Rican students in schools and transition them to college is ASPIRA. In fact, ASPIRA is one of the oldest organizations supporting and promoting the educational opportunities of students of color across the United States. "Aspira" is a Spanish word that means "to aspire," "a desire to succeed." ASPIRA was founded by Puerto Rican educator Antonia Pantoja, who in the 1960s witnessed firsthand the problems of Puerto Rican, African American, and Latino kids in the New York City schools. As in Chicago, New York City Puerto Ricans faced many issues in the schools that resulted in high rates of dropouts, among other concerns.

As a black Puerto Rican, Antonia Pantoja had experienced racism and social exclusion throughout her life. She was born and raised in Puerto Rico, where she became a teacher and union organizer. She migrated to New York City in the 1940s and went on to earn a bachelor's degree from Hunter College and a PhD in social work. Pantoja is today a celebrated leader in the annals of educators who have made a difference in the lives of youth across racial and ethnic backgrounds. Virginia E. Sánchez Korrol writes that, from its inception, ASPIRA "pledged itself to pressure official bodies and mount campaigns that focused on educational issues."[42] Its primary objective was to help youth stay in school and to understand their communities and their needs. Today, ASPIRA has more than seven chapters in cities with large Puerto Rican populations, although it continues to be a multicultural organization that helps students and families across the racial and social classes in large urban centers.

In 1968, ASPIRA held a conference in New York City that brought together African American, Mexican, Puerto Rican, and other non-Latino educators. Set against the decentralization of the New York City schools and the struggle for community control and accountability, the meeting stands today as a historic moment. From there Puerto Ricans analyzed and understood what was needed to best address the educational issues facing young Puerto Ricans. They pledged to renew their campaign for bilingual education and to push for the rights of youth not only to a high school education but, more importantly, to college opportunities. Juan González credits ASPIRA with establishing an enduring legacy of training community leaders who went on to become agents of change during a period of radical organizing in urban communities across the nation. In fact, the website of ASPIRA includes a long list of "Aspirantes," political and cultural figures in the United States today. These include several well-known Illinois Puerto Ricans such as Iris Martinez, Illinois state senator and the first Latina to hold such a position, and Billy Ocasio, former City of Chicago alderman, among many others.

The late Puerto Rican activist Mirta Ramírez took part in the 1968 conference and came back to Chicago determined to start a chapter of ASPIRA there. A dropout who obtained her high school diploma after she had become a mother, Ramírez launched educational groups in the community and eventually brought ASPIRA to Illinois in 1969. ASPIRA became "the first agency in Chicago founded and staffed by Puerto Ricans working for the Puerto Rican community."[43] Mirelsie Velázquez interviewed Ramírez about these early struggles: "I was going to college at the time, and I found the description of ASPIRA in a book . . . so I quit school and worked full time on the ASPIRA Project. . . . I put the board of directors together, I brought the furniture, rented the place, set up the telephones . . . and I hired the first club organizer to go out to the high schools. The significance of that was that no outside agency had been working within high schools."[44]

In 2018, ASPIRA of Illinois celebrated fifty years of educational activism in Illinois. Its mission continues to be "to empower the Puerto Rican community and Latino community through advocacy and the education leadership and development of its youth."[45] The organization provides educational programs structured around a host of topics such as self-esteem, cultural awareness, and leadership abilities. In 1985, it founded Antonia Pantoja High School to address the dropout crisis in the Puerto Rican community further. One educator we talked to in Chicago reflected on the legacy of ASPIRA: "A lot of our elected officials and city leaders credit ASPIRA with helping them to go to college because ASPIRA counseled them and took them on college visits. ASPIRA tutored and mentored them through their leadership clubs. For many, it was the first time that they saw themselves as college material. 'I am college material because this person said they were going to help me get to college.' Also, ASPIRA connected them to their communities, invested students in their communities. That's the ASPIRA model."[46] By 2018, ASPIRA of Illinois had expanded to include four alternative schools.

Alternative Schools

In the current climate of school choice, alternative schools play a significant role. But as one Puerto Rican educator pointed out, in the Puerto Rican community these schools came into existence out of the sheer sense of crisis that was evident in the 1980s and 1990s. Another educator and long-term community member who migrated to Chicago in the 1980s addressed the broader context of their development:

> What is unique about the alternative education model versus other models, at least in Chicago, is that before 1985 the alternative schools that were in the system, like Pedro Albizu Campos, El Cuarto Año, and others, came out of a desire to meet the needs of the crisis with high school dropouts. So, they had that sense of mission and they started with no funding from the Chicago Public Schools. They started by tapping into private dollars for funding. After 1985, funding became available from the Chicago Public Schools. They began providing tuition reimbursements. What is interesting about the alternative schools in the Puerto Rican community is that these schools were not developed because it was the low-hanging fruit or because the funding was available to establish these schools. No, the schools came first before funding was available. I think that says something about the sense of purpose, the steadfast sense of purpose in the Puerto Rican community to address the dropout issue. The community needed alternatives.[47]

Two of the oldest alternative schools in the Puerto Rican community of Chicago are Pedro Albizu Campos High School and Segundo Ruiz Belvis High School. Both have become cherished and celebrated institutions in the community because they have offered hope and opportunities for youth who had been rejected from the city's public school system. As one educator put it in a personal interview, "They were educational lifelines for youth in the community at the time when educational institutions failed to understand the unique needs of Puerto Rican students and it was easier to push them out than to address their needs." Pedro Albizu Campos High was founded in 1972, roughly around the same time as Roberto Clemente High School, as a community response to the high rates of dropouts. Initially, students attended classes in the basement of a local church. With the financial support of the Puerto Rican Cultural Center, the school developed, and today it functions as an important educational institution in the community. Teachers and students are committed to the school because it represents something completely different from what was available in the public education system. Margaret Power reports that by 2015, Pedro Albizu Campos High had grown to 182 students: 86 percent Latino, 12 percent African American, and roughly 4 percent white.[48]

Puerto Ricans and Higher Education in Illinois

In the 1970s and 1980s, students like Felix and Marisa, whose stories appeared at the beginning of this chapter, persevered through their schooling and moved on to attend college. Given that most of the Puerto Ricans lived in the city of Chicago educational institutions near the city offered Puerto Ricans then and now the hope of a college education.

In this context, it is important to point out that Northeastern University has particularly helped Puerto Ricans achieve the dream of a college education. Second- and third-generation Puerto Ricans have graduated from Northeastern, and many of them have gone back to the community as teachers and in the growing nonprofit sector. Puerto Rican students started the Union for Puerto Rican Students and demanded classes and programs to complement their learning. Similarly, Puerto Ricans at the University of Illinois at Chicago organized to demand a Latino cultural center.

Many well-known Puerto Ricans—Luis Gutiérrez, Billy Ocasio, Ada Lopez, José López, Michael Rodríguez-Muñiz—trace their educational successes to Northeastern. Its location near the city has allowed generations of Puerto Rican students to be able to work and go to school, a situation that characterizes many Puerto Rican college students across the nation. Other universities near the city recruited, enrolled, and graduated Puerto Ricans with varying degrees of effectiveness. For example, both Marisa and Felix graduated from Northwestern University.

The story of how Puerto Ricans transition from high school to college is a complex one, let alone how they finish college and go on to pursue postgraduate work, like Felix and Marisa. The view from the classroom is both encouraging and discouraging. Some institutions are more demographically diverse, but Puerto Rican students are not the majority in this educational revolution. It may be instructive to examine what the census data show at the national and state levels. At the national level, Puerto Rican higher educational attainment fell behind that of whites and African Americans. Jennifer Hinojosa and Carlos Vargas-Ramos report that in 2014, only 17.6 percent of Puerto Ricans in the United States held a bachelor's degree or higher, placing Puerto Ricans behind whites (33.6 percent), African Americans (19.7 percent), and even Puerto Ricans on the island (24.1 percent).[49]

The rates for Illinois in 2016 are very similar. The number of Puerto Ricans with a bachelor's degree is much smaller than the Illinois average—19 percent compared with 33 percent for the total population. In that same year, 22 percent of Puerto Rican women had a bachelor's degree or higher in contrast to 14 percent of Puerto Rican men. Puerto Rican educational attainment is lower than for African Americans while identical to that of American Indians or Alaska Natives. Only Mexicans have a lower rate of educational attainment than Puerto Ricans.

Puerto Rican educational attainment (19 percent) is lower than for African Americans (20 percent). American Indians or Alaska Natives (18 percent) and Mexicans (11 percent) have a lower rate of educational attainment than Puerto Ricans. Nonetheless, there have been some improvements since the year 2000 (see table 5.2). The most dramatic changes among Puerto Ricans have been in obtaining a bachelor's degree, which went from 7.4 percent in 2000 to 12.3 percent in 2016, a change of 66 percent. Additionally, more people overall are obtaining graduate degrees; for Puerto Ricans the rate almost doubled, from 3.6 percent in 2000 to 6.2 percent in 2016, a 72 percent change. Still, when compared with non-Hispanic whites, Puerto Ricans lag behind in achieving higher educational levels.

Puerto Ricans, like other immigrants, view education as a path to success. It is well understood that education acts as a predictive marker for everything from one's socioeconomic status and income to the type of employment one is likely to pursue. Education ultimately impacts the quality of life in significant and complex ways, and this is why Puerto Ricans historically have advocated for access to education in their communities.

The opening of Roberto Clemente High School in the 1970s represented a profound accomplishment for Puerto Ricans in the Humboldt Park area. Community members led several sit-ins at the school to raise their concerns about overcrowding and poor-quality education. If it were not for community activism, is very possible that Roberto Clemente High School would not have been built. If it were not for dedicated community members, the school most likely would not have been located on Division Street,

Table 5.1. Race and ethnic origin by educational attainment

	Total	Male	Female
Puerto Rican			
High school graduate or higher	78%	78%	78%
Bachelor's degree or higher	19%	14%	22%
Mexican			
High school graduate or higher	63%	62%	66%
Bachelor's degree or higher	11%	9%	14%
Total population			
High school graduate or higher	88%	88%	89%
Bachelor's degree or higher	33%	33%	33%
White alone			
High school graduate or higher	91%	90%	91%
Bachelor's degree or higher	35%	35%	34%
White alone, not Hispanic or Latino			
High school graduate or higher	94%	93%	94%
Bachelor's degree or higher	37%	37%	36%
Black alone			
High school graduate or higher	85%	83%	87%
Bachelor's degree or higher	20%	17%	23%
American Indian or Alaska Native alone			
High school graduate or higher	78%	77%	78%
Bachelor's degree or higher	18%	19%	17%
Asian alone			
High school graduate or higher	91%	93%	89%
Bachelor's degree or higher	64%	66%	61%
Native Hawaiian and Other Pacific Islander alone			
High school graduate or higher	85%	85%	85%
Bachelor's degree or higher	26%	21%	33%
Some other race alone			
High school graduate or higher	58%	57%	59%
Bachelor's degree or higher	10%	8%	11%
Two or more races			
High school graduate or higher	89%	87%	90%
Bachelor's degree or higher	36%	34%	38%
Hispanic or Latino origin			
High school graduate or higher	64%	63%	66%
Bachelor's degree or higher	14%	12%	15%

Source: Table created by lvis Garcia, from American Community Survey 1-year estimates (2016).

Table 5.2. Percentages of educational attainment among certain populations

Educational attainment	Total population		White		Black		Mexican		Puerto Rican	
	2000	2016	2000	2016	2000	2016	2000	2016	2000	2016
Population 25 years and over	7,973,671	8,665,219	6,144,044	6,421,241	1,064,516	1,154,328	551,757	935,132	84,763	123,373
Less than high school diploma	18.6	11.2	15.0	8.7	27.0	13.8	56.5	36.6	39.7	22.3
High school graduate or GED	27.7	26.0	29.2	26.6	26.1	27.9	22.2	31.9	25.1	28.6
Some college or associate's degree	27.7	28.9	28.0	29.2	32.2	36.7	14.8	20.3	24.3	30.6
Bachelor's degree	16.5	20.9	17.7	22.2	9.6	13.0	4.5	8.1	7.4	12.3
Graduate or professional degree	9.5	13.0	10.1	13.4	5.1	8.6	2.0	3.1	3.6	6.2
High school graduate or higher	81.4	88.8	85.0	91.3	73.0	86.2	43.6	63.4	60.3	77.7
Bachelor's degree or higher	26.1	34.0	28.0	35.6	14.7	21.6	6.5	11.2	10.9	18.5

Source: Created by Ivis García, from the 2000 U.S. Decennial Census and American Community Survey 1-year estimates (2016).

and it certainly would not have carried the name of legendary Puerto Rican baseball player Roberto Clemente. Because Puerto Ricans decided to be politically involved in the education of their children—making demands to board members of Chicago Public Schools, to school districts, and to Mayor Daley's administration—the school has become what it is today, an integral part of the Humboldt Park community. The Community as a Campus project at Clemente is an excellent example of how Puerto Ricans in Humboldt Park have exercised self-help and their right to self-determination by seeking to improve their educational outcomes.

As Mirta Ramírez, the first executive director of ASPIRA in Illinois, stated, "No one is going to help Puerto Ricans. If we want to take advantage of opportunities in this society, we'll have to help ourselves."[50] By 2011, several decades after its founding, ASPIRA had helped nearly a half million Puerto Rican and Latino youth nationwide, 65 percent of them female. Impressively, over 95 percent of ASPIRA-participating youth graduate from high school, and more than 90 percent obtain a college education. In Illinois, four charter schools served about 1,400 students in 2017, and approximately 100 educators work at the ASPIRA Network in Chicago.[51] Reforming education through alternative schools has been a familiar theme in the Puerto Rican community. ASPIRA, Pedro Albizu Campos High , and Segundo Ruiz Belvis High are examples of such efforts.

By highlighting initiatives like Clemente, Community as a Campus, and the alternative school movement in this chapter, we have discussed very broadly the educational struggles faced by Puerto Ricans in Illinois. Parents, activists, community leaders, and students have taken their destiny into their own hands by working to improve the educational conditions and outcomes of Puerto Ricans. Students also realize how their educational aspirations connect to their communities. There are those who attend an alternative school or who return to school to get their GED and find out that education is about something much more substantial. There are also those who, while working, manage to pursue their college degrees, including postgraduate work. Puerto Rican parents, students, and community leaders recognize that education is a way to transform themselves and their communities.

This is why, historically, Puerto Ricans have been changing and improving their quality of life through advocating for access to education: they understand that education has a fundamental role in liberation and democracy. Lourdes, Felix, and Marisa are examples of not only achieving the American dream but being liberated to the point of becoming scholars—able to solve problems, advocate for democracy, and create social change. Educator Karen Chenoweth wrote in a *Washington Post* article in 2018 that "if we as a country are really serious about wanting to improve schools and education, we should be studying Chicago. . . . I know what you are thinking. Chicago? Really? Isn't that the land of dysfunction and gun violence? . . . Underneath all of that is a story of institutional resilience that is worth examining."[52] Puerto Ricans deserve to be placed at the top of this story because theirs is a story of resilience.

6

PUERTO RICAN COMMUNITIES IN ILLINOIS: FROM THE CITY TO THE PRAIRIE AND BEYOND

From the City to the Prairie and Beyond

In *Steel Barrio: The Great Mexican Migration to South Chicago, 1915–1940*, historian Michael Innis-Jimenez makes an important point: the concept of community is foundational to understanding the experiences of immigrants. He points out that "when people share a culture, resources, and the use of physical spaces in a single geographical location, they form community not only through interacting with one another but also by considering themselves part of the group."[1] In fact, Innis-Jimenez's book documents how Mexican immigrants in Chicago built vibrant and viable immigrant communities that still exist today. In keeping with Innis-Jimenez's definition, Puerto Ricans in Illinois have shared space, resources, and a geographic location to constitute themselves as a community. Puerto Ricans have also constructed communities in ways that transcend a geographically specific connection. In other words, for Puerto Ricans, there is the broader sense of community engendered by the Puerto Rican diaspora. From their arrival in Illinois until now, Puerto Ricans have worked hard to become part of established communities in Illinois and have built strong communities of their own, locally and transnationally.

In this chapter, we describe and analyze the development of Puerto Rican communities in Illinois. Several questions guide our analysis: What constitutes the community for Puerto Rican residents of the state of Illinois? How do Puerto Ricans who live in Chicago and other parts of the state construct community? We have known that in the last twenty years there has been a steady movement of Puerto Ricans from Chicago to the suburbs; have they established communities of their own or integrated themselves in what constitutes a community in the suburbs? The oldest and largest Puerto Rican communities are in Chicago, so a significant part of this chapter will revisit how these early barrios came into existence and the struggles Puerto Ricans faced in the process of forming these communities.

The Chicago story is foundational to understanding how Puerto Ricans built and thrived in communities of their own. The story of these communities provides a departure point for us. Puerto Ricans encountered a great deal of prejudice and discrimination in Chicago's housing market. Urban renewal programs pushed out Puerto Ricans from the first barrios. In the 1970s, the largest communities in the city (and state) were West Town, Humboldt Park, and Logan Square. The 1966 Puerto Rican riots along Division Street made the community hyper-visible and marked the neighborhood for decades to come as an area riddled with crime and social problems. But the vision and perseverance of community leaders and the political mobilization of residents led to the neighborhood's transformation into Paseo Boricua. Figure 6.1 shows the street corridor that many Puerto Ricans across the state have come to identify as *un pedacito de patria* (a small piece of motherland).

Again, in keeping with previous chapters, we rely on interviews, demographic data, and the available literature to help us describe and analyze how Puerto Ricans reconstitute themselves within various communities throughout the state of Illinois. We also use interviews collected for this project to explain the meaning of Paseo Boricua for Puerto Ricans living in the suburbs and central Illinois. As we have argued throughout this book, Puerto Ricans are U.S. citizens, but they tend to experience the process of migration, community, and identity formation along the same lines as other Latino immigrants. In fact, as Innis-Jimenez argues, immigrant ethnic communities function as a third space where immigrants attempt to mediate the profound sense of displacement and the pressures of being members of a racialized and marginalized group.

The historical evidence in Chicago suggests that, like Mexicans and other immigrant groups, Puerto Ricans first developed mutual aid associations, credit unions, and alternative communal spaces as an act of self-affirmation and national pride. Community organizing became a way of dealing with the discrimination they encountered in a city that first welcomed them but quickly turned against them and vilified them through racialization processes. In

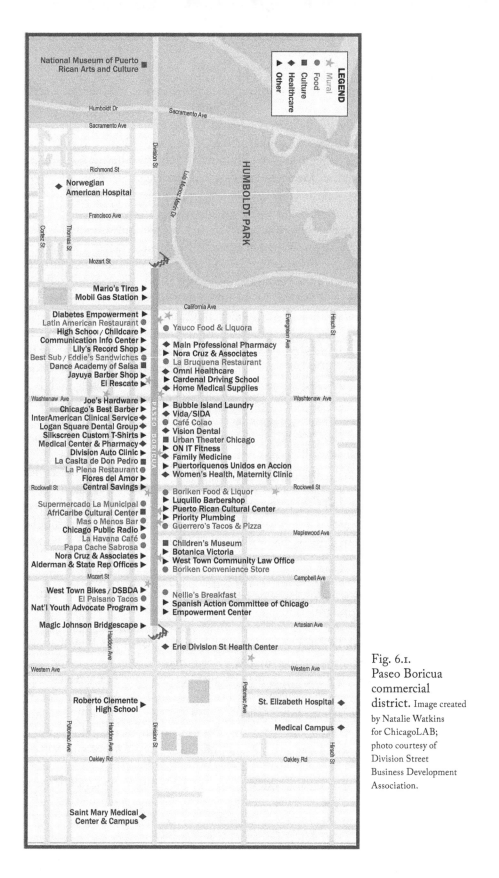

Fig. 6.1.
Paseo Boricua
commercial
district. Image created
by Natalie Watkins
for ChicagoLAB;
photo courtesy of
Division Street
Business Development
Association.

the early stages of community development in Chicago, Puerto Ricans lived alongside other poor and immigrant communities, primarily Mexican Americans and African Americans. In downstate Illinois, a similar process unfolded, as Puerto Ricans have built communities and organizations with other Latino groups, including Mexicans and South Americans. Based on the scholarly work done in Chicago, we know that when Puerto Ricans live next to Mexican Americans and African Americans, ethnic and racial solidarities develop. In Chicago, Mexicans and Puerto Ricans not only lived near each other but also married each other. Now, there is a new generation of Mexi-Ricans born and raised in Chicago.[2] The ethnic and racial solidarity that developed between Mexicans and Puerto Ricans has been sustained through years of community activism. Evidence of that community activism can be seen in the role that Puerto Rican political leaders—Congressman Luis Gutiérrez, a case in point—have played in advocating on behalf of immigrants and immigration reform. Most recently, that solidarity continues to underpin relations between groups as demonstrated by the Chicago for Mexico and Puerto Rico Relief Fund Campaign, an effort to help Mexican victims of the September 2017 earthquake and Hurricane Maria in Puerto Rico, a topic we will discuss later in this chapter.[3]

We warn readers at the outset that we cannot speak of one singular Puerto Rican community. Although Puerto Ricans across the state have many characteristics in common, such as national identity and culture, to reduce their experiences to a singular community would be misleading. This is most evident in Chicago. Although some areas are known as demographically Puerto Rican, the community's diverse views about the political status of the island, for example, represent just one of the many ways that community splits have developed over the years. One informant captured these tensions: "To me, our community is much bigger than Division Street, Humboldt Park, Paseo Boricua. We are part of that, but our community is a diaspora that is dispersed because of social and economic reasons. A community that had been ours for many years because of its affordability and where it was, namely it was close to jobs, is something of the past. It still has some symbolism and some impact in our community, but it is by no stretch of the imagination 'the' only Puerto Rican community."

Ironically, as another of our informants put it, today "Paseo Boricua is an island surrounded by gentrification," a force that threatens to displace yet again Puerto Ricans from the Humboldt Park area. The struggle to save Paseo from the adverse effects of gentrification is epic and deserves a section of its own because it reveals the political power that Puerto Ricans have gained in the city and the importance of identity to place-making among immigrant/migrant communities.

Before going any further, readers must know that in Illinois, Chicago has served as a unique social laboratory for the scientific study of immigrant communities. In fact, sociologists at the University of Chicago developed labels for these seventy-seven communities. More specifically, they were conceived by the Community Research Committee, an interdisciplinary group of scholars who in the 1920s studied and ordered the city. Figure 6.2

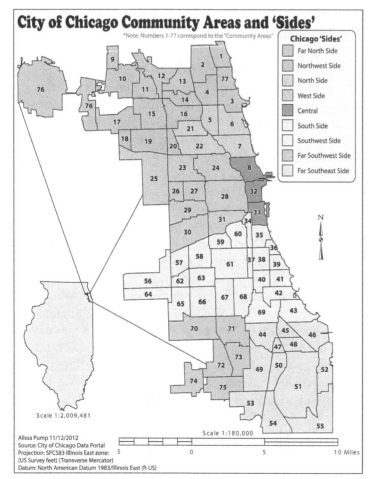

Fig. 6.2. Chicago's seventy-seven community areas. Wikimedia Commons, https://commons .wikimedia.org/wiki /File:Map_of_the _Community_Areas _and_%27Sides%27 _of_the_City_of _Chicago.svg.

shows a map of the city and the names of these communities. These communities reflect the lingua franca of social scientists in the city, but underlying these areas are competing notions of community that overlap—some may say conflict—with one another. The 2012 Puerto Rican Agenda report makes this clear: Puerto Rican residents in Chicago use several overlapping definitions of their community.[4] For example, Humboldt Park refers to community area 23, but it is also the colloquial name of the Puerto Rican neighborhood, which includes Division Street. "La Division" was the name Puerto Ricans used for this broader community.[5] Paseo Boricua—some call it the heart of the community—is the name of the commercial strip, marked by two immense steel flags at either end, that sometimes stands to signify the Puerto Rican community as a whole. Clearly, the concept of the community must be understood as fluid and evolving alongside people's understandings of place.

Early Puerto Rican Barrios

The story of the early barrios was one of struggle, resilience, and displacement, as evidenced by the written accounts generated by poets, writers, and scholars. The story of the early Puerto Rican barrios also lives in the memories of the *familias* (families) that arrived in Chicago in the 1950s and 1960s. We still need future scholars to continue to gather those stories for generations to come. Historian Lilia Fernández writes that "when Puerto Ricans came to Chicago in the 1940s and 1950s, many of them settled in the neighborhoods closest to the city's downtown—the Near West Side and the Near North Side—areas with relatively cheap rents, racially mixed populations, and also the most aged real state in the city."[6] But as families and budgets grew, Puerto Ricans moved north toward what is today Lincoln Park and other communities. Former alderman Ray Colón lived in the South Side of Chicago, in the Woodland area.[7] Sociologist Marisa Alicea writes that she grew up hearing stories that always started with "*cuando nosotros vivíamos en la sesentitres*" (when we lived on sixty-third).[8] Some stories were lighthearted, about getting lost on the way to work or meeting other Puerto Ricans who moved near them, but the stories were regularly punctuated with the difficulties the families faced. Unemployment was always a problem. Racial hostilities on the part of descendants of European immigrants and African Americans were also evident. With the security of a steady job,

Alicea's family was able to move to a house on Eighteenth Street, in the Pilsen area, an area known as a Mexican community still today. Eventually, like many other Puerto Ricans in the city, they found their way to West Town/Humboldt Park, community areas that are still known as primarily Puerto Rican.

Underlying the history of the first barrios is a compelling story of how Puerto Ricans established community organizations, worked to support their families, and navigated Chicago's complex racial landscape. Initially, Puerto Ricans were as seen as racially ambiguous. They did not conform to the racial dichotomy that ruled the city. But that racial ambiguity did not protect them from rejection and racism. In Chicago, Puerto Ricans and Mexicans challenged a deeply rooted, traditionally dichotomous—black and white—racial hierarchy enforced through policy, politics, and geography. Anthropologist Mérida M. Rúa argues that Puerto Ricans and Mexicans came to occupy a "buffer" zone between the black and white binary characteristic of the city.[9] But Puerto Ricans felt the brunt of the racial divide in unique ways. Alicea writes, "As a child I was constantly being yelled at by white Anglo-Americans and European immigrants for sitting on their front steps, walking on their grass, or just simply coming too close to their house. They saw us through a racist lens, which presented images of us as wild, dirty, and dumb children who had to be controlled. This constant surveillance and the arrogant sense of entitlement exhibited when yelling at us about where we could and could not be were aimed at putting us in our place."[10]

In the North Side, Puerto Ricans also encountered white ethnics (Polish, German, Italian, and Russian) who were deeply ambivalent about Puerto Ricans but firmly committed to a racial order that placed themselves at the top. "Whiteness" is an ideological construct (as with any race) and had to be conferred upon the Irish. White ethnics in Chicago had constructed their whiteness in the struggle with other whites, descendants of European immigrants (primarily Irish), and with the large community of African Americans, a community that grew exponentially during the Great Migration. The Great Migration brought to the city working-class and low-income families from the segregated and rural South. Fernández observes that Chicago white ethnics did not reject Puerto Ricans as "universally and unequivocally" as they did African Americans.[11] For example, when Puerto Ricans moved in, they did not move out, but as Alicea's comment shows, whites did not openly accept them. The U.S. Census found that in 1960 there were 581 Puerto Ricans living in Uptown, 1,191 in Lakeview, 2,699 in Near North Side, and 2,181 in Lincoln Park.[12]

Many well-known Puerto Ricans, such as Congressman Luis Gutiérrez, photographer Carlos Flores, and poet David Hernández, grew up in Lincoln Park. In the chapter "When Lincoln Park Was Puerto Rican," Gutiérrez writes that his family lived comfortably, able to afford such luxuries as a color TV, a stereo, and a Chevy Impala station wagon, which they used to visit relatives in Gary, Indiana, and New York City. The family was well off because both parents worked. He describes the racial landscape of the neighborhood he knew as a child: "In Lincoln Park, we had our Puerto Rican world mapped out. We knew every inch of our neighborhood. We knew where to look for cute girls. We knew which guys were just wannabe gang members trying to act tough, and which guys were dangerous. We knew what streets not to cross so you didn't end up in the black neighborhood or the white neighborhood. It was simple."[13]

Puerto Rican photographer Carlos Flores had fond memories of the Lincoln Park community: "As Puerto Ricans became established in the Lincoln Park area, they opened restaurants, barber shops, grocery stores, taverns, clothing stores, record shops, and other smaller businesses."[14] As residents of an early barrio, Lincoln Park Puerto Rican families welcomed their share of recent arrivals. Again, Gutiérrez's memories are helpful. He writes, "In our first apartment down the block at 849 West Willow, I remember about a dozen Puerto Ricans who had just arrived from the island and were living in the basement of the building. Their apartment was smaller than ours, and I thought ours felt cramped, though there was plenty of room for roaches and the mice."[15] Rúa pointedly observes that Puerto Ricans in Chicago have fond memories of Lincoln Park because it evokes a "loss of belonging in order to make sense of the present."[16]

For Puerto Ricans, going to church represented a way to build continuity in their lives, yet many churches in Chicago openly rejected Puerto Ricans as parishioners. Gutiérrez recalls, "St. Michael's wasn't very advanced in how they treated Latinos." He added, "Spanish mass wasn't held in the main sanctuary, but in a common room next to it. On Sunday mornings the place smelled of the beer that was served at wedding receptions the night before."[17] This is an issue that is etched in the memories of these early families. In this respect, Los Caballeros de San Juan (the San Juan Knights) represents one of the first church-based community groups developed in the city. Padilla writes that "Los Caballeros had strong religious connections and its programs and activities were linked directly with the parish church."[18] However, it did not become a national parish, like those of previous European immigrant groups. Instead, it was more like a voluntary organization organized by the Catholic Church of Chicago.

José López, executive director of the Puerto Rican Cultural Center, explains how the formation of parishes aided in the incorporation of European immigrant groups, something that did not happen for Puerto Ricans:

> The stories that people tell—"my grandfather came here with 20 cents in his pocket"—is BS! There was a network of support here that was already established through churches, and some of it was illegal. If I study the rise of Tammany Hall in New York City, what do I find? I find the rise of gangs in the Irish community of New York. You start with the Irish, they had a tavern, in the back they had stolen things. Upstairs you had the brothel. This generated a lot of money. They produced what you might call today an underground economy. Italian gangs controlled their turf, too. What was their role in building community, one must ask? You got to see how they supported the Catholic Church. The church, in turn, built schools, hospitals, and welfare programs. Take now Division Street in Chicago with the Polish community. You have two main churches, St. Stanislaus and Holy Trinity, the two largest churches of the Polish community. What do they do? They developed schools, Holy Family, Holy Trinity, all the schools.[19]

Implicit here is a critique of the popular "bootstrap" model that has been used as a yardstick through which to evaluate the perceived failure of Puerto Ricans to assimilate, as the charge is frequently made. Contained in his assessment is the need to recognize the multiple ways that the exclusion of Puerto Ricans had profound consequences for their adaptation and community formations. To put it differently, the mythical story of assimilation is one of community and mobility for European immigrants and their descendants— the "pull yourself up by your own bootstraps" model—and exclusion of racial others. To be clear, Puerto Ricans recognized that they also needed a network of support and set out to develop it through their families and community groups and in solidarity with other racial groups in the city. Eventually, Puerto Ricans found churches that welcomed them as parishioners. They also built religious communities with Mexican Americans and African Americans, spaces that became transformative for these communities since they energized faith-based, radical political projects.

Alicea writes that it was in 1969 when she participated in her first organized march to protest the discrimination encountered by the Catholic Church. She added, "At Holy Trinity, as in many other churches throughout the city, our Spanish-speaking congregation was forced to hold mass in the basement of the church."[20] The incident that made them walk out of the church was when they were told that they were dirty and messy after a Holy Week procession. The new Latino priest assigned to the church was so frustrated with their mistreatment that he organized them to walk out and join St. Boniface Church instead. She particularly remembered the bright Sunday morning when the walk took place, for it was also the first time they were allowed to attend mass in the main area of the church. Eventually, the Chicago archdiocese closed down St. Boniface, citing financial reasons, even though it had a large Latino congregation.

Los Caballeros de San Juan is credited with helping Puerto Ricans navigate the city. The group developed cultural events, supported dances and baseball leagues, and marked El Día De San Juan (San Juan's Day) as a community celebration. Felix Padilla reminds us that these celebrations eventually became incorporated with the Puerto Rican Parade, an important event that still takes place in the city. Los Caballeros was also instrumental in registering people to vote for John F. Kennedy's presidential race, the beginning of a long history of political participation in the city, a topic we will address later in this chapter. Maura Toro-Morn writes that "gender dynamics played an important role in the early stages of community development,"[21] and so we see alongside Los Caballeros de San Juan the Hijas de Maria (the Daughters of Mary), also a church-affiliated social group that aided in the socialization of daughters and offered women a space to support each other through the struggles of making homes in Chicago. Puerto Rican women played an important role in the development of the early barrios, a role that has yet to be fully recognized by written accounts.

Puerto Rican scholar Mérida Rúa writes, "Puerto Ricans were, in effect, expelled from Lincoln Park—which once had a prominent Puerto Rican presence prior to becoming one of Chicago's hottest real estate markets—three miles north of the central business district and near the lakefront."[22] A family she interviewed had to sell their home because they could not afford the "high-end property demands," and they no longer fit in with the changing racial order. Urban renewal displaced not only Puerto Ricans but other residents of color and lower-income families, too. But their displacement from Lincoln Park was not without a struggle. José (Cha-Cha) Jiménez and others helped organized youth resistance against displacement by turning the Young Lords, a youth gang, into a full-fledged community organization in the Lincoln Park barrio. As Gutiérrez pointed out earlier, the neighborhood had its share of white ethnic, Puerto Rican, and black gangs. Puerto Rican youth had to navigate this space carefully because they were outnumbered in every respect. David Hernández, Chicago's most celebrated Puerto Rican poet, was a youth worker at the time with the Commission of Youth Welfare, a city agency charged with intervening in the gang problem, or as he put it, "keeping the kids out of trouble." He noted in an interview with Julie M.

Fig. 6.3. José (Cha-Cha) Jiménez. Photo courtesy of the Puerto Rican Cultural Center.

Schmid that the people who first appreciated his poetry were the gang groups, and that is why he became "The Minister of *La Gente* (the People)."[23] His experiences with police violence and harassment turned him into a community advocate, and his poetry made him a storyteller.

Historically, immigrant youth have used gangs as a rite of passage in urban centers, a topic we already discussed as it profoundly shaped the educational chances of young Puerto Ricans in the city. In 1959, Jiménez and seven others formed a Young Lords youth gang to face the antagonisms they encountered in the streets by other white ethnic youth. Their turf wars, life of petty crime, and harassment by the police landed many of the members in jail. In fact, Jiménez had already served time in jail when he came back to his neighborhood to find Puerto Ricans evicted and pushed out by urban renewal. In prison, he had read about the civil rights movement, the Black Power movement, and Pedro Albizu Campos, an important figure in the nationalist movement in Puerto Rico. As these young men awakened politically to the issues that shattered their lives, the city was already an important theater for the social and political movements of the time.

Their transformation from a street gang to a pan-ethnic radical group is beyond the scope of this chapter,[24] but it is important to point out that the Young Lords became an important voice—some may say a radical voice—resisting displacement and promoting an inclusive, multiracial consciousness in the Lincoln Park barrio and beyond. Their motto—self-determination for all Latinos—exemplified a pan-Latino political consciousness. This pan-Latino solidarity was done in conversation with Mexican American youths who were also members of the Young Lords. The group's increased militancy and policies demanding equality and reparations made members targets of the Chicago Police Department, who infiltrated the group and eventually led to its decline. The Young Lords' legacy of struggle expanded to include chapters in New York, where journalist Juan González was one of its founding members. Other chapters were created by Chicanos in San Diego and Hayward, California, and by Puerto Ricans in Milwaukee.

It is well known that the banking industry redlined poor communities, denying them loans to buy homes. To address this problem, Puerto Ricans established a Puerto Rican credit union to help families secure money to buy homes and develop businesses.

Even when Puerto Rican families had two income earners, the low wages they received meant that many were unable to afford to rent apartments in the area, and numbers were forced out of their homes in Lincoln Park. They continued to move west of the city, close enough to work, searching for affordable housing. This is how they landed in three community areas: West Town, Humboldt Park, and Logan Square, which we address in the next section.

From La Division to Paseo Boricua: An Island Enclave

From the 1960s through the 1980s, West Town, Humboldt Park, and Logan Square became the communities with the most significant Puerto Rican populations in the city. But population density alone did not make the Puerto Rican community. Working-class families moved in with the hope of finding a place where they could raise their children and establish themselves. A popular bumper sticker captured their feelings: *Aquí luchamos, aquí nos quedamos* (Here we struggle, here we stay). As Puerto Ricans settled in these three community areas, Division Street emerged as the commercial heart. Like in Lincoln Park, bodegas (grocery stores), barber shops, and *mercados* (markets) sprouted along the avenue. The San Juan Theatre was also located on Division Street. Clemente Community Academy High School is nearby, too, and not far is Humboldt Park. Division Street was also the site of the 1966 Puerto Rican riots, a topic we address more fully later in this section. In this respect, we must return to Michael Innis-Jimenez's concept of community, because it is evident that what developed along Division Street—later affectionately known as "La Division"—was a spatially, culturally bounded community for Puerto Ricans connected to key events that defined their collective presence in the city. You could say this is how Division Street became La Division. The colloquial use of "La Division" evoked the community they built through the 1970s.

Today, the Puerto Rican commercial and business center is known as Paseo Boricua. The story of how La Division became Paseo Boricua is one of struggle, belonging, and claiming space.[25] It is a story drawn from the pages of Chicago's history as the quintessential immigrant city, one that continues to unfold as we write this book since gentrification and displacement constitute significant problems for the remaining families in the communities that intersect along Paseo Boricua, problems we address in the next section. Division Street, made famous by Studs Terkel's 1967 classic, *Division Street: America*, is a main thoroughfare in Chicago running east to west. At one point, the street unfolded like a poem about the struggle of belonging in a segregated city: first, there were the Cabrini-Green projects, once relics of the racial segregation that African Americans encountered in the city; ran through Little Polonia; and then landed on Paseo Boricua. Gentrification has wiped out all of that history from the buildings but not from the memories of those who lived there and faced displacement then and now.

In the 1960s and 1970s, these communities were themselves in the midst of social transformations as industrial employment declined in the city and white ethnic residents exited in droves to the suburbs, a process known as white flight.[26] Humboldt Park, for example, began as a Polish immigrant community. As Poles left, landlords did not see a need to renovate or upgrade buildings. According to Alicea, "Landlord disinvestment from the neighborhood and the city's neglect of the area, coupled with the problems Puerto Ricans faced securing jobs that paid well, meant that gangs, drugs, violence, and poverty proliferated in the community."[27]

Similar issues were evident in Logan Square, once home to immigrants from Germany, Norway, and Poland, as well as some Russian Jews. The construction of the Kennedy Expressway and the promise of better homes and schools enticed these white ethnics and their families to move to the suburbs. This process went on for many years, resulting in a severe deterioration of the housing stock in Logan Square. Realtors knew that properties were riddled with housing code violations and that they needed substantial repairs, yet they sold them to Puerto Ricans. One of the families Mérida Rúa interviewed for her research bought a house in Palmer Square (a subarea of Logan Square). Rúa points out that the work of building community fell in the hands of Puerto Rican women: "When Ana told me how she and her family *sufrieron* [suffered] in Palmer Square, she did not describe the bleak or irredeemable community but told a story of community activism: 'little by little, we worked hard to raise the neighborhood.' Successive small acts set in motion the transformation of this neighborhood of urban decay into one of pride with a sense of place."[28]

When we conducted interviews with Puerto Rican families in the northern suburbs of Chicago, it was evident that they had strong memories of the time they had lived in La Division. When Maura Toro-Morn asked interviewees about whether they go to Paseo Boricua, they quickly replied, "Do you mean La Division?" One family was particularly adamant that they had no desire to visit the community; they had left La Division for the suburbs to escape the social problems that threatened them. Puerto Ricans in central Illinois who did know about the struggles in the area but had come to know it as Paseo Boricua were more positive about going there.[29]

Sociologist Nilda Flores-González writes in her seminal essay "Paseo Boricua: Claiming a Puerto Rican Space in Chicago" that when she first became aware of the community, she was "elated to find a place with familiar sounds and smells." She describes what, in fact, made La Division a typical ethnic community: "Puerto Rican music, in all its forms, blared from loudspeakers outside Lily's Record Shop. *Pasteles*, *lechon*, *alcapurria*, and other favorite dishes of the Puerto Rican cuisine could be ordered at La Bruquena Restaurant, or across the street. . . . I was immediately transported to my childhood and adolescent days in Rio Piedras. . . . I immediately felt connected to La Division, yet I remained cautious because La Division had a bad reputation, especially among those of us who did not live in the community."[30]

The labeling of La Division as "problem community" was a process that took place over the course of many years through the racialization of Puerto Ricans as an undesirable minority group and the vilification of the community as crime-ridden and dangerous. Police harassment was rampant, and it went back to the first barrios. Terkel offers one example, the story of Carlos Alvarez. One interaction with the police had profound consequences for him and his family. Alvarez was a night watchman in a city museum. One day, as he came off his shift, he was stopped by the police. Officers did not believe that he worked in the museum. Instead, they harassed him, pushed him around, broke his arm, and jailed him. When he went before the judge he tried to explain himself, but he had limited English skills, and at a time when it was customary to judge without assigning counsel or a translator, his civil rights were violated. He was found guilty and ended up losing his job.[31] Los Caballeros de San Juan knew of the frequent problems and encounters with the police and tried to intervene.

The spark for the 1966 riots began shortly after Mayor Richard J. Daley designated the first week of June as "Puerto Rican

Week." The weeklong events culminated—as they still do today—in Humboldt Park. Historian Lilia Fernández reconstructed the events: "That night police allegedly answered a call about youths fighting in the street. As they approached a group of men, they proceeded to chase two of them down an alley. In the pursuit, Office Thomas Munyon shot and then arrested a 20-year-old man, Aracelis Cruz, claiming he had drawn a gun. Witnesses dispute the accusation."[32]

Crowds gathered near the scene, and the police tried to disperse onlookers. When people refused to move along, though, the police brought the German shepherds, a practice used across the country for addressing unrest in black protests and neighborhoods. Rodríguez-Muñiz writes that one dog bit a Puerto Rican man, and the crowd exploded in anger.[33] Puerto Ricans also protested in front of the police station and demanded the release of Cruz and others who had been arrested. The community was outraged at the long-term mistreatment and harassment by the police going back to the early barrios. All of these issues, of course, were

Fig. 6.4. Cristian Roldan's mural of the 1966 Division Street Riots, corner of Division Street and Washtenaw Avenue, Chicago. Photograph by Ivis García.

known only to Puerto Rican residents because local newspapers typically did not cover them, and when they did they frequently took the side of the police. The coverage in the *Chicago Tribune* was particularly egregious since editors blamed Puerto Ricans for their inability to conform and assimilate, like European immigrants had done in the past.[34]

Puerto Ricans rioted for three days along Division Street, congregating near the entrance of Humboldt Park. Religious and community leaders intervened, trying to convince the rather large crowd estimated at around three thousand to return to their homes. In the end, sixteen people were injured, forty-nine arrested, and fifty buildings destroyed.[35] The riot, Rodríguez-Muñiz argues, represented the rebellion of a people exhausted by racial profiling, police violence, and poverty. Their protest signified a resistance to "their internal colonial reality" and the assertion of their identity as Puerto Ricans, "the spark that produced a new political consciousness." Rodríguez-Muñiz grew up in Chicago and learned about the riots from his grandparents, mother, and uncles who had migrated from Puerto Rico and lived in Humboldt Park. He writes, "They recounted being racially profiled and roughed up by police officers, having doors slammed in their face by white landlords, and put in closets by white teachers for speaking Spanish. On one occasion of racial violence, white neighbors set their building on fire, forcing my grandmother to jump out of the window and my uncle, then about six years old, to be thrown to the firemen below."[36]

In the aftermath of the riot, the mayor called for meetings with clergy, Puerto Rican leaders, and the police to address the problems Puerto Ricans faced in the city. The mayor appointed Claudio Flores, publisher of the Puerto Rican newspaper *El Puertorriqueño*, to lead a special committee of the Chicago Commission on Human Relations. The University of Chicago also commissioned a study of the race relations in West Town. The city held hearings for five months where Puerto Ricans explained the problems they faced, yet the report reduced the issue to cultural differences and to the failure of Puerto Ricans to assimilate. At the same time, the federal agency in charge of the War on Poverty had been in Chicago studying the poverty in the city.[37]

It is well known that the riots marked a radical shift for Puerto Ricans in Chicago. It led to the creation of new groups and the transformation of others. For example, the Spanish Action

Committee of Chicago, the Latin American Development Organization, and the Puerto Rican Cultural Center were formed in the aftermath of the riots. As we showed in the previous chapter, community activism was also channeled in addressing educational issues. Given the scope of this book and this chapter, it is difficult to summarize the thirty years between the riots and the 1990s, when Paseo Boricua came into existence. But it is important to mention that Puerto Ricans created their path to inclusion in the ethnic and racial landscape of the city through affirming a national identity as Puerto Ricans and in solidarity with Mexican Americans and African Americans. Their involvement in the mayoral campaign and rise to power of Harold Washington, the first black mayor of the City of Chicago in the 1980s, represents a crucial political moment for Puerto Ricans. Puerto Ricans exercised their political muscle in the voting booth and began to elect political leaders to the city council and state legislative positions in Springfield. Luis Gutiérrez very proudly remembers the day in 1986 when he was sworn in as the first Puerto Rican alderman in the city, representing the Twenty-Sixth Ward.[38] He was elected to Congress in 1992 and went on to serve twelve terms, representing Illinois's Fourth District, and became one of the best-known Illinois Puerto Ricans in the nation.

After Gutiérrez decided to run for Congress, Mayor Daley nominated Billy Ocasio to serve as the alderman for the Twenty-Sixth Ward. Ocasio, a Puerto Rican born and raised in Chicago's Humboldt Park, was one the visionaries of Paseo Boricua. With the support of Mayor Daley, he convened a diverse group of leaders—today known as the Puerto Rican Agenda, a not-for-profit organization composed of community leaders and educators from across the city of Chicago—with the purpose of developing an economic base of businesses and restaurants to consolidate what could have been known as "Little Puerto Rico." The notion of "Little Puerto Rico" was intended to follow the ethnic enclave model that has proven successful for other immigrants in the city. Prosperous ethnic enclaves are Chinatown, Greektown, Little Italy, and La Villita. According to Ocasio, after the installation of the flags of steel, the commercial vacancy on Division Street went from 70 percent vacant to almost no vacancy. The area has become popular among city dwellers, and it attracts consumers from different social classes from the suburbs as well as the city.[39] In 2008, the Division Street Business Development Association found 114 business in the area, many owned by young Puerto Ricans, first-time business owners.[40] In 2012, restaurants represented 17 percent of all businesses in Paseo.[41] A survey conducted by the Puerto Rican Agenda report during Fiesta Boricua found that, on average, people come to Paseo to eat at least once a week.[42] It remains to be seen whether the business dimension of Paseo remains a viable opportunity for local entrepreneurs.

The two gateways in the shape of two flags in Paseo serve to defend and claim "collective ownership" as opposed to "individual ownership" over space, even when the majority of Puerto Ricans are not owners but renters.[43] Paseo has played an even stronger role in the fight against gentrification. The neighborhood is an example of "Latino Urbanism," which is a form of urbanism that produces and appropriates space with the purpose of resisting marginalization, gentrification, and uneven development. In this particular case, Puerto Rican leaders wanted the gateways to act as a physical and mental barrier against outsiders. As a community leader explained to Ivis García, "My view is that you need the mechanism to go out there and to tell them and say, 'We have a map, we are here,' and then another mechanism is of just keeping people [the gentrifiers] out."[44] The erection of the flags in 1995 was one of the first steps in marking the community as a Puerto Rican space, and it coincided with its naming as Paseo Boricua. The steel flags, each fifty-nine feet tall, come with a narrative of their own. They were installed at both ends of Paseo Boricua, the segment of Division Street that runs between Western and California Avenues and marks the center of Humboldt Park's Puerto Rican community. The flags were intended to help define and claim the space as Puerto Rican. Though they were initially criticized by some residents as "too expensive" and "too little, too late," the flags have become essential, well-loved symbols in the fight against gentrification.

In 2016 the community marked the fiftieth anniversary of the Division Street Riots with the unveiling of a mural that paid homage to the history of Puerto Ricans: their displacement from the island, migration to Chicago, mistreatment, and survival in the city. Cristian Roldán, with the help of other young people in the community, painted the mural on the corner of Division Street and Washtenaw Avenue—the battleground of a rapidly gentrifying space. The artistic rendition became a public interpretation and reinterpretation of the community's history, a way to remember what happened and how the community responded. The mural has multiple layers of meaning, connecting the island and Chicago, claiming space, and affirming identity. The mural is also a reminder that cultural and national pride was both the antidote to the dehumanization Puerto Ricans faced and the political strategy that energized community struggles then and now.

Gentrification and Displacement

Puerto Ricans have struggled against the forces of gentrification in three of the communities that they claimed as home: West Town, Humboldt Park, and Logan Square. The 2012 Puerto Rican Agenda report found that 47 percent of the total number of Puerto Ricans in the city were distributed throughout the neighborhoods of Logan Square, Hermosa, Humboldt Park, Belmont, Cragin, West Town, Avondale, Portage Park, and Montclare, with smaller groupings in Austin and Irving Park. The other 53 percent of Puerto Ricans were dispersed across the city.[45]

Humboldt Park, West Town, and Logan Square today may be nominally Puerto Rican since there has been such a sharp decline in the number of Puerto Ricans who actually live in the community, but the struggle to keep it a Puerto Rican community is fierce and multifaceted. Anthropologist Jesse Mumm helps us understand how the current wave of gentrification enveloped these communities, arguing that they are near communities that are already gentrified, thus making the housing stock desirable for developers. The city also wanted to attract middle-class white families and professionals after decades of white flight. Mumm writes that "outside investors saw a set of beautiful buildings embodying the best historic architecture of the city. . . . The one problem that remained . . . was that in the eyes of far too many white people outside the neighborhood—Humboldt Park meant poverty, pathology, gangs, drugs, danger, and Puerto Ricans."[46] By the mid-1990s, the slow trickle of middle-class whites into West Town and Logan Square meant rising rents, removal of cultural landmarks, and the relocation of essential services and businesses. We know that this problem has been at the forefront of Puerto Rican families since the 1980s because the *Chicago Tribune* has covered this gentrification as front-page news.[47]

Initially, residents of Humboldt Park, Logan Square, and West Town relied on face-to-face discussions and informational meetings to combat gentrification. In a 1999 article, José López, executive director of the Puerto Rican Cultural Center, said an outsider should "come in as 'a learner,' rather than one who has 'the truth.'" Zenaida Lopez, the owner of a popular bakery, said in the same article, "Division Street and Humboldt Park are synonymous with being Puerto Rican." She implored newcomers to "learn about the history of Puerto Rico, of Puerto Ricans in Chicago and this community." Invitations were often even more direct. An organizing committee in 1999 placed fliers in gentrifying areas that read, "You are invited to discuss how we can live together."[48]

What explains these efforts to push back against gentrification? Residents often described a feeling of attachment to their neighborhood that transcended mere fondness. "I think we're the only Latino family left on the block," Johan Khalilian said in a 2007 article, adding, "I wanted to stay here in the neighborhood I grew up in." Caleb Sjoblom, director of Rogers Park Community Development Corporation, said, "It's important to fight gentrification for those who have been in the neighborhood and are being forced out."[49] Zenaida Lopez agreed. "What I see happening, if we don't take a stand, is that Roberto Clemente High School will disappear. I see it as Wicker Park High in a few years, with no Puerto Ricans there."[50] This is why keeping control over Clemente and making it a school of choice has been one of the main goals of the Community as a Campus Initiative, discussed in the previous chapter.

Second- and third-generation Puerto Ricans grew up hearing the stories of eviction from Lincoln Park and feel a palpable sense of loss when faced with the current problem of gentrification in Humboldt Park. "We're a floating community," Xavier Burgos, a twenty-year-old student at Northeastern Illinois University, said in 2006. "We've been pushed out of Lincoln Park and Wicker Park. The process of gentrification is denying our history in the same way that the process of colonialism has on the island."[51] A Loyola University study released that same year described gentrification as a "block-by-block process that [residents] liken to removing their community piece-by-piece."[52] Alejandro Molina of the Puerto Rican Cultural Center equates gentrification with violence as white professionals who have no roots in the community push lower-income minorities out of their homes. "These people, they hide in their trendy hipster stores, but there's no sense of themselves being in a community," he said. "All of a sudden, it's condos, and it's not for us."[53]

Gentrification is not only about removing Puerto Ricans as residents but about removing the cultural symbols of their struggle, too. For example, murals, like homes and buildings, have been targeted for destruction. In 2008, the *Chicago Tribune* reported that the Near Northwest Neighborhood Network (NNNN) planned to buy a 3,100-square-foot city-owned lot fronting a historic mural for one dollar. The NNNN planned to spruce up the property, valued at $353,000, with trees, benches, and a wooden shelter around the mural. "That lot and the mural will do a lot to enhance current redevelopment in the North Avenue business quarter," Eluid Medina, executive director of the NNNN, said.[54] Puerto Rican leaders mobilized to counter the development and the fight to save the mural paid off. This situation helped call attention to the state of other murals in the neighborhood and to the organizing efforts to preserve them.

Culture and identity have become ways to make claims for space and belonging. In response to soaring rents that threaten to push out a "shrinking" Puerto Rican community, plans for the 25,000-square-foot National Museum of Puerto Rican Arts and Culture in the former Humboldt Park Stables took shape.[55] The development of the museum represents a particular strategy against gentrification: defining Humboldt Park as the Puerto Rican capital of the Midwest. Today, it remains the only museum in the mainland United States dedicated exclusively to the island's heritage.

Congressman Gutiérrez, who remembers the city using the Humboldt Park Stables as a garbage transfer station, said the opening of the museum represented the start of a significant chapter in the neighborhood's history. "It's almost as if, 20 years ago, they were saying you don't deserve our respect," he said. "Today, we're saying you must respect this place. Not only must you respect it, we'll show you the most beautiful parts of our community, the arts and the culture." Fittingly, the theme chosen for the museum's first exhibit was gentrification.[56]

Most efforts to fight gentrification take place at a small scale. A student-led effort at Roberto Clemente Community Academy and Pedro Albizu Campos High School, for example, focused on planting flowers in front of businesses on Division Street.[57] The project succeeded not only in beautifying the community but in helping students build stronger relationships with their peers. *Hoodoisie*, a live podcast sponsored by the Urban Theater

Company, visited Paseo Boricua in 2017 as part of its series on gentrification.[58] The show provided a platform for community activists and artists to discuss topics like displacement, activism, and identity. Other strategies for combating gentrification include tutoring and mentoring children and teens, creating art projects, and providing tax rebates for longtime homeowners.[59] And at one time, under Ocasio's leadership as alderman, a down-zone ordinance was applied that reduced the number of new units that could be built on any given lot. This gave more power to the aldermanic office in redevelopment areas.[60]

The struggle for Puerto Ricans and community organizers is not over. The onset of the Great Recession in the first decade of the twenty-first century brought a host of new challenges for renters and homeowners in Humboldt Park and other neighborhoods. Foreclosures abounded. "I walk two blocks, and I see six houses for sale," Melissa Rivera told the *Chicago Tribune* in 2007. "I look at the mailboxes and see last names that are not Hispanic. I feel like we're losing our community."[61] Residents at the time described feeling looked over, pushed out, and forgotten. "They don't even want to know who we are," Angela Reyes said of the people moving to Humboldt Park. "If you had enough gall to . . . purchase a home and live here, why not make an effort to get to know the residents?" Both women joined a march of more than one hundred residents protesting gentrification.[62]

In the aftermath of the 2008 recession, things became even more difficult in many ways. In 2014, Redfin reported that median home sale prices were up 62 percent from the previous year in Humboldt Park.[63] Popular media outlets called it an "up-and-coming neighborhood," buzzwords familiar to locations on the verge of rapid upscaling. The next year, the 606 opened, a new elevated trail system that had been in the works for more than a decade. The route cut through Humboldt Park and Logan Square on its way to wealthy Bucktown. Mayor Rahm Emanuel hailed the trail system as "a good thing . . . for the people who have property here. Increased housing values are not a bad thing."[64]

But what about the people who rent? Only 35 percent of units in Logan Square and Humboldt Park are owner-occupied. Roberto Maldonado, alderman for the Twenty-Sixth Ward, was looking at property tax abatements and rent control to assist low-income residents of both neighborhoods. "At the beginning, when [the 606] was being discussed, [the residents] thought it would be a nice amenity for the community and they supported it," he said. "I told them, 'Be careful; this is going to drive up rents and assessed values.' Now they are worried about the impact to long-term residents and other residents."[65] In 2017 Maldonado and Proco "Joe" Moreno, alderman for the First Ward, were drafting an ordinance that would increase the demolition fee for residential properties and charge a deconversion fee when multiple unit buildings are converted into single family homes. The aldermen also hoped to curb destruction of low-income housing as luxury housing was taking its place around the 606.[66]

The closure of school buildings in 2013 has been also worrisome for community members. In Chicago's gentrifying communities like Logan Square, West Town, and Humboldt Park, former school buildings have been transformed into luxury condos and charter schools.[67] In response to this threat, Community as a Campus advocated for Alexander Von Humboldt Elementary School to become a "teachers' village," to include housing for teachers with amenities such a coffee shops, meeting places, and public spaces.[68] With the collaboration of the Illinois Facilities Funds, the Puerto Rican Cultural Center, and the RBH Group and the support of Alderman Moreno, Community as a Campus was able to secure the space.[69] Von Humboldt will be repurposed into a mixed-use and mixed-income community with affordable and market-rate housing, as well as a café, classrooms, and a community space.[70]

Ultimately, the fight against gentrification is a battle to change attitudes. Middle- and upper-class whites returning to Chicago often are not aware of the impact they have on neighborhoods dominated by Puerto Ricans, other Latino populations, and blacks. Alejandro Molina recalled seeing one transplant who made papier-mâché protest art and drove a car with an Obama bumper sticker. "This young man is probably left of center, he's probably anti-war, he's probably college-educated, yet he has no clue that he's contributing to the displacement of a community," he said.[71] José López encouraged people to be more thoughtful about their housing decisions. "I cannot tell anyone where they should or should not live," he said. "However, I think that if . . . there is a historically defined area, that you would want to respect that and that you would want to look and validate what it has created, rather than coming and erasing it."[72] Since their arrival in the city, gentrification has been a problem that has shaped the community

Fig. 6.5.
¡Humboldt Park
Is Not for Sale!
campaign, 2011
postcard. Courtesy
of the Puerto Rican
Cultural Center.

experiences of Puerto Ricans. It is important to point out that long-term community organizations have also faced a host of problems that have threatened their existence. As we concluded the research and writing for this book, a community-wide effort formed to save La Casa Puertorriqueña, which organized the Puerto Rican Parade and has offered a host of services. This important chapter in the recent history of the community is an illustration of the political power and concerted effort that took place to protect one of the oldest organizations in Humboldt Park.

Keeping La Casa Puertorriqueña

La Casa Puertorriqueña has been a cherished institution for Puerto Ricans since its founding as a cultural center dedicated to promoting the culture, heritage, and history of Puerto Rico. It has also provided educational opportunities and programming such as music lessons, art classes, and other activities to help preserve and promote Puerto Rican culture. In fact, the history of the community center deserves a book of its own. It is beyond the scope of this section to address the complexity of the case, but it is relevant as an example of the political capital that Puerto Ricans accrued in the city and of their desire to sustain community institutions for generations to come.

Members of the Puerto Rican Agenda learned that the building that housed La Casa Puertorriqueña was for sale. The Puerto

Rican Agenda set to investigate how a building with no mortgage and an organization with tax-exempt status was in bankruptcy court. Over several months much was revealed about the workings of the organization and its financial troubles, mismanagement, and precarious condition. In a press conference on August 14, 2018, the cochair of the Puerto Rican Agenda at the time, Jessi Fuentes, announced that the Puerto Rican Agenda would mobilize to save La Casa Puertorriqueña. The same press conference revealed that the office of the attorney general had investigated the Puerto Rican Parade Committee of Chicago because of the mismanagement of funds. With only two weeks to go from the day of the press conference, the Puerto Rican Agenda resolved to prevent the sale of La Casa Puertorriqueña. Senator Iris Martinez communicated directly with Attorney General Lisa Madigan's office to voice her concerns over how the state had handled the problems, with La Casa coming close to being lost and the property sold to developers gentrifying the community. While the building was in the process of being sold to the highest bidder to pay outstanding debts, the bankruptcy judge was unaware of the potential fraud and pending investigation. Martinez said, "They have to stop this at bankruptcy court, so we can continue to find other options. We have community organizations working together that want this building, because is this the property of the Puerto Rican community; not anyone else's."[73]

In January 2019, nearly half a year after the press conference, Paul Roldán, president and CEO of the Hispanic Housing Development Corporation, informed Ivis García that the Puerto Rican Agenda had secured the money and was about to sign the paperwork to purchase La Casa Puertorriqueña. This entailed a settlement of more than $900,000 in debt accrued by the Puerto Rican Parade Committee. Roldán added, "The plan is to demolish the building and build affordable housing for families." The corporation recently had also purchased the empty lot between Division and California, just steps away from the lot of La Casa Puertorriqueña, at 1237 North California Avenue. "We are going to build an eight-story building on that corner; is going to be huge [sic]," Roldán expressed with excitement. Hispanic Housing, along with the Puerto Rican Agenda, was trying to secure as much property as possible in the face of gentrification. This new project would become part of a new effort of Alderman Roberto Maldonado to designate the area as a Special Service Area called "Puerto Rico

Town." Although the area has had several names—from its early days as La Division, to the Paseo Boricua of the 1990s, and now under its new designation, Puerto Rico Town—this space and its institutions have served as an important place for Puerto Ricans in Illinois to gather to affirm culture and identity.

In the Prairie: Communities beyond Chicago

At the beginning of this chapter we asked whether Puerto Ricans outside of Chicago have established communities of their own and have integrated themselves into established communities in the suburbs. We find that the experiences of Puerto Ricans outside of Chicago and the suburbs contrast sharply with the organized community groups, cultural spaces, museums, and restaurants that exist in the city. Drawing on interviews and fieldwork observations, we conclude that there is no other spatially bounded space like Paseo Boricua outside of Chicago. That does not mean that Puerto Ricans do not feel part of their communities. On the contrary, it is evident from our interviews that Puerto Ricans belong to more than one community at once, something that is true for those in Chicago as well.

In the absence of the population density that characterizes the community experiences of Puerto Ricans in Chicago, in central Illinois Puerto Ricans have constituted and reconstituted themselves as members of various communities. Puerto Ricans in central Illinois have a sophisticated understanding of themselves as members of local, transnational, and diaspora communities. Their trajectories engender this understanding—we could also say they engender migrations through these communities. They also understand how their collective story is connected to the story of the more substantial Latino immigration in the country. As Puerto Ricans in central Illinois spoke about community, they extended the definition of community to mean more than a group of people bounded by a shared culture and national identity; the concept of community that is evident through the interviews also threads through the life-cycle stages. In other words, it became less a shared sense of community bounded by nationality and more the presence of people—networks of friends—connected by family, faith, and everyday experiences as immigrant/migrants in a predominantly white community. For many of the Puerto Ricans in central Illinois, other residents of Latin America—but primarily Mexicans and Central Americans—came together to form the community. Social class mattered here, too, in that educated and professional Puerto Ricans developed a community of interest with other immigrants from Latin America with similar professional and social-class interests. In cities where Puerto Ricans were part of a larger Hispanic/Latino community, the concept of community extended to include others who were not Puerto Rican. One could say that the experiences of Puerto Ricans in central Illinois mirror those evident in the early stages of community formation in Chicago when Puerto Ricans and Mexicans came together, bound by family, work, and immigration experience, to form various communities.

We also learned that community had multiple meanings for Puerto Ricans. One woman who had recently arrived in central Illinois commented, "First, Puerto Ricans lived dispersed throughout these communities, and frequently they didn't know each other unless they knew each other through work. Although several corporations in the area are known to hire Puerto Ricans, that alone did not promote a sense of community." The famous phrase that goes, "Will it play in Peoria?" also applies to the development of Puerto Rican communities in downstate Illinois. Ironically, in Peoria we found a large but dispersed Puerto Rican community that meets once a year. One respondent described the event that has been happening for ten consecutive years: "This woman from Puerto Rico got us together. She came up with the idea, and everyone is like, let's do it. She rented the park for several hours on July 4th. We all bring food, *arroz con habichuelas*, *pernil*, just the whole array of food. I usually play the music. We have games for kids, games for the adults. After that, we go to my friend Roberto's house, swim in his swimming pool. Then we all drive downtown to watch the fireworks." In Peoria there is also a group of Puerto Ricans who meet to play salsa and dance. One member of the Puerto Rican community described to us how, when he first arrived in the city, he tended to hang out with his African American friends who became his family. He has continued those relationships but has now also joined this Puerto Rican group. Other Puerto Ricans described how they formed community through connections with other Latino groups made up of other newcomers to the state.

In towns with large universities, those institutions themselves are spaces for the development of communities. One professor told us, "When a large group of students landed at the University of

Illinois, students bonded among themselves, invariably some fell in love, married, and had children with other Puerto Ricans and/or Latinos. Some stayed in these university towns to start their careers in academia or other jobs."[74]

Many Puerto Ricans outside of Chicago have formed organizations like the Waukegan Puerto Rican Society and the Aurora Puerto Rican Cultural Council, to mention two. They have also opened a number of businesses and contributed to their region's vibrant economy. A growing number of second-generation Puerto Ricans living in Illinois have stayed connected to these organizations and their culture through events, restaurants, parades, and festivals.

When Hurricane Maria hit Puerto Rico, a number of Puerto Rican organizations and restaurants outside of Chicago led fundraising efforts. For example, the Puerto Rican Society in Waukegan raised $5,236 in one night from about one hundred individuals, including local elected officials. As they continued the campaign, they raised a total of $30,000. One of their goals was to buy two hundred solar lights.[75] The money they raised went to various Puerto Rican municipalities and local organizations such as Casa Pueblo, a well-known Puerto Rico nonprofit, and Caritas de Puerto Rico, a Catholic charity. Members of the Puerto Rican Society traveled to Puerto Rico to personally deliver the checks.

After Maria: The Bonds of Community and Diaspora

In early September, category 5 Hurricane Irma skirted Puerto Rico, causing massive failure to the island's infrastructure and leaving the entire island without electricity for two weeks. Just as the island's electricity grid was restored, on September 20 Hurricane Maria crisscrossed the island, wreaking massive devastation on the battered economy and producing material scarcity and widespread emotional trauma. There may be many arguments and heated conversations about the meaning of Paseo Boricua for Puerto Ricans in Illinois. But one thing is undeniable: in the aftermath of the most devastating hurricane to hit the island in the last hundred years, it was the Puerto Rican diaspora that responded with force, determination, and without hesitation. We next describe the efforts of the Puerto Rican community of Chicago to offer aid in the aftermath of Hurricanes Irma and Maria and how these efforts have strengthen the bonds of community.

On September 22, 2017, an Emergency Task Force composed of members of the Puerto Rican Agenda hosted a fundraiser at the Segundo Ruiz Belvis Cultural Center for essential needs; over four hundred people attended and raised about $70,000 to go to local organizations in Puerto Rico. Within two days, the Emergency Task Force also purchased shipping-ready pallets of emergency supplies, secured transportation courtesy of Custom Trucking Company, and loaded the first cargo plane, underwritten by United Airlines.[76] Congressman Gutiérrez and Mayor Emanuel personally delivered supplies for distribution across the island, arriving in San Juan on September 25 (five days after Maria) and received by Mayor Carmen Yulín Cruz.[77] The same United Airlines plane brought to Chicago, free of charge, three hundred evacuees from Puerto Rico. Their families received the evacuees with a big *parranda* (music festivity) at O'Hare International Airport.

The Puerto Rican Agenda organized efforts to provide relief in Puerto Rico through a program called "3 R's for Puerto

Fig 6.6. Blue tarps covering homes in Saturce, Puerto Rico, after Hurricane Maria.
Photograph by Ivis García.

Rico Campaign: Rescue, Relief, and Rebuild." The Puerto Rican Agenda work was conducted in collaboration with people from the island to "bring Puerto Rico into the twenty-first century on the infrastructure and economy side" and to help "it be a self-determined Puerto Rico," as stated by cochair Cristina Pacione-Zayas, one of the main organizers of the relief efforts. The Puerto Rican Agenda continued its campaign from October 19 to October 21, 2017, commissioning Congressman Gutiérrez to purchase and distribute a second and third donation of pallets, this time in areas outside of San Juan—including Aibonito, Barranquitas, Comerío, Toa Baja, Jayuya, Bayamón, and Loíza. At the beginning of November, given the need to stimulate Puerto Rico's local economy, the Emergency Task Force of the Puerto Rican Agenda changed its strategy to apply donations for purchasing pallets directly on the island instead of in Chicago and shipping them to Puerto Rico.

By April 11, 2018, Pacione-Zayas and the Puerto Rican Agenda had raised $300,000 in emergency supplies and micro-grants for thirty *municipios* (municipalities). Moreover, the agenda received a grant from Chicago Community Trust for a total of $100,000 to continue its efforts, which included micro-grant distribution in Puerto Rico as well as support for the resettlement of evacuees in Chicago. Members of the Puerto Rican Agenda opened a Multi-Agency Resource Center in the Humboldt Park Fieldhouse sponsored by 311 (the City of Chicago's emergency services) and Mayor Rahm Emanuel's administration. The resource center was a one-stop destination for recently arrived evacuees where they could learn about city services. Families and individuals were paired with a case manager who provided them with support for relocating to Chicago, from enrolling their kids in school to finding affordable housing. The Puerto Rican Agenda helped to bring together a community development system composed of social service organizations, housing, schools, universities, hospitals, and city agencies to welcome Puerto Rican refugees to Paseo, Chicago, and, more broadly, Illinois. By May 2018, the efforts of the Puerto Rican Agenda were felt by many in Puerto Rico and those making Chicagoland their new home, either temporarily or permanently. After Hurricane Maria, Puerto Ricans were not passively waiting for the federal government. Puerto Ricans on the island cleaned up and started to rebuild. Puerto Ricans in the diaspora said *presente* (present) at a moment of crisis. The physical

Fig 6.7. Members of the Puerto Rican Agenda in Comerío, Puerto Rico. Photographer unknown; Ivis García, personal collection.

distance of those living in Chicago and Illinois did not erase the pain from Hurricane Maria or their sense of loyalty to and love of Puerto Rico—if anything, it strengthened it.[78]

It is evident that Puerto Ricans have built strong and vibrant communities by themselves and in conversation with other groups that have been marginalized. Historically, one way marginalized groups cope with subordination and dehumanization is by affirming their humanity through their identities. Puerto Ricans affirmed their identity and pride as a way to survive in the city and as a way to stay connected to their families and communities in Puerto Rico. They affirmed their humanity through their dedication to work, their families, and their communities. Second- and third-generation Puerto Ricans born and raised in Chicago also learn to navigate this ethnic and racial landscape, some more effectively than others.

Although Puerto Ricans were displaced from Lincoln Park, Old Town, Lakeview, Uptown, and other neighborhoods due to urban renewal and government-sponsored gentrification, they moved farther west to West Town, Logan Square, and Humboldt Park. Festivals, restaurants, and organizations characterize Paseo Boricua on Division Street, which became the heart of the community. Paseo Boricua, the National Museum of Puerto Rican Arts and Culture, and other organizations were born from the gentrification struggle. But this struggle has also paved the way for a stronger and more resilient community identity. Paseo Boricua, Division Street, and Humboldt Park have become some of the most recognized Puerto Rican communities in the country. Moreover, they have also become the center of public debates surrounding opposition to displacement.

The Puerto Rican national and political identity (as a colonized space) has also become a tool to challenge gentrification. Puerto Ricans frequently view the arrival of non-Hispanic white newcomers as a form of colonization and as undermining their sense of community. Non-Hispanic white newcomers often encounter hostility from Puerto Ricans, the same hatred that children like Marisa Alicia encountered as a child when Puerto Ricans first settled in the area. Their resentment, however, is not unfounded. For decades Puerto Ricans have been subjected to violence and stigmatization, as demonstrated when a policeman shot an unarmed Puerto Rican man at the first Puerto Rican neighborhood parade in 1966, setting off the Division Street Riots.

The year 1966 marked changes for Puerto Rican Chicago. Because of the riots, the Chicago Commission on Human Relations, as well as politicians, started to do something about the problems in the Puerto Rican community, among them poverty, housing discrimination, and police brutality. Federal and local funds were allocated for government services and to start not-for-profit organizations and many community-based projects that would not have been possible were it not for the riots, such as Community Action Programs, the Chicago Committee on Urban Opportunity, Neighborhood Youth Corps, and Head Start. Through popular protest, Puerto Ricans found that they had the power of creating social change. The Division Street Riots were vital to generating a sense of community, even when today the percentage of Puerto Ricans in the area has decreased dramatically. These spatial claims have been and continue to be a vehicle for community organizing in the diaspora as demonstrated recently by the community efforts after the storms.

7

CONCLUSION: THE PARADOX OF BELONGING

Since its founding a little more than two hundred years ago, Illinois has been forged by demographic and migration processes that have also shaped the country's population growth. These processes have not been smooth; there have been many conflicts over land, resources, and labor, intended and unintended exclusions, and many painful lessons along the way.[1] This book offers evidence that Puerto Ricans are important to the demographic growth occurring in Illinois. Puerto Ricans arrived in the middle decades of the twentieth century and have made their mark in the history of the state since then. The incorporation of Puerto Ricans at various levels of the political establishment represents one example. As we documented in chapter 6, Harold Washington's run and tenure as the first black mayor of the City of Chicago overlapped with the incorporation of Puerto Ricans into Illinois politics. It is well known that his political rise was possible through a politically progressive coalition between African Americans, Latinos, and whites. Mayor Washington appointed Latinos, a number of them Puerto Ricans, to important city posts, launching many into larger political careers.[2] Luis Gutiérrez, who campaigned and worked closely with Mayor Washington, was appointed in 1984 as deputy superintendent in the Department of Streets and Sanitation. He then went on to run for alderman. From 1986 to 1993, Gutiérrez represented the Twenty-Sixth Ward, and his tenure helped marshal resources and political capital for Puerto Rican community groups. In the 1990s, the creation of the Fourth District led to Gutiérrez's election to Congress, a position he occupied until 2019, when he retired. Billy Ocasio, today CEO and president of the National Museum of Puerto Rican Arts and Culture, was tapped to replace

Gutiérrez and served a tenure in the city council, representing the Twenty-Sixth Ward as well.

When the larger history of the political power of Latinos in the state of Illinois is written, Puerto Rican Miguel del Valle will play a prominent role as the first Latino senator in the Illinois General Assembly, defeating Edward Nedza in the Democratic primary. He was also the first Latino to occupy the position of assistant majority leader in the Illinois Senate. Today he is still an outspoken advocate for Latino representation in the legislative and judicial branches of government. He was the cochair of the Illinois Legislative Latino Caucus and the first Latino member of the Illinois Legislative Black Caucus. His leadership in redistricting cases in 1981, 1991, and 2001 led to the creation of Latino majority districts on the city, county, and state levels. Puerto Rican women have also played a significant role in the more recent political history of Puerto Rican representation in the legislature. In 2020, Cristina Pacione-Zayas was appointed to represent the Twentieth District after Iris Martinez was elected clerk of the Circuit Court of Cook County. We must also mention the political campaigns of two Puerto Rican women in the City of Chicago, Jessica Gutiérrez and Rossana Rodríguez-Sánchez, who played an important part in the Latino political incorporation in the state as well. For one of these young women, the fruit does not fall far from the tree, as Jessica Gutiérrez, daughter of Congressman Gutiérrez, ran but lost the aldermanic election for the Thirtieth Ward. Rossana Rodríguez-Sánchez won the Thirty-Third Ward aldermanic position by thirteen votes.[3] Puerto Rican incorporation into the political landscape of Chicago politics is historic and measurable.

Puerto Ricans have worked hard to form strong and stable communities in Chicago and beyond. As discussed in chapter 3, there are Puerto Ricans in every county throughout the state, with significant concentrations in Elgin, Aurora, Rantoul, and Bloomington-Normal. This book has shown how they struggled to belong, working hard to support and raise their families and making meaningful contributions to their communities and the state. Puerto Ricans have crafted their sense of belonging, one that is different from other Latino ethnic and racial groups in the state and the nation because of the colonial condition that has characterized United States–Puerto Rican relations.

Belonging for Puerto Ricans has meant living—and some might say dying—in a transnational existence.[4] Belonging has been a paradoxical process for many reasons, but principally because of the prejudice and discrimination that Puerto Ricans have encountered along the way. They are demographically present but remain invisible to the average Illinoisan. Even in the current historical moment, when stories about the 2017 hurricane season and the deepening economic crisis on the island saturate the news, we still maintain that the average Illinoisan knows little about Puerto Ricans, their struggles, and their political, economic, and social contributions to the state. We hope this book makes the lives and experiences of Puerto Ricans more visible and helps combat the vast lack of knowledge that exists about Puerto Ricans in Illinois. As one popular bumper sticker in Chicago reads, *Aquí luchamos, aquí nos quedamos* (Here we struggle, here we stay).

As we look back and reflect about the research and writing of this book, we cannot help but also recognize the extraordinary historical moments we are currently witnessing with respect to Puerto Rico, U.S. Puerto Rican communities, and more specifically Puerto Ricans in Illinois. These events have impacted the narrative we offered here. First, as we mentioned in earlier chapters, the hurricane season of 2017 has forever marked the history of the island, where life is now described as before Maria and after Maria. It also marked the research and writing of this book because what we had initially proposed to write had to be changed to account for the devastation and new migrations in the aftermath of these events. It is clear now that these catastrophes institutionalized the role of the Puerto Rican diaspora as a source of emotional support, economic help, and political mobilization. In this respect, Chicago's participation in the recovery process has been historic, as money and materials collected by various organizations continue to pour into the island steadily.[5] The Puerto Rican Agenda, in particular, is an organization that must be praised because of the breadth of resources, aid, and political capital it has marshaled toward recovery efforts across the towns most affected. As we concluded this book, news and reports about the recovery efforts and new political developments continued to take place and the estimated number of those who died was still being debated.

The Struggle Continues

We cannot end this book without writing about an event that took place in Chicago. In fact, we can state categorically that the Puerto Rican community in Chicago—and broadly the entire diaspora community—was shocked to its core when a cell phone video showed the mistreatment and verbal harassment of a young Puerto Rican woman, Mia Irizarry, merely for wearing a T-shirt with a Puerto Rican flag. The event took place at Caldwell Woods in the Cook County Forest Preserves. In the age of viral videos showing violence, hate crimes, and blatant discrimination against African Americans and other people of color, this video of Irizarry's racial harassment by a white man will be analyzed for many years to come. It placed Chicago's Puerto Rican community at the heart of national conversations about new forms of xenophobia and racism and reaffirms a point we made at the beginning of this book: while Puerto Ricans have worked hard to belong by creating thriving communities, the average Illinoisan knows very little about those struggles and that history. The incident also shows how Puerto Ricans are placed in the larger narrative of "immigrants," even though they are technically migrants, and, like other immigrants, continue to be perceived as "foreigners" and "non-citizens." The thirty-six-minute video filmed by Irizarry herself and posted to her personal Facebook page in early July 2018 has been viewed more than two million times. The details of the story add a sobering note to our conclusion, but it is imperative that our readers recognize its magnitude and how it rippled through Puerto Ricans in the diaspora.

As Mia Irizarry gathered her family for a birthday celebration at the Cook County Forest Preserves in the city's northwest side, an inebriated white man approached her with questions about her T-shirt. He first asked her if the flag on her shirt was the Texas flag. The man, later identified as sixty-two-year-old Timothy G. Trybus, became very agitated and physically threatening. Trybus got in Irizarry's face and pointed a finger at her, asking, "Are you a citizen? Then you should not be wearing that." He continued, "I would like to know if she is an American citizen? Why is she wearing that shit? You are not going to change us. You know that. The world is not going to change the United States of America. Period." A Forest Preserves police officer, later identified as Patrick Conner, stood nearby doing nothing. Irizarry recorded the incident while expressing to the officer loudly and clearly that she was feeling threatened by the man. "Officer, I feel uncomfortable," Irizarry said in a quiet voice. "Officer, I feel highly uncomfortable, can you grab him . . . please officer," but she received no response. "Officer, I'm renting this area, and he is harassing me about the shirt that I am wearing. I paid for a permit for this area. I do not feel comfortable with him here. Is there anything you can do?" The officer walked away and is seen intervening only when the men in her family got involved. We know that after a prolonged period, Trybus was asked to leave. Eventually, a Cook County police patrol arrived to address the situation. Once the video went viral, it was clear what had transpired. Trybus was arrested and charged with a hate crime. Conner, a ten-year veteran of the Forest Preserves, was placed on desk duties during the period of the investigation and eventually resigned. We have watched the video multiple times, and we are both shaken to the core witnessing it. It represents a sobering moment at a time in our history when there are a number of reports about whites calling the police on people of color for innocuous things, like selling candy or using an expired coupon. Trybus took this a step further and deputized himself to police a Puerto Rican woman's body by telling her that she should not wear the Puerto Rican flag. The statement, "You are not going to change us," is packed with meaning in the current xenophobic climate articulated most prominently by former president Donald Trump.

The response from the local community was swift and pointed. The Puerto Rican Agenda and other community leaders and politicians—including District Eight Cook County Board commissioner Luis Arroyo Jr. and state senator Iris Martinez, among

Fig. 7.1. Mia Irizarry at a press conference with Cristina Pacione-Zayas, cochair of the Puerto Rican Agenda. Photographer unknown; Ivis García, personal collection.

others—quickly mobilized to offer Irizarry support and demanded action. Political leaders wrote petition letters asking for the officer's formal resignation or for him to be fired. Even Puerto Rican governor Ricardo Rosselló weighed in on the issue in a CNN interview. "I was shocked, appalled, and disgusted. This was an attack of one American citizen on another American citizen. Puerto Ricans have been part of the United States. We've been fighting wars with other fellow Americans. We are proud U.S. citizens. People need to understand that."[6] Congressman Gutiérrez wrote a letter to the Civil Rights Division at the Department of Justice in which he stated, "I understand this incident on a gut level because almost the same thing happened to me when I was a freshman in Congress. I was denied entry into the Capitol complex by U.S. Capitol Police despite being a Congressman with identification because my daughter was carrying a Puerto Rican flag and the officer doubted that I could be a Member of Congress."[7]

Congressman Gutiérrez first shared this story in his autobiography, *Still Dreaming*, which we feature prominently in this book. Although he has retired from Congress and moved to Puerto Rico, his involvement and connection to the Puerto Rican community will continue for years to come. The events that Gutiérrez and Irizarry faced have been labeled microaggressions, part of the range of behavior that people of color confront in the current age of color-blind racism. What is most poignant in the exchange are the implicit undertones about belonging: "You are not going to change us" says the white man, gathering the collective anxieties of whites that underlie the current moment. Indeed, the issue of belonging is central to who we are as a society, who we are as a community, and the future of our state. Belonging is embracing and accepting the contributions of everyone who is part of your community.

As we search to articulate ways to capture the process of belonging, one more example from Chicago must be mentioned. As discussed earlier, Chicago is now home to the National Museum of Puerto Rican Arts and Culture, the only museum in the United States, outside of Puerto Rico, devoted to the preservation and promotion of Puerto Rican arts and culture (see figure 7.2). An exhibit in the museum titled "The Humboldt Park Stables: A Transition into the Future" captures in glorious detail how the building evolved from its European roots, which are engraved in the still-evident architecture of the building, to what is today a place where Puerto Ricans gather to celebrate the arts and the artistic contributions of Puerto Ricans in the diaspora. In one room of the museum, we learn and celebrate the legacy of Danish immigrant Jens Jensen, who was superintendent of Humboldt Park in 1895. In fact, his office has been preserved with precise details—his desk, his papers. Jensen, the exhibit reminds us, became the "Dean of American landscape architecture." One quote on the walls of his office is particularly evocative: "Nature and Art are to go hand in hand crowned with the highest attainment possible by human conceptions, thereby adding to the prestige and good nature of any city, making life in these piles of brick and mortar worth living." Puerto Ricans have worked hard to build a community that celebrates art, culture, poetry, food, and history and integrates them into the city, thereby contributing in significant ways. The building is itself evidence of such contributions. They rescued the stables from destruction, and now it is a museum. Puerto Rican leaders and a range of professionals worked hard to integrate the local architecture, history, and cultures it represented. The structure today is evocative and offers evidence of how the cultures and influences that have successively occupied the space can be harmonized to create a new space of

Fig. 7.2. National Museum of Puerto Rican Arts and Culture. Photograph by Maura Toro-Morn.

belonging, a hopeful message for our current era. In a way, the building in all its complexity—first developed under European immigrants and now renovated and given a new life by Puerto Ricans—is an answer to the racist's rant of Mr. Trybus: we will not change you, we will transform you!

Key Findings and Themes

The migration of Puerto Ricans entails what Jorge Duany describes as *a vaivén* (a coming and going) that makes Puerto Ricans belong to both places at once. The tendency has been to perceive *a vaivén* as the strategy of working-class Puerto Ricans, Yet it is clear that across generations and social classes Puerto Ricans engage in *a vaivén* of sorts, with the notion of Puerto Rico as their homeland. To be sure, Puerto Ricans in Illinois come and go as they gain, lose, or change employment. Life course and family-driven events shape movement, too, such as marriage, divorce, and the arrival of children or grandchildren. Moving may also entail taking care of sick parents and dealing with other end-of-life issues. Migration continues to be a strategy to resolve not only the economic problems facing poor and working-class families but the educational aspirations of young Puerto Ricans, too.

The stories of the early arrivals offer a view of the difficulties Puerto Ricans faced in establishing themselves and their families in Illinois. Those who arrived after Hurricane Maria confronted difficulties of their own, too. It is evident that migration to Illinois has been very diverse, as it has included contract workers who came to do domestic and industrial work as well as Puerto Rican students and professionals. As shown in chapter 5, many leave Puerto Rico to further their education in Illinois and then end up staying. Puerto Ricans have maintained their relationship to the island through remittances but also by visiting and taking care of family and friends or moving back and forth. Hurricane Maria showed multidirectional flows. Many Puerto Ricans in the diaspora mobilized their networks for solidarity by providing emergency relief and leading recovery efforts on the island, while Puerto Ricans left the island in despair and as a direct consequence of the hurricane.

Family is the foundation of the immigrant experience because it is one unit that frequently mediates and initiates migration, feels the push and pull of movements, and becomes a safe place for immigrants/migrants to be themselves away from home.

Sociologists have pointed out that the family is an important institution where profound changes regarding gender, work, and inclusion and exclusion are evident. As we have shown, Puerto Rican families reconstitute themselves between Puerto Rico and Illinois in complicated ways. The Puerto Rican family is foundational to understanding adaptation processes.

Throughout our research and interviews, we examined the reception of Puerto Ricans in the state, whether they had settled in Chicago or other parts of Illinois. Some felt welcomed, but it was clear that knowledge about Puerto Ricans and the colonial situation of Puerto Rican was minimal. In Chicago, given the Puerto Rican density and the historical presence, Puerto Ricans encountered a great deal of prejudices and discrimination at work, at school, and in their communities. Puerto Ricans in downstate Illinois also reported their share of prejudice and discrimination. Yet, in the last fifty years, it is evident that Puerto Ricans have contributed in complex ways to the social, economic, and cultural life of the state.

Our research revealed various challenges that Puerto Rican students face in order to stay in school, from gang involvement to teenage pregnancy. Although sociological research suggests that Puerto Rican women had more parental monitoring, especially from their mothers, certain cultural taboos, such as not talking about or having sex before marriage, contributed to a higher likelihood of young girls challenging parental authorities and a high rate of teenage pregnancy. Meanwhile, the cultural approval of letting young men be relatively free might have contributed to their engagement in risky behaviors, such as skipping school, joining gangs, and selling and using drugs. Although society, for the most part, presented these two limiting stereotypes for Puerto Rican youth in the popular media—teenage mothers and gang members—other Puerto Rican youth have become star athletes, good students, and success stories of their own. Affirming a Puerto Rican identity different from the one depicted in the media has been one of many mechanisms used by young men and women to adapt and succeed. School and community groups and organizations aided in the process of affirming positive images of Puerto Ricans, although their mistreatment by teachers and administrators coupled with the structural reality of the grossly underfunded schools has led to gender and social class disparities in educational attainment.

Students, parents, and community involvement in education has been vital to affirming identity and community development. In the 1970s, working-class Puerto Rican parents pushed educators and school administrators to serve the new Spanish-speaking populations. They advocated for bilingual programs that would ease the transition of young people and for more resources, such as bilingual teachers, more books, and fewer overcrowded classrooms. Students were also crucial in these struggles. Parents and students fought for a new school, Roberto Clemente, which is today an important institution along Division Street. While the new school solved the issue of overcrowding, the school dropout rates became a serious problem. Community leaders and educational advocates created alternative schools such as Pedro Albizu Campos High School and Segundo Ruiz Belvis High School to address the issue of dropouts. The alternative Puerto Rican school movement recognized that the lack of cultural understanding by white teachers was problematic and contributed to the reproduction of students' marginalization. Community

Fig. 7.3. Pedro Albizu Campos statue in Paseo Boricua. Photograph by Ivis García.

leaders proposed educational materials that emphasized Puerto Rican history, culture, and pride. These efforts promoted a cultural consciousness among graduates that continues today.[8]

As one graduate of Pedro Albizu Campos High School stated, "In this school the first thing we as students are taught is to think, and at the same time [we study] our Puerto Rican heritage."[9] The founding of ASPIRA in Illinois is part of this process. ASPIRA created programs that were supportive of moving students from kindergarten through grade 12 and then to college. More recently, Community as a Campus represents another stage of this long history to promote educational success. CAAC is also invested in increasing graduation rates of all students and encouraging the transition to college. CAAC works from the assumption that educational success requires the involvement of community members, parents, students, teachers, and administrators.

Puerto Ricans have built strong and vibrant communities in the face of discrimination and marginalization. The 1966 Division Street Riots marked a crucial turning point in the Puerto Rican community. Community organizations developed to meet the needs of Puerto Ricans in West Town, Logan Square, and Humboldt Park, key Puerto Rican communities at the time. Some examples are the Community Action Programs, the Chicago Committee on Urban Opportunity, the Neighborhood Youth Corps, and the Head Start Program. Although gentrification first pushed Puerto Ricans out of Lincoln Park, Lakeview, and Old Town, their claim to Paseo Boricua—recently renamed Puerto Rican Town—became a way to affirm identity and community. Today, Paseo Boricua is a lively commercial corridor with diverse businesses, murals, and community groups. Paseo is the heart of the community. This is how the Humboldt Park Stables were transformed from a dumping site to the National Museum for Puerto Rican Arts and Culture, the only one of its kind in the United States. Paseo Boricua and the museum were both born from the gentrification struggle. Although the battle against gentrification is an ongoing one, Puerto Ricans in Chicago have been agents of change and community organizers.

Puerto Rican leaders in the community do not hesitate to mobilize their community power to address local and national issues. The campaign to release political prisoner Oscar López Rivera represents an example of that community power.[10] Another is the way Puerto Rican leaders and elected officials drew on the hard-earned political capital of over fifty years of political engagement at the level of city politics to mobilize and aid in the aftermath of the 2017 hurricane season. Puerto Ricans in Waukegan, Bloomington-Normal, Urbana-Champaign, and other communities outside of Chicago led efforts to assist families who needed food, water, and power. Puerto Ricans in Illinois communities have started organizations and advocated for policy changes. They have been elected and appointed to local, regional, and national positions as politicians, legislators, and policy makers. Their contributions will be felt for years to come.

A book as ambitious as this one is not without its limitations. Although we tried to interview people in all of the significant

Fig. 7.4. Oscar López Rivera mural. Photograph by Ivis García.

Puerto Rican communities, time and access did not allow us to talk to people in Aurora, Joliet, Cicero, and Des Plaines, among other places. Furthermore, both of us have more connections in Chicago, which is one reason the city figures so prominently. Yet, Chicago's status in the history of Puerto Ricans in Illinois is, without debate, an important one. They have lived and worked in the city for over sixty years. Their population density has made Chicago the most important Puerto Rican ethnic enclave and economic center not only in Illinois but also in the Midwest and, arguably, the nation. Although there might be more Puerto Ricans in New York City and Philadelphia, their communities tend to be more dispersed across land mass with no clearly defined commercial center. That is not the case in Chicago, as Paseo Boricua is a commercial and artistic hub of the community. Moreover, politically Chicago has been the center for critical political campaigns on the island, from the struggle to free Puerto Rican political prisoners (such as Oscar López Rivera) to the movement to get the marines out of Vieques, to name a few. Chicago has also supported the island in the aftermath of hurricanes by welcoming storm refugees and by sending relief and keeping the island's plight at the forefront of community organizing.

This is the first book about Puerto Ricans in Illinois, but we hope that other researchers can take the work produced here as a point of departure to continue to study their experiences. We hope that second- and third-generation Puerto Rican academics take on the task of considering the experiences of Puerto Ricans in Illinois from their perspective, too. One book cannot address it all. The Puerto Rican community is complex and diverse and deserves to be studied by future researchers. We are hopeful that a new generation of storytellers will take on this critical task.

In the end, we have offered a nuanced and sophisticated understanding of Puerto Rican history and migration to Illinois with the hope that it pays tribute to the hard work of the families and individuals who today call Illinois home. In our view, Puerto Ricans embody the promise of a community. This book is a tribute to all Puerto Ricans in Illinois who have worked, lived, loved, and died there. Puerto Ricans have indeed made significant contributions to making the state of Illinois more diverse and inclusive.

Notes

Bibliography

Index

NOTES

1. Introduction

1. Biles, *Illinois*.

2. Innis-Jimenez, *Steel Barrio*, 10.

3. Lemann, *Promised Land*.

4. Dropp and Brendan, "Nearly Half of Americans Don't Know Puerto Ricans Are Fellow Citizens." Historian Daniel Immerwahr in his book *How to Hide an Empire* writes that for a greater part of the twentieth century, maps did not show the territories and colonies the United States had acquired in the aftermath of the Spanish-American War, making invisible the people who lived there. He concludes that most people in this country know very little of the history and influence the United States had in these territories.

5. Center for Puerto Rican Studies, *Puerto Ricans in Illinois*, 1.

6. Cintrón et al., *60 Years of Migration*.

7. Cintrón et al., *60 Years of Migration*.

8. American Community Survey, *Socioeconomic Characteristics*, 2016: ACS 1-Year Estimates Selected Population Profiles.

9. Alicea and Toro-Morn, "Puerto Rican Chicago *Dice Presente*."

10. Duany, *Puerto Rican Nation on the Move*.

11. The literature about Puerto Ricans in Chicago has grown a lot over the years. The first study about Puerto Ricans was conducted by Elena Padilla. Her dissertation at the University of Chicago was republished in Merida Rúa's *Latino Urban Ethnography and the Work of Elena Padilla*. The work of Felix Padilla represents an important chapter of this body of work. In 2001 there was a special issue of *Centro*, the leading journal in the field of Puerto Rican studies, published by the Center for Puerto Rican Studies at Hunter College and edited by Gina Pérez. It featured the work of Nilda Flores-Gonzalez, Maura Toro-Morn, Marisa Alicea, Irma Olmedo, Ana Ramos-Zayas, and Merida Rúa. In 2016 Maura Toro-Morn, Ivis Gárcia Zambrana, and Marisa Alicea edited a second volume of *Centro*, "Puerto Rican Chicago Revisited," in commemoration of the fiftieth anniversary of the Division Street Riots, a watershed moment in the history

of the community. This volume featured the work of Margaret Power, Yadira Nieves-Pizarro, Jesse Mumm, Mirelsie Velázquez, Frances Aparicio, Michael Staudenmaeir, and Michael Rodríguez-Muñiz. Other notable publications in the field include Pérez, *Near Northwest Side*; Ramos-Zayas, *National Performances*; and Cruz, *City of Dreams*. More recently, see the work of historian Lilia Fernández, *Brown in the Windy City*.

12. Toro-Morn, "Class and Gender Dimensions."

13. Toro-Morn, "Migration and Gendered Webs of Obligation."

14. García-Zambrana, "Puerto Rican Identity."

15. Cintrón et al., *60 Years of Migration*.

16. See the introduction to the issue: Toro-Morn, García-Zambrana, and Alicea, "*De bandera a bandera* (From flag to flag)."

17. Duany, *Puerto Rico*, 2.

18. Thomas, *Puerto Rican Citizen*.

19. Alicea and Toro-Morn, "Puerto Rican Chicago *Dice Presente*."

20. Grosfoguel, *Colonial Subjects*, 77.

21. American Community Survey, *Socioeconomic Characteristics*, 2016: ACS 1-Year Estimates Selected Population Profiles.

22. American Community Survey, *Socioeconomic Characteristics*, 2016: ACS 1-Year Estimates Selected Population Profiles.

23. Cohn, "Census History."

24. Vidal-Ortiz and Martinez, "Latinx Thoughts."

25. Vidal-Ortiz and Martinez, 393.

26. Padilla, *Latino Ethnic Consciousness*.

27. Taylor et al., *When Labels Don't Fit*.

28. García Zambrana and Bachman, *Making the Case for Change*.

29. Cruz, *City of Dreams*.

30. García Zambrana, *Making the Case*.

31. García Zambrana, *Making the Case*.

32. American Community Survey, *Population Estimates* 2015: ACS 1-Year Estimates Selected Population Profiles.

2. Island Paradox

1. Grosfoguel, *Colonial Subjects*.

2. For a detailed history of these events, see Immerwahr, *How to Hide an Empire*.

3. Duany, *Puerto Rican Nation on the Move*.

4. Denis, *War against All Puerto Ricans*, 11.

5. Rouse, *Taínos*.

6. Duany, *Puerto Rico*, 143.

7. González, *Harvest of Empire*.

8. Godreau, *Scripts of Blackness*.

9. Duany, *Puerto Rican Nation on the Move*, 161.

10. Llorens, *Imagining the Great Puerto Rican Family.*

11. Velázquez Vargas, "Marco Said I Look Like Charcoal," 953.

12. Acosta-Belen, *Puerto Rican Woman*, 3.

13. Suárez Findlay, *Imposing Decency*, 20.

14. Immerwahr, *How to Hide an Empire*, 72. Immerwahr notes, "The peace treaty negotiated in Paris was between Spain and the United States alone. Spain sold the Philippines for $20 million. Puerto Rico and Guam (a Micronesian Island, valuable as a Mahan-style base) came free. Because of the amendment anti-imperialists had passed, the United States couldn't annex Cuba. But it could occupy it, placing the country under military control until a suitable government could be installed—a government suitable to Washington, that is. No representative from Cuba, Puerto Rico, the Philippines or Guam had a say in any of this."

15. Quoted in Duany, *Puerto Rican Nation on the Move*, 88.

16. Suárez Findlay, *Imposing Decency*, 28.

17. Suárez Findlay, 29.

18. For a detailed analysis of these cases, see Burnett and Marshall, *Foreign in a Domestic Sense*, 20.

19. "Puerto Ricans Call for Aid Amid Catastrophe."

20. Franqui-Rivera, *Soldiers of the Nation.*

21. Denis, "After a Century of American Citizenship, Puerto Ricans Have Little to Show for It."

22. Alicia Pomada, "Puerto Rico, School Language Policies."

23. Toro-Morn, "*Yo era muy arriesgada.*"

24. Alba Acevedo, "Género, trabajo asalariado y desarrollo industrial en Puerto Rico."

25. Ortiz, *Puerto Rican Women and Work.*

26. M. Rivera, "Development of Capitalism in Puerto Rico," 37.

27. Boris, "Needlewomen under the New Deal in Puerto Rico."

28. Boris, 48.

29. History Task Force, *Labor Migration under Capitalism.*

30. Sánchez Korrol, *From Colonia to Community*, 55.

31. For an autoethnographic account of this period, see Cintrón, "Sociales de Mayaguez."

32. González, *Harvest of Empire*, 83.

33. González, 84.

34. As cited in Wagenheim and Jimenez de Wagenheim, *Puerto Ricans*, 157.

35. Wagenheim and Jimenez de Wagenheim, 175.

36. Suárez Findlay, *We Are Left without a Father Here*, 33.

37. Toro-Morn, "Family in Puerto Rico," 449.

38. Cited in Martín, "How Hurricane Maria Exposed Puerto Rico's 'Colonial Boom and Bust.'"

39. Duany, *Puerto Rican Nation on the Move*, 73.

40. Acevedo, "Daughter of Bootstrap," 138–40.

41. Rios, "Export-Oriented Industrialization."

42. Rios, 333.

43. Santiago, *When I Was Puerto Rican*, 122.

44. Rios, "Export-Oriented Industrialization," 331.

45. Acevedo, "Industrialization and Employment."

46. Amott and Matthaei, *Race, Gender, and Work*, 283.

47. Duany, *Puerto Rico*, 95.

48. Pantojas-García, "Is Puerto Rico Greece in the Caribbean?," 57.

49. González, *Harvest of Empire*, 283.

50. For a detailed discussion of "la crisis Boricua," see Mora, Davila, and Rodriguez, *Population, Migration, and Socioeconomic Outcomes*.

51. Toro-Morn and García, "Gendered Fault Lines."

52. Meléndez and Venator-Santiago, "Puerto Rico Post–Hurricane Maria."

53. Corkery, "Let Us Help You."

54. Exemplars of this new work are Duany, "Orlando Ricans"; and Silver and Velez, "'Let Me Go Check Out Florida.'"

55. Vargas-Ramos and Meléndez, *State of Puerto Ricans 2013*.

56. See https://oversightboard.pr.gov/.

57. Mora, Davila, and Rodriguez, *Population, Migration, and Socioeconomic Outcomes*, 168.

58. See https://oversightboard.pr.gov/natalie-jaresko/.

59. Godreau, *Scripts of Blackness*, 23.

60. Coto, "Month after Maria Hit, 80% of Puerto Rico Still without Power."

61. Bonilla, "Why Would Anyone in Puerto Rico Want a Hurricane?"

3. Migration to Illinois

1. See Toro-Morn, "Gender, Class, and Family and Migration."

2. All informants in this chapter have been given pseudonyms to protect their anonymity, in keeping with IRB protocols.

3. Hinojosa, Román, and Meléndez, Puerto Rican Post-Maria Relocation by States.

4. Duany, Puerto Rican Nation on the Move.

5. Pérez, Near Northwest Side Story, 130.

6. Mastony, "Elgin, Aguada Share Family Ties."

7. Informant interview.

8. Informant interview.

9. Stanley, "First Latina Appointed Will County Judge."

10. Aurora Puerto Rican Cultural Council website, accessed July 19, 2018, http://auroraprcc.wixsite.com/aprcc.

11. Chicago Tribune, "Mayor Slates Race Parley for Waukegan."

12. This quote and the five that follow are from informants' interviews.

13. Institute for Latino Studies, Bordering the Mainstream.

14. Fleischer, "Immanuel Lutheran Church."

15. Rúa, Grounded Identidad, 30.

16. Rúa, 15.

17. Elena Padilla was the youngest of the group. As an anthropologist, she studied with the leading scholars at the time from 1944 to 1947. Her doctoral dissertation was the first empirical study about Puerto Ricans in Chicago. Rúa argues that she needs to be seen as a pioneer in the field of urban ethnography.

18. Ricardo Alegría was the first director of the Institute of Puerto Rican Culture and founding member of the Museum of the Americas in San Juan.

19. Muñoz Lee was the daughter of Puerto Rico's first popularly elected governor, Luis Muñoz Marín.

20. According to Rúa, the children of Ángel Quintero and Milton Pabón became prominent researchers at the University of Puerto Rico and leading figures in the field of Puerto Rican studies.

21. Rúa, Grounded Identidad, 12.

22. Again, all interview subjects have been given pseudonyms to protect their anonymity, in keeping with IRB protocols.

23. Toro-Morn, "Gender, Class, and Family and Migration"; Fernández, Brown in the Windy City; Pérez, Near Northwest Side Story. In Illinois, the work of Felix Padilla, Marisa Alicea, Maura Toro-Morn, Lilia Fernández, Wilfredo Cruz, and Gina Pérez has helped trace larger outlines of working class migrations to Illinois. More recently, Lisa Ortiz's dissertation at the University of Illinois, Urbana-Champaign, "Rantoul es como Jayuya," represents evidence that migrations to Illinois continue and that rural settings have been added as a site of settlement.

24. Pérez, Near Northwest Side Story, 56.

25. Cruz, City of Dreams.

26. Toro-Morn, "Gender, Class, and Family and Migration."

27. Alicea, "'Cuando Nosotros Vivíamos . . .'"

28. Pérez, Near Northwest Side Story, 73.

29. Pérez, 82.

30. Pérez, 82.

31. Pérez, 75, 76.

32. Pérez, 83.

33. Miraftab, Global Heartland, 66.

34. Miraftab, 69.

35. Vazquez Paz, Poemas Callejeros

4. Family and Work Experiences of Puerto Ricans in Illinois

1. Interview published in Cruz, City of Dreams, 70.

2. Toro-Morn, "Yo era muy arriesgada," 26.

3. Informant interview.

4. Informant interview.

5. Otterstrom and Tillman, "Income Change and Circular Migration."

6. American Community Survey, Socioeconomic Characteristics, 2016: ACS 1-Year Estimates Selected Population Profiles.

7. American Community Survey, Socioeconomic Characteristics, 2016: ACS 1-Year Estimates Selected Population Profiles.

8. Padilla, Puerto Rican Chicago.

9. Gutiérrez, Still Dreaming, 25.

10. García and Rúa, "'Our Interests Matter.'"

11. Padilla, Puerto Rican Chicago, 73.

12. As mentioned in chapter 3, local newspapers and city politicians praised Puerto Rican families for their hard work and healthy families. In fact, the model Puerto Rican family that they admired in the Chicago Tribune—hardworking husband and stay-at-home mom—directly exposed the dominant view of the family at the time, which rested on the problematic notion of the separate spheres we deconstructed above. The reality for Puerto Rican families on the island and now in Illinois is far more complicated than that.

13. Padilla, Puerto Rican Chicago, 73.

14. Toro-Morn, "Gender, Class, and Family and Migration."

15. Quoted in Gutiérrez, Still Dreaming, 25.

16. Toro-Morn, "Yo era muy arriesgada," 27.

17. Aranda, Emotional Bridges to Puerto Rico, 103.

18. Rúa, Grounded Identidad, xiii.

19. Alicea, "Cuando Nosotros Vivíamos . . . ," 171.

20. Flores, "Capturing the Images of Chicago's Puerto Rican Community," 135.

21. Gutiérrez, Still Dreaming, 25.

22. Toro-Morn and Alicea, Gendered Geographies of Home.

23. Toro-Morn and Alicea, 203.

24. Toro-Morn and Alicea, 203.

25. Rúa, Grounded Identidad.

26. Olmedo, "Puerto Rican Grandmothers," 105.

27. Quoted in Rúa, Grounded Identidad, 7.

28. Toro-Morn, "Yo era muy arriesgada," 38.

29. Toro-Morn, 38.

30. Cintrón et al., 60 Years of Migration.

31. American Community Survey, Socioeconomic Characteristics, 2016: ACS 1-Year Estimates Selected Population Profiles.

32. Blatt and Drew, Illinois Commission in the Elimination of Poverty.

33. García Zambrana and Bachman, Making the Case for Change.

34. Olmedo, "Puerto Rican Grandmothers," 105.

5. Educational Struggles Then and Now

1. Padilla and Santiago, *Outside the Wall*, 43.
2. Padilla, *Struggle of Latino/Latina University Students*, 24.
3. Alicea, "Cuando Nosotros Vivíamos . . . ," 177.
4. Meléndez and Vargas-Ramos, *Puerto Ricans at the Dawn of the New Millennium*, 45.
5. Franceschi, *Chicago's Puerto Rican Story*.
6. Gutiérrez, *Still Dreaming*, 77.
7. González, *Harvest of Empire*, 91.
8. Franceschi, *Chicago's Puerto Rican Story*; Padilla, *Puerto Rican Chicago*, 212.
9. Olmedo, "Puerto Rican Grandmothers," 111.
10. Padilla, *Puerto Rican Chicago*.
11. U.S. Commission on Civil Rights, *Hearing before the United States Commission on Civil Rights*.
12. Rodríguez-Muñiz, "Riot and Remembrance."
13. Fernández, *Brown in the Windy City*, 73.
14. Velázquez, "Looking Forward, Working for Change," 138.
15. Velázquez, *"Brincamos el charco y ahora que."*
16. Ruiz, "Chicago."
17. Neal, "Power Seekers."
18. Mermigas, "Public TV Focuses on the Students."
19. *Chicago Tribune*, "Report Plans Progress for Tuley High School."
20. Boyce, "School Name for Settler, Polio Doctors."
21. Padilla, *Puerto Rican Chicago*.
22. Kyle and Kantowicz, *Kids First—Primero Los Niños*.
23. Garza, "Bringing Drama to the School Reform Story."
24. W. Smith, "'Safe Zone' Aims to Give Gangs a Lesson."
25. *Chicago Tribune*, "How Many . . . Have to Die?"
26. Chicago Public Schools, "Stats and Facts," http://cps.edu/About_CPS/At-a-glance/Pages/Stats_and_facts.aspx.
27. Cintrón et al., *60 Years of Migration*.
28. Chicago Public Schools, *High School Progress Report*, Roberto Clemente Community Academy High School, 2015, https://www.cps.edu/schools/schoolprofiles/clemente-hs.
29. Pérez, *Near Northwest Side Story*, 167.
30. Informant interview.
31. García, *Respect Yourself*.
32. Pérez, *Near Northwest Side Story*, 129.
33. "Young Lords, Puerto Rican Liberation, and the Black Freedom Struggle."
34. Padilla and Santiago, *Outside the Wall*.
35. Informant interview.

36. Flores-González, *School Kids/Street Kids*.

37. Cintrón et al., *60 Years of Migration*.

38. Flores-González, *School Kids/Street Kids*, 61.

39. Informant interview.

40. Informant interview.

41. Flores-González, *School Kids/Street Kids*, 131.

42. Sánchez Korrol, *From* Colonia *to Community*, 231.

43. Veláquez, "Looking Forward, Working for Change," 142.

44. Velázquez, 142.

45. ASPIRA of Illinois website, https://www.aspirail.org.

46. Informant interview.

47. Informant interview.

48. Power, "Puerto Rican Nationalism in Chicago," 51.

49. Hinojosa and Vargas-Ramos, *Almanac of Puerto Ricans*, 19.

50. Shojai, "Latins Form Group to Develop, Train Spanish Leaders."

51. Pérez, *Near Northwest Side Story*.

52. Strauss, "To Learn about Improving Urban Public Schools, We Should Study Chicago."

6. Puerto Rican Communities in Illinois

1. Innis-Jimenez, *Steel Barrio*, 10.

2. Rúa, *Grounded* Identidad.

3. National Museum of Mexican Art website, http://nationalmuseumofmexicanart .org/relief.

4. Cintrón et al., *60 Years of Migration*.

5. Flores-Gonzalez, "Paseo Boricua."

6. Fernández, *Brown in the Windy City*, 132.

7. Mumm, "When the White People Come."

8. Alicea, "'Cuando Nosotros Vivíamos . . . ,'" 170.

9. Rúa, *Grounded* Identidad.

10. Alicea, "Cuando Nosotros Vivíamos," 173.

11. Fernández, *Brown in the Windy City*, 134.

12. Padilla, *Puerto Rican Chicago*, 82.

13. Gutiérrez, *Still Dreaming*, 33.

14. Flores, "Capturing the Images of Chicago's Puerto Rican Community," 135.

15. Gutiérrez, *Still Dreaming*, 20.

16. Rúa, *Grounded* Identidad, 53.

17. Gutiérrez, *Still Dreaming*, 29.

18. Padilla, *Puerto Rican Chicago*, 126.

19. Informant interview.

20. Alicea, "Cuando Nosotros Vivíamos . . . ," 175.

21. Toro-Morn, *Boricuas En Chicago,* 139.

22. Rúa, *Grounded* Identidad, 53.

23. Schmid and Hernández, "MELUS Interview," 149.

24. For more detailed information about the Young Lords, see Fernández, *Brown in the Windy City*; and Lazu, "Chicago Young Lords."

25. Flores-Gonzalez, "Paseo Boricua."

26. Betancur, "Settlement Experience of Latinos in Chicago."

27. Alicea, "Cuando Nosotros Vivíamos . . . ," 173.

28. Rúa, *Grounded* Identidad, 243.

29. Informant interview.

30. Flores-Gonzalez, "Paseo Boricua," 8.

31. Terkcl, *Division Street.*

32. Fernández, *Brown in the Windy City*, 163.

33. Rodríguez-Muñiz, "Riot and Remembrance, " 208.

34. See Fernández, *Brown in the Windy City*, for a detailed analysis.

35. Fernández, 166.

36. Rodríguez-Muñiz, "Riot and Remembrance," 210.

37. Staudenmaier, "War on Poverty," 180.

38. Gutiérrez, *Still Dreaming.*

39. García, "Puerto Rican Business District."

40. Division Street Business Development Association, "Path to New Strategies."

41. García, "Puerto Rican Business District."

42. Cintrón et al., *60 Years of Migration.*

43. García, "Paseo Boricua."

44. García, "Paseo Boricua."

45. Cintrón et al., *60 Years of Migration.*

46. Mumm, "Gentrification in Color and Time," 88.

47. *Chicago Tribune*, "Gangs, Jobless Plague West Town."

48. Anderson, "Community Clings to Its Roots."

49. Fitzsimmons, "Logan Square Diversity Gets a Hand with Lottery."

50. Anderson, "Community Clings to Its Roots."

51. Olivo, "Prisoners' Plight on Display."

52. Briggs, "2 Sides Detailed in City's Housing Boom."

53. Kassanits, "Riot Fest and the Gentrification of Humboldt Park."

54. *Almada*, "To the Rescue of Humboldt Mural."

55. Olivo, "Puerto Rican Culture to Have a New Showcase."

56. Olivo, "Puerto Rican Culture to Have a New Showcase."

57. Armanni and Carter, "Roberto Clemente Community Academy."

58. J. Rivera, "Hoodoisie Live Podcast Visits Urban Theater Company."

59. Anderson, "Community Clings to Its Roots."

60. Ropiy v. Hernandez, accessed July 22, 2018, http://www.illinoiscourts.gov/opinions /appellatecourt/2005/1stdistrict/december/html/1050283.htm.

61. G. Smith, "Humboldt Park Residents Feel Sting of Foreclosures."

62. G. Smith, "Humboldt Park Residents Feel Sting of Foreclosures."

63. Holliday, "Humboldt Park Hotter Than Ever."

64. Byrne, "Critics Hammer Emanuel's Affordable Housing Plan."

65. Byrne and Trotter, "Chicago's New 606 Park Stirs Gentrification Fears."

66. Shropshire, "Ald. Maldonado and Ald. Moreno."

67. García, "Community Participation as a Tool."

68. García, "Community Participation as a Tool."

69. García, "Community Participation as a Tool."

70. García, "Community Participation as a Tool."

71. Olivo, "Puerto Rican Culture to Have a New Showcase."

72. Olivo, "Puerto Rican Culture to Have a New Showcase."

73. Bloom, "La Casa Puertorriqueña Demolition Stalled after City Finds 'Possible' Asbestos."

74. Informant interview.

75. Sanchez Olson, "Post-Hurricane Aid for Puerto Rico Presses On."

76. NBC Chicago, "Cargo Plane Filled with Supplies Heads from Chicago to Puerto Rico."

77. Pathieu, "Hurricane Relief Supplies Headed to Puerto Rico from Chicago."

78. Alicea and Toro-Morn, "Puerto Rican Chicago *Dice Presente*."

7. Conclusion

1. Biles, Illinois.

2. Biles, Harold Washington.

3. Hernandez, "Rossana Rodríguez-Sánchez Outs Ald. Deb Mell."

4. Alicea, "'Chambered Nautilus'"; Rúa, Grounded Identidad.

5. Alicea and Toro-Morn, "Puerto Rican Chicago Dice Presente."

6. Cullinane and Jackson, "Man Harasses a Woman for Wearing a Puerto Rico Shirt."

7. S. Smith, "Woman Harassed for Wearing Puerto Rico Shirt."

8. Power, "Puerto Rican Nationalism in Chicago."

9. Power, 57.

10. Nieves-Pizarro, "Free Oscar Lopez Rivera!"

BIBLIOGRAPHY

Acevedo, Luz del Alba. "Daughter of Bootstrap." In *Telling to Live: Latina Feminist Testimonios*, edited by Latina Feminist Group, 138–40. Durham: Duke University Press Books, 2001.

———. "Género, trabajo asalariado y desarrollo industrial en Puerto Rico: La división sexual del trabajo en la manufactura." In *Género y trabajo: La industria de la aguja en Puerto Rico y el Caribe*, edited by María Del Carmen Baerga, 161–212. Rio Piedras: University of Puerto Rico Press, 1993.

———. "Industrialization and Employment: Changes in the Patterns of Women's Work in Puerto Rico." *World Development* 18, no. 2 (1990): 231–55. https://doi .org/10.1016/0305-750X(90)90049-4.

Acosta-Belen, Edna. *The Puerto Rican Woman: Perspectives on Culture, History and Society*. 2nd ed. New York: Praeger, 1986.

Alicea, Marisa. "'A Chambered Nautilus': The Contradictory Nature of Puerto Rican Women's Roles in the Social Construction of a Transnational Community." *Gender and Society* 11, no. 5 (1997): 597–626.

———. "'Cuando Nosotros Vivíamos . . .': Stories of Displacement and Settlement in Puerto Rican Chicago." *Centro: Journal of the Center for Puerto Rican Studies* 8, no. 2 (January 2001): 167–95.

Alicea, Marisa, and Maura Toro-Morn. "Puerto Rican Chicago *Dice Presente*: Preliminary Reflections on Community Responses to Hurricanes Irma and Maria." *Latino Studies Journal* 16, no. 4 (2018): 548–58.

Almada, Jeanette. "To the Rescue of Humboldt Mural." *Chicago Tribune*, January 13, 2008. https://www.chicagotribune.com/news/ct-xpm-2008-01-13-0801100305-story.html.

American Community Survey. *Population Estimates*. 2015: ACS 1-Year Estimates Selected Population Profiles. Washington, D.C.: U.S. Census Bureau, 2016. https://factfinder.census.gov/.

———. *Selected Population Profile in Puerto Rico*. 2017: ACS 1-Year Estimates Selected Population Profiles. Washington, D.C.: U.S. Census Bureau, 2018. https:// factfinder.census.gov.

———. *Socioeconomic Characteristics.* 2015: ACS 5-Year Estimates Selected Population Profiles. Washington, D.C.: U.S. Census Bureau, 2016. https://factfinder.census.gov/.

———. *Socioeconomic Characteristics.* 2016: ACS 1-Year Estimates Selected Population Profiles. Washington, D.C.: U.S. Census Bureau, 2017. https://factfinder.census.gov/.

Amott, Teresa, and Julie Matthaei. *Race, Gender, and Work: A Multicultural Economic History of Women in the United States.* Boston: South End Press, 1991.

Anderson, Jon. "Community Clings to Its Roots." *Chicago Tribune*, October 12, 1999. https://www.chicagotribune.com/news/ct-xpm-1999-10-12-9910120172-story.html.

Aranda, Elizabeth. *Emotional Bridges to Puerto Rico: Migration, Return Migration, and the Struggles of Incorporation.* Lanham, Md.: Rowman and Littlefield, 2006.

Armanni, Varela, and Kennedy Carter. "Roberto Clemente Community Academy and Pedro Albizu Campos High School Beautify Paseo Boricua." *La Voz del Paseo Boricua*, June 2015.

Betancur, John J. "The Settlement Experience of Latinos in Chicago: Segregation, Speculation, and the Ecology Model." *Social Forces* 74, no. 4 (1996): 1299–1324. https://doi.org/10.1093/sf/74.4.1299.

Biles, Roger. *Harold Washington: Champion of Race and Reform in Chicago.* Urbana: University of Illinois Press, 2018.

———. *Illinois: A History of the Land and Its People.* DeKalb: Northeastern Illinois Press, 2005.

Blatt, Amber, and Kimberly Drew. *Illinois Commission in the Elimination of Poverty: Annual Report.* Chicago: Heartland Alliance for Human Needs and Human Rights, 2017.

Bloom, Mina. "La Casa Puertorriqueña Demolition Stalled after City Finds 'Possible' Asbestos." Block Club Chicago, October 4, 2019. https://blockclub chicago.org/2019/10/04/la-casa-puertorriquena-demolition-stalled-after-city -finds-possible-asbestos/.

Bonilla, Yarimar. "Why Would Anyone in Puerto Rico Want a Hurricane? Because Someone Will Get Rich." *Washington Post*, September 22, 2017. https://www. washingtonpost.com/outlook/how-puerto-rican-hurricanes-devastate-many-and -enrich-a-few/2017/09/22/78e7500c-9e66-11e7-9083-fbfddf6804c2_story.html.

Boris, Eileen. "Needlewomen under the New Deal in Puerto Rico, 1920–1945." In *Puerto Rican Women and Work: Bridges in Transnational Labor*, edited by Altagracia Ortiz, 33–54. Philadelphia: Temple University Press, 1996.

Boyce, Katherine. "School Name for Settler, Polio Doctors." *Chicago Daily Herald*, October 23, 1974.

Briggs, Johnathon. "2 Sides Detailed in City's Housing Boom." *Chicago Tribune*, January 2, 2006.

Burnett, Christina Duffy, and Burke Marshall, eds. *Foreign in a Domestic Sense: Puerto Rico, American Expansion, and the Constitution.* Durham: Duke University Press, 2001.

Byrne, Greg, and John Trotter. "Chicago's New 606 Park Stirs Gentrification Fears." *Chicago Tribune*, June 6, 2015. http://www.chicagotribune.com/news/local /breaking/ct-606-bloomingdale-trail-gentrification-met-20150605-story.html.

Byrne, John. "Critics Hammer Emanuel's Affordable Housing Plan; Aldermen Advance It." *Chicago Tribune*, September 25, 2017. http://www.chicagotribune .com/news/local/politics/ct-rahm-emanuel-affordable-housing-pilot-met -20170925-story.html.

Center for Puerto Rican Studies. *Puerto Ricans in Illinois, the United States, and Puerto Rico, 2014*. New York: Hunter College, CUNY, 2016. https://centropr .hunter.cuny.edu/sites/default/files/PDF/STATE%20REPORTS/6.%20IL-PR -2016-CentroReport.pdf.

Chicago Public Schools. "Stats and Facts." September 25, 2017, http://cps.edu/About _CPS/At-a-glance/Pages/Stats_and_facts.aspx.

———. *High School Progress Report*. Roberto Clemente Community Academy High School, 2015. https://www.cps.edu/schools/schoolprofiles/clemente-hs.

Chicago Tribune. "Gangs, Jobless Plague West Town." September 19, 1982.

———. "How Many . . . Have to Die?," February 19, 2013.

———. "Mayor Slates Race Parley for Waukegan." September 4, 1966.

———. "Report Plans Progress for Tuley High School." November 23, 1969.

Cintrón, Ralph. "Sociales de Mayaguez." *Comparative American Studies: An International Journal* 5, no. 2 (2007): 205–20. https://doi.org/10.1179/147757007X204411.

Cintrón, Ralph, Maura Toro-Morn, Ivis García Zambrana, and Elizabeth Scott. *60 Years of Migration: Puerto Ricans in Chicagoland*. Chicago: Puerto Rican Agenda, 2012. http://www.puertoricanchicago.org/.

Cohn, D'Vera. "Census History: Counting Hispanics." *Pew Research Center Social and Demographic Trends* (blog), March 3, 2010. http://www.pewsocialtrends.org /2010/03/03/census-history-counting-hispanics-2/.

Corkery, Michael. "Let Us Help You, Hedge Funds Tell Puerto Rico." *New York Times*, September 12, 2014. http://dealbook.nytimes.com/2014/09/12/puerto-rico -finds-it-has-new-friends-in-hedge-funds/.

Coto, Danica. "A Month after Maria Hit, 80% of Puerto Rico Still without Power." *Daily Hampshire Gazette*, October 19, 2017. http://www.gazettenet.com/Stumbling -in-the-dark-13224765.

Cruz, Wilfredo. *City of Dreams: Latino Immigration to Chicago*. Lanham, Md.: University Press of America, 2007.

Cullinane, Susannah, and Amanda Jackson. "A Man Harasses a Woman for Wearing a Puerto Rico Shirt, Saying It's 'Un-American.'" CNN, July 10, 2018. https://www.cnn.com/2018/07/10/us/illinois-puerto-rico-park-officer/index.html.

Denis, Nelson. "After a Century of American Citizenship, Puerto Ricans Have Little to Show for It." *The Nation*, March 2, 2017. https://www.thenation.com/article /after-a-century-of-american-citizenship-puerto-ricans-have-little-to-show-for-it/.

———. *War against All Puerto Ricans: Revolution and Terror in America's Colony*. Rev. ed. New York: Nation Books, 2016.

Division Street Business Development Association (DSBDA). "Path to New Strategies." Unpublished manuscript, 2008.

Dropp, Kyle, and Nyhan Brendan. "Nearly Half of Americans Don't Know Puerto Ricans Are Fellow Citizens." *New York Times*, September 26, 2017. https://www.nytimes.com/2017/09/26/upshot/nearly-half-of-americans-dont-know-people-in-puerto-ricoans-are-fellow-citizens.html.

Duany, Jorge. "The Orlando Ricans: Overlapping Identity Discourses among Middle-Class Puerto Rican Immigrants." *Centro: Journal of the Center for Puerto Rican Studies* 22, no. 1 (2010): 84–115.

———. *The Puerto Rican Nation on the Move: Identities on the Island and in the United States*. Chapel Hill: University of North Carolina Press, 2002.

———. *Puerto Rico: What Everyone Needs to Know*. New York: Oxford University Press, 2017.

Fernández, Lilia. *Brown in the Windy City: Mexicans and Puerto Ricans in Postwar Chicago*. Chicago: University of Chicago Press, 2012.

Fitzsimmons, Emma Graves. "Logan Square Diversity Gets a Hand with Lottery." *Chicago Tribune*, October 28, 2007. https://www.chicagotribune.com/news/ct-xpm-2007-10-28-0710270662-story.html.

Fleischer, Denise. "Immanuel Lutheran Church—Sharing Closet Open." *Journal and Topics* (Chicago), October 25, 2017. https://www.journal-topics.com/2017/10/25/page/5/?post_type=oht_article.

Flores, Carlos. "Capturing the Images of Chicago's Puerto Rican Community." *Centro: Journal of the Center for Puerto Rican Studies* 13, no. 2 (2001): 134–65.

Flores-Gonzalez, Nilda. "Paseo Boricua: Claiming a Puerto Rican Space in Chicago." *Centro: Journal of the Center for Puerto Rican Studies* 8, no. 2 (2001): 7–23.

———. *School Kids/Street Kids: Identity Development in Latino Students*. New York: Teachers College Press, 2002.

Franceschi, Antonio, dir. *Chicago's Puerto Rican Story*. PBS, 2018. http://www.newfilmproduction.com/documentary.html.

Franqui-Rivera, Harry. *Soldiers of the Nation: Military Service and Modern Puerto Rico, 1868-1959*. Lincoln: University of Nebraska Press, 2018.

García, Ivis. "Community Participation as a Tool for Conservation Planning and Historic Preservation: The Case of 'Community as a Campus' (CAAC)." *Journal of Housing and the Built Environment*, June 2018. https://doi.org/10.1007/s10901-018-9615-4.

———. "Paseo Boricua: Identity, Symbols, and Ownership." *América Crítica* 1, no. 2 (2017): 117–38.

———. "The Puerto Rican Business District as a Community Strategy for Resistance Gentrification in Chicago." *PLERUS* 25, no. 1 (2015): 79–98.

García, Ivis, and Mérida M. Rúa. "'Our Interests Matter': Puerto Rican Older Adults in the Age of Gentrification." *Urban Studies*, November 2017. https://journals.sagepub.com/doi/10.1177/0042098017736251.

García, Lorena. *Respect Yourself, Protect Yourself: Latina Girls and Sexual Identity*. New York: NYU Press, 2012.

García-Zambrana, Ivis. "The Puerto Rican Identity: Reconstructing Ownership in the Face of Change." PhD diss., University of Illinois at Chicago, 2015. https://indigo.uic.edu/handle/10027/19798?show=full.

García Zambrana, Ivis, and Anna Bachman. *Making the Case for Change: Report Series*. Chicago: Nathalie P. Voorhees Center for Neighborhood and Community Improvement and the Illinois Latino Family Commission, 2014. https://www.voorheescenter.com/publications.

Garza, Melita. "Bringing Drama to the School Reform Story." *Chicago Tribune*, January 18, 1993.

Godreau, Isar P. Scripts of Blackness: Race, Cultural Nationalism, and U.S. Colonialism in Puerto Rico. Urbana: University of Illinois Press, 2015.

González, Juan. *Harvest of Empire: A History of Latinos in America*. Rev. ed. New York: Penguin Books, 2011.

Grosfoguel, Ramón. *Colonial Subjects: Puerto Ricans in a Global Perspective*. Berkeley: University of California Press, 2003.

Gutiérrez, Luis. *Still Dreaming: My Journey from the Barrio to Capitol Hill*. New York: W. W. Norton, 2013.

Hernandez, Alex. "Rossana Rodríguez-Sánchez Outs Ald. Deb Mell by Just 13 Votes as Final 33rd Ward Count Comes In." *Block Club Chicago*, April 16, 2019. https://blockclubchicago.org/2019/04/16/rossana-rodriguez-sanchez-ousts-ald -deb-mell-by-just-13-votes-as-final-33rd-ward-count-comes-in/.

Hinojosa, Jennifer, and Carlos Vargas-Ramos. *Almanac of Puerto Ricans in the United States*. New York: Centro Press, 2017.

Hinojosa, Jennifer, Nashia Román, and Edwin Meléndez. *Puerto Rican Post-Maria Relocation by States*. Research Brief, Center for Puerto Rican Studies, Hunter College, CUNY. Centro RB-2018-03, March 2018. https://centropr.hunter.cuny .edu/sites/default/files/PDF/Schoolenroll-v2-3-3-2018.pdf.

History Task Force. *Labor Migration under Capitalism: The Puerto Rican Experience*. New York: Monthly Review Press, 1979.

Holliday, Darryl. "Humboldt Park Hotter Than Ever When It Comes to Real Estate: Redfin." DNAinfo Chicago, August 4, 2014. https://www.dnainfo.com /chicago/20140804/humboldt-park/humboldt-park-named-americas-hottest -neighborhood-redfin.

Immerwahr, Daniel. *How to Hide an Empire: A History of the Greater United States*. New York: Farrar, Straus and Giroux, 2019.

Innis-Jimenez, Michael. *Steel Barrio: The Great Mexican Migration to South Chicago, 1915–1940*. New York: New York University Press, 2013.

Institute for Latino Studies. *Bordering the Mainstream: A Needs Assessment of Latinos in Berwyn and Cicero, Illinois*. Notre Dame: University of Notre Dame Institute for Latino Studies Communications Group, 2002.

Kassanits, Jessica. "Riot Fest and the Gentrification of Humboldt Park." *Chicago Monitor*, September 10, 2014. http://chicagomonitor.com/2014/09/does-riot-fest -support-gentrification/.

Kyle, Charles L., and Edward R. Kantowicz. *Kids First—Primero Los Niños: Chicago School Reform in the 1980s*. Springfield, Ill.: Institute for Public Affairs, 1992.

Lazu, Jacqueline. "The Chicago Young Lords: (Re)Constructing Knowledge and Revolution." *Centro: Journal of the Center for Puerto Rican Studies* 25, no. 2 (2012): 28–59.

Lemann, Nicholas. *The Promised Land: The Great Black Migration and How It Changed America*. New York: Vintage Books, 1992.

Llorens, Hilda. *Imagining the Great Puerto Rican Family: Framing Nation, Race, and Gender during the American Century*. Lanham, Md.: Lexington Books, 2014.

Martín, Carlos. "How Hurricane Maria Exposed Puerto Rico's 'Colonial Boom and Bust.'" *Urban Institute*, October 12, 2017. https://www.urban.org/urban-wire/how -hurricane-maria-exposed-puerto-ricos-colonial-boom-and-bust.

Mastony, Colleen. "Elgin, Aguada Share Family Ties." *Chicago Tribune*, August 8, 2003. http://articles.chicagotribune.com/2003–08–08/news/0308080244_1 _aguada-puerto-rican-parade-puerto-rico.

Meléndez, Edwin, and Carlos Vargas-Ramos, eds. *Puerto Ricans at the Dawn of the New Millennium*. New York: Centro Press, 2014.

Meléndez, Edwin, and Charles R. Venator-Santiago. "Puerto Rico Post–Hurricane Maria: Origins and Consequences of a Crisis." *Centro: Journal of the Center for Puerto Rican Studies* 30, no. 3 (2019): 1–10.

Mermigas, Diane. "Public TV Focuses on the Students." *Chicago Daily Herald*, September 17, 1977.

Miraftab, Faranak. *Global Heartland: Displaced Labor, Transnational Lives, and Local Placemaking*. Indianapolis: Indiana University Press, 2016.

Mora, Cristina. *Making Hispanics: How Activists, Bureaucrats, and Media Constructed a New American*. Chicago: University of Chicago Press, 2014.

Mora, Marie T., Alberto Davila, and Havidan Rodriguez. *Population, Migration, and Socioeconomic Outcomes among Island and Mainland Puerto Ricans*. Lanham, Md.: Lexington Books, 2018.

Mumm, Jesse. "Gentrification in Color and Time: White and Puerto Rican Racial Histories at Work in Humboldt Park." *Centro: Journal of the Center for Puerto Rican Studies* 28, no. 2 (2016): 88.

———. "When the White People Come: Gentrification and Race in Puerto Rican Chicago." PhD diss., Northwestern University, 2014.

NBC Chicago. "Cargo Plane Filled with Supplies Heads from Chicago to Puerto Rico." NBCChicago.com, September 25, 2017. https://www.nbcchicago.com /news/local/Cargo-Plane-Filled-With-Supplies-Heads-from-Chicago-to-Puerto -Rico-447634863.html.

Neal, Steve. "The Power Seekers: Chicago's Mayoral Race." *Chicago Tribune*, February 13, 1983.

Nieves-Pizarro, Yadira. "Free Oscar Lopez Rivera! New Coverage of United States Domestic Human Rights Issues." *Centro: Journal of the Center for Puerto Rican Studies* 28, no. 2 (2016): 68–87.

Olivo, Antonio. "Prisoners' Plight on Display." *Chicago Tribune*, May 31, 2006. http://articles.chicagotribune.com/2006–05–31/news/0605310171_1_oscar-lopez -rivera-carlos-alberto-torres-rican.

———. "Puerto Rican Culture to Have a New Showcase." *Chicago Tribune*, May 23, 2006. http://articles.chicagotribune.com/2006–05–23/news/0605230131_1_puerto -rican-arts-puerto-rico-museum.

Olmedo, Irma M. "Puerto Rican Grandmothers Share and Relive Their *Memorias*." *Centro: Journal of the Center for Puerto Rican Studies* 13, no. 2 (2001): 105.

Ortiz, Altagracia, ed. *Puerto Rican Women and Work: Bridges in Transnational Labor.* Philadelphia: Temple University Press, 1996.

Ortiz, Lisa. "*Rantoul es como Jayuya*: (De)valued Migrations, Education, and *Progreso* within Media, Puerto Rico, and the Rural Midwest." PhD diss., University of Illinois, Urbana-Champaign, 2018. http://hdl.handle.net/2142 /101792.

Otterstrom, S. M., and B. F. Tillman. "Income Change and Circular Migration: The Curious Case of Mobile Puerto Ricans, 1995–2010." *Journal of Latin American Geography* 12, no. 3 (2013): 33–57. doi:10.1353/lag.2013.0039.

Padilla, Felix. *Latino Ethnic Consciousness: The Case of Mexican Americans and Puerto Ricans in Chicago.* Notre Dame: University of Notre Dame Press, 1985.

———. *Puerto Rican Chicago.* Notre Dame: University of Notre Dame Press, 1987.

———. *The Struggle of Latino/Latina University Students: In Search of a Liberating Education.* New York: Routledge, 1997.

Padilla, Felix, and Lourdes Santiago. *Outside the Wall: A Puerto Rican Woman's Struggle.* New Brunswick: Rutgers University Press, 1993.

Pantojas-García, Emilio. "Is Puerto Rico Greece in the Caribbean? Crisis, Colonialism, and Globalization." *Fletcher Forum of World Affairs* 40, no. 1 (Winter 2016): 57.

Pathieu, Diane. "Hurricane Relief Supplies Headed to Puerto Rico from Chicago." ABC7 Chicago, September 25, 2017. http://abc7chicago.com/2451885/.

Pérez, Gina. *The Near Northwest Side Story: Migration, Displacement, and Puerto Rican Families*. Berkeley: University of California Press, 2004.

Pomada, Alicia. "Puerto Rico, School Language Policies." *Encyclopedia of Bilingual Education* (online). SAGE Publications, April 5, 2010. http://aliciapousada .weebly.com/uploads/1/0/0/2/10020146/puerto_rico_school_language_policies _encyclopedia_of_bilingual_education.pdf.

Power, Margaret. "Puerto Rican Nationalism in Chicago." *Centro: Journal of the Center for Puerto Rican Studies* 28, no. 2 (2016): 36–67.

"Puerto Ricans Call for Aid amid Catastrophe: 'We're American Citizens. We Can't Be Left to Die.'" Democracy Now! September 26, 2017. https://www.youtube .com/watch?v=QrYPjM2UB9U.

Ramos-Zayas, Ana Yolanda. *National Performances: The Politics of Class, Race, and Space in Puerto Rican Chicago*. Chicago: University of Chicago Press, 2003.

Rios, Palmira. "Export-Oriented Industrialization and the Demand for Female Labor: Puerto Rican Women in the Manufacturing Sector, 1952–1980." *Gender and Society* 4, no. 3 (1990): 321–37.

Rivera, Janeida. "The Hoodoisie Live Podcast Visits Urban Theater Company." *La Voz del Paseo Boricua*, March 2017.

Rivera, Marcia. "The Development of Capitalism in Puerto Rico and the Incorporation of Women into the Labor Force." In *The Puerto Rican Woman: Perspectives on Culture, History, and Society*, 2nd ed., edited by Edna Acosta-Belen, 30–45. New York: Praeger, 1986.

Rivera-Batiz, F., and C. E. Santiago. *Island Paradox: Puerto Rico in the 1990s*. New York: Russell Sage Foundation, 1998.

Rodríguez-Muñiz, Michael. "Riot and Remembrance: Puerto Rican Chicago and the Politics of Interruption." *Centro: Journal of the Center for Puerto Rican Studies* 28, no. 2 (2016): 204–17.

Rouse, Irving. *The Taínos: Rise and Decline of the People Who Greeted Columbus*. New Haven: Yale University Press, 1993.

Rúa, Mérida M. *A Grounded Identidad: Making New Lives in Chicago's Puerto Rican Neighborhoods*. New York: Oxford University Press, 2012.

———. *Latino Urban Ethnography and the Work of Elena Padilla*. Champaign: University of Illinois Press, 2009.

Ruiz, Noraliz. "Chicago: Home to the Puerto Rican Cuatro, Centro de Estudios Puertorriqueños." *Voices* (blog), November 5, 2014. https://centropr.hunter.cuny .edu/centrovoices/arts-culture/chicago-home-puerto-rican-cuatro.

Sánchez Korrol, Virginia E. *From Colonia to Community: The History of Puerto Ricans in New York City, 1917–1948*. Berkeley: University of California Press, 1994.

Sanchez Olson, Yadira. "Post-Hurricane Aid for Puerto Rico Presses On with Waukegan Fundraiser." *Lake County News-Sun*, December 8, 2017. http://www. chicagotribune.com/suburbs/lake-county-news-sun/news/ct-lns-lake-puerto-rico -fundraiser-st-1208–20171207-story.html.

Santiago, Esmeralda. *When I Was Puerto Rican: A Memoir.* Cambridge, Mass.: Da Capo Press, 2006.

Schmid, Julie M., and David Hernández. "A MELUS Interview: David Hernández, Chicago's Unofficial Poet Laureate." *MELUS* 25, no. 2 (2000): 147–62. https://doi. org/10.2307/468224.

Shojai, Carolyn. "Latins Form Group to Develop, Train Spanish Leaders." *Chicago Tribune*, March 16, 1969.

Shropshire, Carolyn. "Ald. Maldonado and Ald. Moreno Want to 'Put a Brake' on Gentrification along the 606." *La Voz del Paseo Boricua*, March 2017.

Silver, Patricia, and William Velez. "'Let Me Go Check Out Florida': Rethinking Puerto Rican Diaspora." *Centro: Journal of the Center for Puerto Rican Studies* 29, no. 3 (2017): 98–125.

Smith, Gerry. "Humboldt Park Residents Feel Sting of Foreclosures." *Chicago Tribune*, November 4, 2007. http://articles.chicagotribune.com/2007–11–04/news/0711030838 _1_humboldt-park-number-of-foreclosure-filings-puerto-rican-cultural-center.

Smith, Samantha. "Woman Harassed for Wearing Puerto Rico Shirt 'in America' as Officer, Who Resigned Wednesday, Stood by Watching." *Washington Post*, July 12, 2018. https://www.washingtonpost.com/news/morning-mix/wp/2018/07/11 /woman-harassed-for-wearing-puerto-rico-shirt-in-america-as-officer-stands -by-watching/.

Smith, Wes. "'Safe Zone' Aims to Give Gangs a Lesson." *Chicago Tribune*, March 30, 1987.

Stanley, Brian. "First Latina Appointed Will County Judge." *Joliet Herald-News*, January 6, 2015, http://www.theherald-news.com/2015/01/05/first-latina-appointed -will-county-judge/agfng7e/.

Staudenmaier, Michael. "War on Poverty, War on Division Street: Puerto Rican Chicago in the 1960s through the Lens of the Janet Nolan Collection." *Centro: Journal of the Center for Puerto Rican Studies* 28, no. 2 (2016): 180.

Strauss, Valeria. "To Learn about Improving Urban Public Schools, We Should Study Chicago. Yes, Chicago." *Washington Post*, February 2, 2018.

Suárez Findlay, Eileen J. *Imposing Decency: The Politics of Sexuality and Race in Puerto Rico, 1870–1920.* Durham: Duke University Press, 2000.

———. *We Are Left without a Father Here: Masculinity, Domesticity, and Migration in Postwar Puerto Rico.* Durham: Duke University Press, 2014.

Taylor, Paul, Mark Hugo Lopez, Jessica Martínez, and Gabriel Velasco. *When Labels Don't Fit: Hispanics and Their Views of Identity.* Pew Research Center Hispanic

Trends, April 4, 2012. http://www.pewhispanic.org/2012/04/04/when-labels-dont -fit-hispanics-and-their-views-of-identity/.

Terkel, Studs. *Division Street: America*. 1967. Reprint, New York: New Press, 2006.

Thomas, Lorrin. *Puerto Rican Citizen: History and Political Identity in Twentieth-Century New York City*. Chicago: University of Chicago Press, 2014.

Toro-Morn, Maura. "*Boricuas en Chicago*: Gender and Class in the Migration and Settlement of Puerto Ricans." In *Puerto Rican Diaspora: Historical Perspectives*, edited by Carmen T. Whalen and V. Vázquez-Hernández, 128–50. Philadelphia: Temple University Press, 2005. http://www.jstor.org/stable/j.ctt14bto9b.

———. "The Class and Gender Dimensions of Puerto Rican Migration to Chicago." PhD diss., Loyola University, 1993. https://ecommons.luc.edu/luc_diss/3025.

———. "The Family in Puerto Rico: Colonialism, Industrialization, and Migration." In *The Handbook of World Families*, edited by Bert N. Adams and Jan Troost, 440–63. Thousand Oaks, Calif.: SAGE, 2004.

———. "Gender, Class, and Family and Migration: Puerto Rican Women in Chicago." *Gender and Society* 9, no. 6 (1995): 706–20.

———. "Migration and Gendered Webs of Obligation: Caring for My Elderly Puerto Rican Mother in a Transnational Context." In *Critical Gerontology Comes of Age*, edited by C. Wellin, 225–42. New York: Routledge, 2018.

———. "*Yo era muy arriesgada*: A Historical Overview of the Work Experiences of Puerto Rican Women in Chicago." *Centro: Journal of the Center for Puerto Rican Studies* 13, no. 2 (2001): 24–43.

Toro-Morn, Maura, and Marisa Alicea. *Gendered Geographies of Home: Mapping Second and Third-Generation Puerto Ricans' Sense of Home*. In *Gender and U.S. Immigration: Contemporary Trends*, edited by Pierrette Hondagneu-Sotelo, 194–214. Berkeley: University of California Press, 2003.

———, eds. *Migration and Immigration: A Global View*. Westport, Conn.: Greenwood Press, 2004.

Toro-Morn, Maura, and Ivis García. "Gendered Fault Lines: A Demographic Profile of Puerto Rican Women in the United States." *Centro: Journal of the Center for Puerto Rican Studies* 29, no. 3 (2017): 10–35.

Toro-Morn, Maura, Ivis García-Zambrana, and Marisa Alicea. "*De bandera a bandera* (From flag to flag): New Scholarship about the Puerto Rican Diaspora in Chicago." *Centro: Journal of the Center for Puerto Rican Studies* 18, no. 2 (2016): 4–35.

U.S. Commission on Civil Rights. *Hearing before the United States Commission on Civil Rights in New York, New York, February 14–15, 1972*. Washington, D.C.: Government Printing Office, 1973

Vargas-Ramos, Carlos, and Edwin Meléndez, eds. *The State of Puerto Ricans 2013*. New York: Centro Press, 2013.

Vazquez Paz, Johanny. *Poemas Callejeros/Streetwise Poems*. Bilingual ed. Chicago: Mayapple Press, 2007.

Velázquez, Mirelsie. *"Brincamos el charco y ahora que*: Historicizing Puerto Rican Education in Chicago, 1967–1977." PhD diss., University of Illinois at Urbana-Champaign, 2010.

———. "Looking Forward, Working for Change: Puerto Rican Women and the Quest for Educational Justice in Chicago." *Centro: Journal of the Center for Puerto Rican Studies* 28, no. 2 (2016): 138.

Velázquez Vargas, Yarma. "Marco Said I Look Like Charcoal." *Qualitative Inquiry* 14, no. 6 (2008): 949–52.

Vidal-Ortiz, Salvador, and Julianna Martinez. "Latinx Thoughts: Latinidad with an X." *Latino Studies Journal* 16, no. 3 (2018): 384–95. doi:10.1057/s41276–018–0137–8.

Wagenheim, Kal, and Olga Jiménez de Wagenheim, eds. *The Puerto Ricans*. Rev. ed. Princeton: Markus Wiener, 2013.

Whalen, Carmen, and Victor Vasquez. *Puerto Rican Diaspora: Historical Perspectives*. Philadelphia: Temple University Press, 2005.

"The Young Lords, Puerto Rican Liberation, and the Black Freedom Struggle: Interview with José 'Cha-Cha' Jiménez." *OAH Magazine of History* 26 (2012): 61–64.

INDEX

Italicized page numbers indicate figures.

MAURA I. TORO-MORN is a professor of sociology and director of the Latin American and Latino Studies program at Illinois State University. She is a coeditor of *Immigrant Women Workers in the Neoliberal Age* and has published essays in *Latino Studies Journal*, *Centro: Journal of the Center for Puerto Rican Studies*, and the *Journal of Latino/Latin American Studies*.

IVIS GARCÍA, associate professor of landscape architecture and urban planning at Texas A&M University, was the cochair of the Puerto Rican Agenda of Chicago and a Chicago-based oral historian with Centro at City University of New York. She is also a faculty member at the ABCD Institute at DePaul University. She has published her work in *Urban Studies*, the *Journal of Planning Education and Research*, and the *Journal of the American Planning Association*, among other urban planning journals.